To Marjorie
who is making it
happen in Missouri

Al Blank

The Community Tourism Industry Imperative:
The Necessity, The Opportunities, Its Potential

by *Uel Blank*

Venture Publishing, Inc.
State College, PA 16803

Cover Design by Sandra Sikorski
Typesetting by Sandra Cramer
Production Supervisor Bonnie Godbey
Library of Congress Catalogue Number 89-50207
ISBN 0-910251-31-2

Table of Contents

Chapter Six

Chapter Seven

Chapter Eight

Chapter Eleven

Chapter Twelve

PREFACE

To The Community Tourism Industry Imperative: The Necessity, The Opportunities, Its Potential

This book brings into simultaneous focus most of the social science disciplines upon the development and management of the community tourism industry. The primary approach is from the viewpoint of economics. This economic bias is amply justified by the potential economic role that the tourism industry can play in many communities.

Communities are where people live. Thus despite its economic thrust, the book's first concern is with the community's provision of living quality for its residents. Economic considerations—the means for living—are an important part of living quality. At the same time living quality goes far beyond economics. It is pointed out that residents want to feel good about, take pride in and enjoy life in their community. Many factors are involved deserving much better treatment than space and available knowledge could accord them here. A challenge is hereby issued to colleagues to carry the analysis and its synthesis much farther.

More than twenty-five years were required in the making of this book. It grows out of a series of study, research, teaching and practice under teutelage of a variety of systems and people. The principles proposed are drawn from these experiences plus the nascent but growing body of tourism research in the Western World. Perhaps the most basic lesson of all came from long-time experience with the Extension Services of U. S. Land Grant Colleges—how to help people help themselves through information and understandings; and that

there is an astounding creativity to be unleashed thereby!

Much is owed to insights gained from working associations with a large number of individuals. They helped to shape concepts, as well as by direct contributions. At the risk of omitting really important contributors to my upbringing in the tourism/hospitality area I wish to especially acknowledge the following: Ed Alchin, Michigan State University; Robert Anderson, Michigan State University; Gary Ballman, Lakewood Research, Minneapolis; James Burke, Rochester Institute of Technology; Clare Gunn, Texas A & M University; Gladys Knight, Michigan State University; Timothy Knopp, University of Minnesota; Wilbur Maki, University of Minnesota; L. C. Merriam, University of Minnesota; Robert McIntosh, Michigan State University; Robert Olson, University of Minnesota; Lawrence R. Simonson, University of Minnesota; Louis Twardzik, Michigan State University; Raymond Vlasin, Michigan State University and Glen Weaver, University of Missouri.

In addition to academic colleagues my understandings owe much to practitioners with whom I have had opportunity to consult from Nova Scotia to California. These include operators of hospitality services, park managers, chamber of commerce executives, and tourism and other state and federal agency personnel. They provided the inspiration for the many positive examples used to illustrate principles throughout the book. It is my hope that the correct inferences have been drawn, and further that the materials assembled in this publication will assist them and many of their fellow operators in developing the tourism industry.

Certainly not least has been the encouragement and support from my family. My wife Vernie was understandingly patient during periods of intensive work on the text. Grant Blank, Chicago, was helpful in providing numerous sociology references. Rebecca Blank, Princeton University, critiqued portions of the early drafts. Thus this work, like all human endeavor, leans heavily upon the overall human experience, and its collective intellect.

Every community has a tourism industry; every community can have a better tourism industry. Warroad, Minnesota. Photo credit: Uel Blank

ONE

Tourism: The Cinderella Stepchild of Economic Development

A great wall of mythology surrounds the tourism industry. Under the onslaught of systematic tourism study the wall has now sustained minor breaches. But for most of the populace, including many who are direct participants in the industry, the mythology is treated as reality. Before comprehensive progress can be made toward sound development of the tourism industry of a community or a state, the myths must be demolished.

Let us examine some of the prevailing web that comprises the wall of tourism mythology:

"How could anyone, much less an economist, work with anything so frivolous as tourism?" The clear, but usually unspoken, question indicated by the bemused expression on the face of casual acquaintances, when the author tells them that he works with the tourism industry.

"Tourism, of course, will increase in the area."—a frequent comment in newspaper stories analyzing economic prospects of the northern Great Lakes Region.

"We can cut out vacation travel."—remark by a government economic adviser in the period of critical oil shortage of the 1970's.

"I'm not a tourist, I'm traveling on business."—a common reaction of United State's traveling businesspersons.

"I'm not going to jeopardize my business by sharing information with other businesses in the area."—widely-held attitude of operators of smaller restaurants, motels, and resorts.

"But, what would anyone on vacation in our area do if they don't fish?"—question by a state conservation department official.

"Tourism produces nothing!"—remark by a forest management official while comparing uses of a forested area in timber production with recreational use.

"Service industries will not develop the economy."—statement by a nationally syndicated economist.

"We don't want a bell-hop economy!"—comment by a state elected official.

"We want to keep the people who don't live here out of our lakes and out of our area!"—declaration by a local blue-collar worker.

"Tourism has ruined our community."—lament by a citizen of a community that has a relatively large tourism industry.

"Every dollar the tourist spends turns over fourteen times in our community!"—claim by a chamber of commerce executive, in extolling the values of tourism.

The list of such quotes could be continued almost indefinitely.

What is illustrated by the above quotes? They reveal a vast store of misinformation and misunderstanding about the tourism industry on the part of the person on the street, as well as on the part of many so-called experts. Many of the quotes also reveal a prejudicial bias against tourism arising from a number of factors that will be treated later.

Why so much mythology and misunderstanding?

Perhaps the greatest contributory factor is in the nature of the tourism industry itself. Tourism is complex, cross-cutting at least half of the entire economic and social fabric of the community and nation. For that reason it cannot be neatly defined and concisely treated.

Adding to the difficulty of understanding is tourism's newly emergent nature. Only in this century has it been a factor demanding attention. In the United States it received little attention until well after World War II. This means that there has not been time to acquire information about it, nor develop mature attitudes and judgements. Because of this lack of information, many statements about tourism are based on limited personal observation rather than objective, empirical fact.

Psychological factors weigh heavily upon attitudes and judgement about the tourism industry. Prominent among these is the work ethic philosophy that contributed importantly to our nation's physical development in the 19th Century. This ethic put stress upon aggressive action in tangible, physical construction and production. This attitude is examined further in Chapter 5. Suffice it to note here, that we now have command over considerable physical wealth, most people travel extensively, but many retain attitudes regarding these factors that were held by the society a century ago.

A peculiarity of tourism is that it cannot be warehoused, stored and transported as is the case with most physical products. Consumers must be physically in the supplying area. This causes another kind of psychological problem—that of having to share one's home turf with strangers. The United States has large numbers, driven by the frontier spirit—they moved when neighbors got too close. It is easy to understand resentment when non-residents become more numerous in the neighborhood than residents. This occurs in heavily tourism-impacted communities.

The adjustments necessary by communities that are heavily impacted by tourists come slowly. Rather than make the adjustments, many residents simply resent tourists' intrusion. Few recognize the short-sighted nature of this attitude; in today's setting most are tourists. When away from home we all wish to be treated with courtesy. With this treatment comes a price and obligation—that we are good hosts to others when they are visitors in our community.

A wide spectrum of business and employment in many communities is dependent, in part, on tourism. This interrelationship is not well known. Because of this ignorance, many who gain from, and need, the tourism industry, regard tourists as an unnecessary nuisance, or worse.

The highly personalized nature of the tourism experience produces yet another barrier to its widespread understanding. Individuals and families have sharply differing views of what constitutes a satisfactory tourism experience. Some approach tourism as a matter of miles traveled and amounts consumed—the more the better. Others view tourism as the experiencing of nature or human culture, and measured by the heartbeat rather than consumption. These two polar types seldom understand each other's motives or even recognize the other as a legitimate experience. The potential for widely varied travel/tourism experiences, despite the confusion of understanding that it may create, is a great strength. It contributes to a richly varied living quality.

Now let us review briefly some of the "positives" of tourism. We will deal with definitions in Chapter 2, but we need a preliminary understanding of three words: *tourist*—anyone away from the usual place of living and/or work; *tourism*—what tourists do plus the activities in the host community to serve tourists; *tourism industry*—the economic activities generated by tourism.

Every U.S. and Canadian community has a tourism industry. Some communities fail to even recognize that they have tourism. In others it is the major means of community income. Tourists are attracted to some places because of the unusual natural features. Travelers also go to other communities because of business operations there, because of superior health care facilities, or because of some other man-made feature or service.

Nearly every business providing goods or services at retail is a part of the tourism industry. This fact derives from the need of travelers to purchase nearly everything when they are away from home that they would buy if they were at home. However, compared to home purchases, the proportions in which travelers buy will be very different. Also, among the classes of businesses, the proportions of sales to tourists compared to residents will vary widely. Most motel sales are to tourists. Dentists perform most of their services for residents—pity the poor traveler with a toothache, but some are thus unfortunate!

Tourism produces jobs, profits, rents, and taxes just as do most other economic activities. Tourism becomes an economic activity when a business or operation sells something to a traveler. Simply having travelers in the community is not enough—someone must sell them something. This means that the sales package available for travelers to buy is important to tourism's role as an economic component in the community.

Over a wide range, tourism and most other industries are complements. Travel is necessary to the operation of most modern businesses. In addition, everyday economic activities can be travel attractors for people who enjoy seeing an economy that differs from their own. Thus factories, forests, mines and agriculture can attract sightseeing travelers. This observation flies in the face of much prevailing thought—that the community must choose between factories and tourism, or mining and tourism. With the proper governmental and private infrastructure in place, not only can competitive aspects be minimized, but each can contribute to the other. Why not eat your cake and have it too?

Everyone (almost) is a tourist. Because of high levels of personal income and other factors producing mobility, the travel market is broad. This means that opportunities for tourism industry development are extensive.

Among the most important considerations that a community has regarding its tourists are these: *The community attracts visitors by its complex of businesses, governmental headquarters, pleasures, amenities, shopping, and human or personal services. It then has opportunity to serve these travelers, thus generating jobs, profits, rents and taxes from the tourism industry.*

Although all communities have a tourism industry now, most could greatly improve that industry:

— It can add income to the community.
— It can improve the living quality of residents.
— It can better serve its visitors—the traveling public.

This book aims at assisting communities in attaining these ends.

ORGANIZATION AND USE OF THIS BOOK

This book is intended for use by both students and practitioners of the science and art of developing the tourism industry of a community. It brings to bear the major principles of tourism industry development, illustrating them by actual examples or composite examples. Once student and practitioners understand principles, they are equipped to treat problems. Each problem solution requires different operating techniques. These techniques change over time, and must be learned with each new application. For that reason very little "how to" procedures are treated here except to illustrate the principles.

The specific focus is upon community tourism industry development and management in developed countries. *Communities* are the destination of most travelers. Therefore *it is in communities that tourism happens.* Because of this, *tourism industry development and management must be brought effectively to bear in communities.*

Most communities, large and small, have a drastically underdeveloped and undermanaged tourism industry. Through tourism development they have opportunity for a better balanced, more viable economy, and improved living quality for their citizens. This is the book's main aim.

The claims that some communities are over-impacted and negatively impacted by tourism are recognized. Some of these claims are true. But "over development" as well as "under development" come about for the same basic reasons: lack of adequate information, and lack or loss of control. The principles explained in this book apply to and can assist in both situations.

The book fills a major informational gap for operators of private tourism services and facilities. Since communities are the primary destinations of tourists, virtually everyone related to the travel and recreation industries needs to understand communities and how they function in the provision of tourism and recreation experiences. This is true whether the individual is dealing mainly with lodging, food or recreational services, the provision of transportation services, or intermediary services such as travel agencies and travel brokers.

A firm grasp of the principles of community tourism industry development and management is equally essential for officials and employees in governmental and quasi-governmental agencies at all levels. It is particularly applicable to those in

convention and tourism bureaus, chambers of commerce, and resource-managing agencies. In addition, officials of city and county government will find the insights contained herein useful.

The book has four major divisions:

Chapters 1, 2 and 3 are primarily definitional. They deal with the ramifications and details of "What is tourism?" and "What is a tourist destination area?"

Chapters 4 through 7 treat the principles of functioning relationships between the tourism industry: the rest of the overall economy; the community psychology and mindset; the community's internal economy; and the community's resources.

Chapters 8, 9 and 10 are transitional. They continue discussion of principles of functioning relationships. They also move in the direction of treating the principles of actions needed to bring about desired tourism industry results, dealing with linkages to markets, managing information, and systems for achieving project action.

Chapters 11 and 12 discuss how a community can take control. They discuss principles of how a community can stimulate its network of decision-makers to make plans and generate positive action, thereby bringing the creativity of the community to bear upon community tourism industry development.

Questions and suggestions for additional reading appear at the end of chapters 2 through 12. These are intended to help in review of the material discussed. They can also help direct the reader in further exploration of the many facets of community tourism industry development and management. The exploration can be fascinating and rewarding.

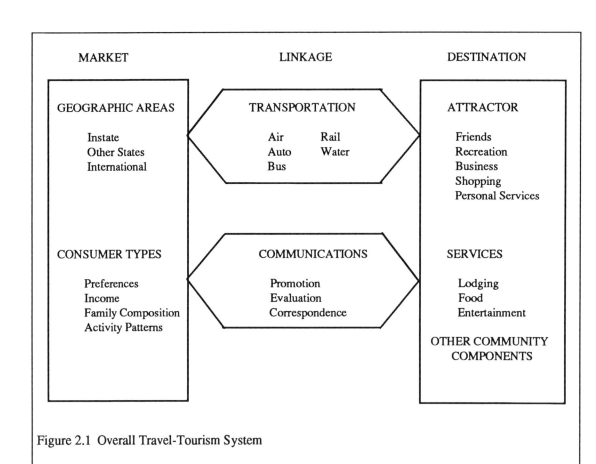

MARKET   LINKAGE   DESTINATION

GEOGRAPHIC AREAS

    Instate
    Other States
    International

TRANSPORTATION

    Air   Rail
    Auto   Water
    Bus

ATTRACTOR

    Friends
    Recreation
    Business
    Shopping
    Personal Services

CONSUMER TYPES

    Preferences
    Income
    Family Composition
    Activity Patterns

COMMUNICATIONS

    Promotion
    Evaluation
    Correspondence

SERVICES

    Lodging
    Food
    Entertainment

OTHER COMMUNITY
COMPONENTS

Figure 2.1 Overall Travel-Tourism System

/hat, Really, is This Thing—Tourism?

s chapter and the next are mainly definitional.
:ir purposes are to explain in detail the overall
rism-travel system, and the community tourism
tem, or as we will call it, the community tourist
:tination area.

DEFINITIONS

have said that a *tourist* is anyone away from his
ier usual place of living and/or work. We have
cribed *tourism* as a comprehensive term,
ompassing acts by tourists as well as activities of
se serving tourists.

The definition of *tourist* needs further treatment.
)uld the reader look up "tourist" in a standard
tionary, most will find a definition such as "a
son traveling or making a tour for pleasure or
ure." The definition is inappropriate for this text
ch approaches tourism as an economic industry
ie community. When using the latter approach,
has two choices: Two or more words can be
d such as "tourists and visitors" or "tourists and
elers." Alternatively, the definition of "tourist"
be expanded to include anyone traveling away
n home or the usual work place for any purpose.
reasingly tourism professionals use the latter
nition.

For those treating tourism as an economic
vity, tourists' important feature is that they
nd money in a host community away from
ie. Travel purpose is not a part of the initial
nition. Travel purpose is important, however,

when segmenting the market (Chapter 9), and when
developing attractions and services that appeal to
specific tourist segments (Chapters 3, 9, 10, 11, and
12). When applied to a specific setting, travel
distance must also be a part of the definition of
"tourist" (Chapter 8). How far is "away?" In each
case "distance" depends upon the purposes for
which tourists are enumerated.

Tourism is a complex system consisting of
three major parts:

— *The tourist* or the people who travel. From
the viewpoint of the tourism industry that
is selling to them, it is *the market*.
— *The destination* or the place to which tourists
travel. In tourism industry terms it is an
area that has a cohesive travel appeal and
that can be marketed to specific tourist
segments.
—*The linkage(s)* or the communication and
transportation means that allow information and people flows between the market
and the destination.

Figure 2. 1 pictures a tourism system in simplified graphic form. The system's several components will be discussed in detail after we have
explained other terms that are closely associated
with tourism.

The *tourism industry* is made up of all those
economic activities that take place because
tourists travel. These activities generate employment, profits, rents and taxes, and nearly all parts of

the community that provide goods and services at retail are directly involved (Fedler, 1987).

The *hospitality industry, or hospitality services,* includes those businesses and services making it possible for tourists to live away from home. In its most exclusive sense it includes only food and lodging services. Travel and recreational services may sometimes be included. The term "tourism industry" has broader meaning since it includes all economic activities generated by tourists.

Travel is the activity of moving from one geographic location to another. Tourism includes all travel except short-distance, vicinity travel, and regular commuting to work or school. Sometimes a "distance from home" qualification is placed upon travel in order for it to be considered as tourism travel. The most frequently used distance limitations are 50 and 100 miles from home.

Recreation is activity, usually undertaken in unobligated time, with pleasure as a primary purpose. It is important to note that travel for other purposes than recreation is included in the tourism industry.

Leisure as used here means time unobligated for making a living or the performance of necessary personal operations. Leisure can be viewed in a more sophisticated way. In its classical meaning leisure includes those things undertaken as an end in themselves and not done as a means to some other end (Kaplan, 1975; MacCannell, 1976).

Person-trip is one measure of tourism activity that counts each person one time for every trip taken. The time away from home is not material. Three persons traveling together for four days is counted as three person-trips.

Tourists' expenditures is another measure of tourism activity used extensively in this book. It is a simple accounting of all money spent by tourists in a community, and/or at all travel points. The reader should be aware that many other measures of tourism exist.

TOURISM SYSTEM COMPONENTS

Now let us consider in greater detail the parts of a tourism system shown in Figure 2.1.

The Market

The market consists of all people who come as tourists to a given community. For most purposes, both potential as well as actual tourists are considered to be the tourism market for that community.

Markets can be viewed as geographic segments: Those travelers from within the home state, those from out-of-state, those from other countries. Geographic parts of the United States may make up travel market segments: The Northeast, Midwest, Pacific states, etc.

Market segments may also be considered as different socio-economic and demographic classes of travelers. Travelers may be metropolitan dwellers or non-metropolitan dwellers. They may be of college age, "baby boomers" with their families, or they may be retirees. They may also be segmented by income and occupation.

Perhaps the most important market segmentation system is by preferences—what do the travelers want to do and see? What means of lodging and food services do they patronize? This aspect of the market, and its relationship to a community's tourism industry is discussed in greater detail later in this chapter.

Chapter 9 continues the discussion of markets and market analysis.

The Destination

The destination area is the place to which travelers (tourists) journey. To the extent that people travel to every community of the United States, every community is a destination. Chapter 3 treats the many parts of a tourist destination. Here we highlight two key components: the *travel attractor*—this is the feature of the destination community that induces people to travel there; and *hospitality services*—these make it possible for travelers to live temporarily in the community.

The Linkage

The linkage connects the market and the destination. It has two major components. The *information/communication system* is the means whereby communication and information flow back and forth. Advertising is a part of communication; it flows from the destination to the market. Market evaluation is a communication from the market to the destination even though it may have been initiated by the destination. Other communication includes personal correspondence by mail and telephone, weather information, and newspaper, radio, television, and magazine stories. Usually, the more communication, the more travel between areas. In other words, communication supplements and stimulates travel.

The transportation linkage provides the physical means for travelers to get from their home area to the destination area. It can consist of every possible means of travel including air, highway, rail and water, plus combinations of these. Travel between areas is highly dependent upon travel costs. Increasingly these costs are related to traveler time, effort and experiences, rather than simply miles of distance, or dollar costs. Thus the quality of the transportation services and travel technology play increasing roles. A destination that is 2000 miles distant, but easily reachable by air, may be more viable as a destination than one only 500 miles away that requires more time and effort to reach by automobile and mostly on two-lane roads. From another point of view, the experience of traveling may itself contribute a major part to the overall experience of a given trip away from home. This contribution of the traveling act may derive from the mode of travel—a first airplane flight, or an ocean voyage; from the area traveled through—

sightseeing; and from the specific activities participated in.

WHY DO TOURISTS TOUR?

The tourism industry of most communities weaves together many parts to form a complex, richly patterned tapestry. One way to help understand a community's tourism industry is to analyze why tourists come.

A broad classification of all 1987 United States tourists by travel purpose is show in Table 2.1.

Table 2.1
United States Travel:
Person-Trips by Purpose 1987

Purpose	Million person-trips	Percent
Personal travel	191	16
Vacation travel	782	66
Business/Convention	211	18
Total	1,184	100%

Source: U.S. Travel Data Center, 1988

Overall travel patterns are interesting, but they are of limited value to the individual community. Overall data provide the background, but they cannot replace data about the specific individual destination area. Table 2.2 reveals a surprising variety in the purposes for travel to the four different United States cities for which data are shown. In Chapter 3, those community components satisfying given travel purposes or needs are labeled "attractors." These attractors are the mirror images of travelers' purposes. The attractions' mix will be unique to each community as indicated in Table 2.2. This variety underscores need for individualized, accurate data about the travel pattern for each separate destination area.

Table 2.2
Purposes for Traveling to Selected U.S. Cities 1977
(percentage of person-trips)

Purpose	Wilmington North Carolina	Portland Oregon	Orlando Florida	Cleveland Ohio
Visit friends and relatives	27%	29%	18%	38%
Business/Convention	10	30	12	27
Outdoor recreation	47	3	6	2
Entertainment/Sightsee	10	13	53	14
Personal	2	17	5	13
Shopping	0	3	1	0
Other	4	5	5	6
	100%	100%	100%	100%

Source: U.S. Census of Travel, 1977, Bureau of Census, U.S. Department of Commerce

While recognizing the above-noted differences among communities, a generalized discussion of purposes for travel further explains the tourism phenomenon.

Population

In the United States, more travel away from home is made to visit friends and relatives than for any other purpose. Thus, if a community has a large population, this almost automatically guarantees a large tourism industry. Unfortunately, this traveling segment is often dismissed with, "They stay and eat with relatives; why bother with this group?"

Recent studies have shown why those who visit friends and relatives in the community should not only be considered, but carefully nurtured as a part of the community's tourism industry. They may spend relatively small amounts in hotels, but they may generate large aggregate expenditures. Local residents like to show off their home city to visitors, and commonly take them to see the sights and to eat out (Blank, 1982). In addition, many who are visiting friends take advantage of being in a new

community to shop. Table 2.3 documents this pattern for one city, showing nearly one-third of this class of tourists' expenditures in restaurants, and 40 percent or more in retail stores. In metropolitan areas, expenditures by people traveling there to visit friends and relatives may be as large as one-fourth that of all tourists' expenditures combined (Blank, 1979).

Business Travel

Travel for business purposes is generated when people must leave home to purchase business supplies, when they travel as sales people to stimulate sales, when they need to confer about management, provide technical consultation and many other related travel reasons. "But," you may protest as do many, "this is not tourism travel, these people are not on the road for fun, this is obligatory travel!" True, but the purpose doesn't really matter. These people are away from home, and in order for them to travel and live away from home they must be serviced by the community's hospitality firms.

Table 2.3
Expenditure Patterns of Tourists by Selected Purposes for Travel
to Minneapolis-St.Paul, Minnesota

Expenditure Pattern	Principal Purpose for Travel to Minneapolis-St.Paul				
	Business	Convention/ Conference	Shop	Recreation/ Entertainment	Visit Friends & Relatives
Lodging	18%	25%	1%	11%	3%
Food & Beverage	19	29	2	19	29
Transportation & Travel	14	12	2	13	19
Entertainment & Recreation	3	7	-	40	8
Purchases	46	27	95	17	41
Total	100%	100%	100%	100%	100%

Source: Blank, U. & M. Petkovich *Minneapolis-St.Paul's Travel-Tourism.* University of Minnesota, Minneapolis, 1979.

What is the difference to a hotel owner whether room rentals and meal purchases are made by people traveling for business or pleasure? Either expenditure generates jobs, profits, rent and taxes for the host community. This is part of the complementarity between the community's tourism industry and other types of economic activity. The operation of most of today's businesses requires travel; for this travel to take place there must be hospitality and other retail services in your community—each supports the other.

The business travel proportion varies considerably with the nature of the community, as shown in Table 2.2. Usually, in the larger metropolitan centers, travel for business purposes will make up a larger percentage of all tourism than it will in smaller communities.

Convention/Conference Travel

Most larger cities work aggressively at booking conventions. Some recognize only conventions as

their tourism industry, or at least the only part of it that merits a marketing effort. Conventions represent an identifiable clientele to which a specific marketing effort may be directed. They also have a large impact upon the profits of major hospitality firms; thus these firms not only support community efforts by a convention bureau, but may also mount strong individual convention sales efforts. Convention goers are recognized as relatively large spenders per person (Laventhol and Horwath, 1986), and this spending benefits not only hospitality firms but the community generally. In addition, the favorable national publicity received by a city as the meeting site for a prestigious organization can attract the attention of other groups plus that of investors.

For each large group gathering, hundreds of smaller conferences and consultations occur in every larger community. These usually occur without conscious selling effort on the part of the community, but the expenditures made by their participants contribute positively to the tourism industry as do expenditures by those who attend larger gatherings.

Choice of a convention site is often partly contingent upon the amenities of the community. Group members base decisions of whether or not to attend a specific convention not only upon the conference agenda, but also upon the appeal of the convention's location to them. The community's appeal may also induce other family members to travel with the conventionnaire—with greatly expanded tourism impact potential. Recognizing this, an increasing number of cities give attention to their general attractiveness and ability to provide things for visitors to see and do.

Personal Business

Every person needs at one time or another to attend to financial or legal matters, to see a doctor, and other personal matters. While nationwide travel for personal reasons runs in the range of eight to twelve percent of all person-trips, there are communities in which the ability to attract people for personal reasons is paramount.

High quality personal services—legal, medical, educational, and financial—can be important attractors of travel. Related are such things as the seat of government, and headquarters for churches and other organizations. To the extent that these services attract from beyond the local area, they are direct generators of community tourism income in their own right. As in the case of business-to-make-a-living travel, these travel attractors must be complemented with appropriate and adequate hospitality/travel services in order to generate the full potential from them in terms of community tourism income.

Rochester, Minnesota illustrates the case as one of the more concentrated tourist centers in the United States. Its attracting power bases upon the national fame of the Mayo Medical Clinic and its many supporting facilities and hospitality services. Not only do people come who have medical

problems, but family members often accompany them. Periods of stay may extend for days and even weeks, and the business of providing a place to live for both the sick and the well generates substantial community income in additional to their expenditures for medical care.

Shopping

In common with personal services, shopping serves people as a part of the "trade center" function of a community. Thus, most shopping is done relatively close to home. For that reason only a relatively small number of those who travel far enough to be classed as a tourist indicate "shopping" as their primary reason for travel. But, like convention goers, this relatively small number are "big spenders" (Kent, 1983). Some studies have found them to spend at a rate that is three times that of the average tourist to metropolitan areas (Blank, 1979). The expenditure pattern of tourists who are traveling to shop differs radically from that of most others in that by far, most of their expenditures—up to 95 percent—are made for retail purchases, and not in traditional hospitality businesses (see Table 2.3).

While only a relatively few tourists travel mainly in order to shop, a high proportion of all tourists do some shopping. This activity pattern arises for at least two reasons: Many travel with shopping as a secondary objective, especially those who visit friends in metropolitan areas. Also, tourists need and must buy, while they are traveling, almost everything that they need while at home—the proportions are, of course, different.

Travel to Participate in Outdoor Recreation

Seventy-seven percent of the U.S. population lives in urban areas. Many of them like to get outside the city into a more bucolic setting. And they are joined in most outdoor recreation activities by citizens who live in rural areas. These activities include those in which participation is substantial such as hiking, hunting, boating, swimming, fishing, bicycling, golfing, downhill skiing, snowmobiling, ice fishing, cross-country skiing, and sunbathing on the beach. They extend to more exotic activities including mushroom hunting, spelunking, and rock climbing.

In the United States about *12 percent* of all tourism trips are for outdoor recreation. But in outstate areas of New England, the Middle Atlantic, and the Upper Great Lakes states, as much as one-third of the tourists' person-trips may be to engage in outdoor recreation. Much of this travel is highly dependent upon the quality of the natural resource. Some of the activity may consist of harvesting the natural resource such as hunting and fishing. Some may be non-consumptive, such as nature photography. Some requires special equipment such as power boats or cross-country motor bikes, and use of these latter often requires special access, as well as regulation to avoid infringing upon other outdoor recreation activities. Expenditures for outdoor recreation may range from thousands of dollars for exotic photography, skiing or fishing trips, to only pennies for those who bird watch in nature preserves.

Sightseeing Travel

Most travelers do some sightseeing. In this regard the activity is like shopping, but otherwise the two differ greatly. Sightseeing often takes the form of a family driving vacation with visits to national and state parks, unusual communities, and other points of interest as the objective. Such a travel pattern involves only short stays in each place and may include a number of different destinations. A recent study of the U.S. pleasure travelers found that 41 percent rated a touring trip, which is mostly sightseeing, as "very important" (Tourism Canada, 1986).

Few destinations can be classified as mainly "sightseeing areas" with people going there for that purpose more than any other. One example is the 470-mile Blue Ridge Parkway with its varied vegetation, spectacular overlooks, nature interpretation and adjacent foot trails. The Parkway had an estimated 22 million visits in 1987. Routes along water are also often used for sightseeing. The 150-mile U.S. Highway Number 61 along Lake Superior in Northeastern Minnesota attracts a high proportion of sightseers. This route leads along spectacular rock escarpments, along beaches strewn with water-worn pebbles, and past ancient lava flows; it provides a view of myriads of waterfalls and access to quaint fishing villages. Thirty percent of all tourists to the area indicate "sightseeing" as their major reason for coming (Blank, 1984).

Cultural and Entertainment Travel

We have already noted that when people travel to visit friends and relatives, their hosts often take them to see the sights and experiences of the destination area. In addition, a substantial number travel with cultural/recreational/ entertainment experiences as the major purpose for the trip. Such travel may include going to a show on Broadway, to see a football game, to a theme park, or to view and experience the site of Custer's Last Stand at Custer Battlefield National Monument, near Billings, Montana.

Increasingly communities stage special events and festivals. These contribute to celebration of life in the community. They may also act as major tourist attractions. A series of events may be spaced throughout the year to help maintain the flow of tourists' travel.

Travel Nodes and Travel Routes

Travel routes come to a focus in large population centers. Thus, many travelers are at least physically in communities of all kinds by inadvertence—they can't help it if the road goes there, or the plane stops there.

What is the value to a community if 3,000,000 tourists pass by on the freeway annually? If they fail to stop, these visits may have negative value—noise and air pollution, and a safety hazard. As a group these community visitors spend relatively little—mostly for automobile service, and food. They do respond to attractive services, especially if available at a natural "break point" in travel. One such point is Effingham, Illinois, at the intersection of Interstates 57 and 70, where a substantial service to interstate travelers has developed. Effingham lies at a sufficient distance from large communities where travelers might originate that they are ready for a stop when they reach there. Effingham is one of many locations where travelers can be observed to stop in large numbers at midpoints along the route between major centers.

An objective in serving this tourism segment is to provide a refreshing stop. To be avoided at all costs—any appearance of a "tourist trap."

Some other aspects of travel nodes, both interstates and airports, are examined in Chapter 8.

SUPPLY AND DEMAND: THE PRINCIPLES

We have seen that the tourism industry is an economic activity, producing employment, profits, rents and taxes for the community just as do most other economic activities. Tourism is also an economic good, following the principles of supply and demand in the same manner as other economic goods. Those principles are reviewed here since there is frequent need to refer to tourism demand and supply.

Tourism demand consists of a schedule of amounts of the tourism goods and services of a community that will be purchased at a schedule of prices. It is not a single fixed quantity. Figure 2.2 illustrates such a schedule. At price P_1 (high) a given quantity, Q_1, will be purchased. At price P_2 (low) a larger quantity, Q_2, will be purchased, assuming that consumers' tastes, incomes and other characteristics are the same in both instances.

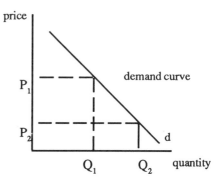

Figure 2.2 Demand for a Community's Tourism Services

Curve d is called a demand curve. Note that it is down-sloping to the right. This illustrates the law of diminishing marginal utility. As more tourism goods are purchased, each added unit is worth progressively less to the tourist. Along curve d the ratio between the change in price and resulting change in the quantity purchased changes; this is part of the concept of price elasticity which is discussed in Chapter 9.

Figure 2.3 illustrates the case in which demand changes. Curve d^1 is a higher curve than d, meaning that more of the community's tourism will be purchased at every price level. It is important to distinguish between shifts to different price levels along the same demand curve and a change to a higher level of demand. Demand can change because tastes, incomes and other consumers' characteristics change. There may be instances in which price is raised from P_1 to P_2 (a higher price), and the quantity of the community's tourism taken remains the same at Q_2. This apparent contradiction in the validity of the demand curve is actually caused by demand shifting up to d^1. Had prices remained at P_1, a larger quantity, Q_2, of tourism goods and services would have been purchased.

The community's tourism supply is another major part of the concept that must be included. Supply is also a schedule of the quantity of tourism goods and services, and the corresponding prices, that producers of lodging, food, entertainment, etc., are willing to supply. The curve in Figure 2.4 is up-sloping to the right since it usually costs relatively more to produce each added unit. Thus tourism service suppliers still provide an amount Q_1 at price P_1. In order to produce a larger amount Q_2, they must have a higher price P_2.

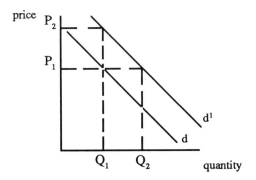

Figure 2.3 Change in Demand for a Community's Tourism Services

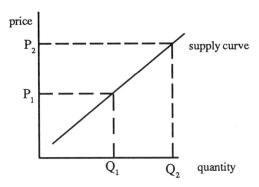

Figure 2.4 A Community's Tourism Supply Response

By putting the supply and demand curves together we can determine the actual amount of community tourism goods and services that will be purchased. This we have done in Figure 2.5. The point at which the two curves intersect determines the equilibrium quantity, Q_e, that will be purchased, and its equilibrium price, P_e. If the price is higher at P_1 (high), suppliers are willing to produce more, but consumers will not buy that much. If the price is at P_2 (low), tourists will gladly purchase more than Q_e, but producers will not make it available at that price.

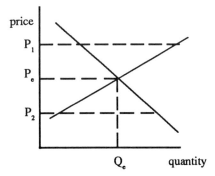

Figure 2.5 Determination of Equilibrium Price and Quantity

Figure 2.6 illustrates the case in which supply relationships change. The supply curve shifts down from s to s^1. In the current setting such a situation could result from technological changes in transportation that reduce cost of travel to and purchasing the tourism of a given community. It can also be due to a change in the overall nature of the community's tourism product, or to structural and technological changes in the producting/supplying firms. As the supply curve s shifts down to s^1 the equilibrium amount of tourism purchased will increase from Q_1 to Q_2, and the price will drop from P_1 to P_2. Alertness may be required on the part of observers to avoid interpreting increased usage that results from changes in supply as an increase in demand.

In summary, tourists travel less when travel costs are high. However, due recognition should be given to price elasticities (Chapter 9). If travelers perceive what is offered to be something that they desire intensely, they may purchase even at high price levels (Clawson, 1966).

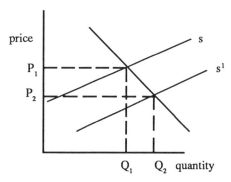

Figure 2.6 Change in Tourism Services Purchased Due to Change in Supply Costs (or Change in Transportation Costs)

TOURISM INDUSTRY CHARACTERISTICS

What especially distinguishes tourism from other industries and their products? We have seen that tourism is an economic good, obeying the traditional rules of economics as do other economic goods. In some of its characteristics it is unique, but it has other attributes similar to those of other major industries (Walsh, 1986). Here we examine briefly tourism's salient features, both that set it apart and that it shares.

—The tourism product that is produced and consumed is mainly an experience. This means that it is intangible, and its evaluation by tourists is like that of many intangibles—more in the eye of the beholder, rather than fully objective.

—The tourism product is produced as it consumed. This is due to its mostly intangible nature; it cannot be stored or transported. To view the matter from the perspective of a supplier: Nothing

is so perishable as a lodging room-night or capacity in a theater; it must either be sold or it is lost.

—The customer must be present physically to "consume" the tourism product. This follows from the fact that the experience can be neither stored or shipped. This characteristic of tourism transforms the supplying community into a hosting community—it must be able both psychologically and physically to deal directly with people. Since it is serving people when they are having fun, its hosting must be positive and up-beat.

—A community's tourism is viewed by the consumer as one single product—an experience. But it is produced as many different products: An airplane ride, a night's lodging, a meal, a museum tour, a golf game, and/or a fishing attempt. All contribute to the experience, and serious flaws in the delivery of any one product can greatly downgrade the image of the total experience in the mind of the tourist (Schmoll, 1977).

—The tourism industry is not one class or type of firm in the sense in which businesses are classified into a Standard Industrial Classification (SIC) by the U.S. Census of Business. Rather the tourism industry consists of different proportions of a large number of firm types. Almost all operations that provide goods and services at retail make sales directly to tourists. A motel may make 90 percent of its sales to tourists; conversely a few percent of a hardware store's sales may be to tourists. This is one of the really unique features of tourism, and makes it particularly difficult to get accurate comprehensive data.

—A relatively high proportion of small entrepreneurships are included among the firms that are heavily engaged in the tourism industry. Tourism shares this characteristic with a number of other industries such as construction. On the negative side, this characteristic means that there may be many inexperienced business managers involved in tourism. On the positive side, this makes tourism an important bastion and generator of free enterprise.

—While there are many small businesses involved in tourism, there are also large firms. These large firms handle a high proportion of the tourism dollars in some destination areas.

—Many community tourism operations are capital intensive. That is, they require a relatively large amount of capital for construction, equipment and/or land relative to their cash flow. This may create a debt, interest and tax problem for tourism managers thus involved.

—Most tourism operations are personal service intensive. This follows from the intangible nature of the product; a relatively small amount of physical goods exchanges hands. A closely related characteristic is that people provide much of the tourism product in the form of services to tourists. This aspect of the industry is relatively less easily impacted with technological innovations.

—Many parts of the tourism industry are highly seasonal in nature. Travel is related to the ebb and flow of seasons, the school year, and even the specific weather. At the same time, nearly all other industries have seasonal fluctuations.

—High amenity areas that become tourist destinations tend to be taken over by the state or nation as owners. In such communities a high proportion of the private tourism-related investments may also be made by nonresidents. This ownership by agencies outside the local community may reduce the local community's control of its own destiny (Rosenow, 1979). This and related factors are sometimes referred to as a "dependency" status. This book's major thrust aims at treating means for the local community to develop and exercise the capacity for positive management of its own tourism industry.

—Tourism interrelates directly with almost the full warp and woof of the society and economy. It is necessary to most industries, and also dependent upon them. Tourism is also compatible, over a broad range, with nearly all types of industries (McNulty, 1985).

These characteristics of the tourism industry will be discussed from various perspectives in the chapters that follow.

ME IN THE TOURISM INDUSTRY? A CLASSIFICATION OF FIRMS

The cutting edge of the local community's tourism industry consists of those who make sales to tourists. It has been noted that every firm that sells goods and services at retail is directly a part of the tourism industry—that is, they will make some sales directly to tourists. These sales are made because tourists buy, while away from home, about everything that they buy at home.

In response to the above paragraph one may legitimately ask, "If all retail businesses gain from tourism, then why do the hotels and resorts in my community appear to work at tourism, while the hardware stores do little or nothing?" Good question, and part of the answer is simple: The hotels and resorts get a high proportion of their income from travelers, therefore they know that for them to make profits there must be travelers in the community; this is less true of hardware stores. Beyond this response the answer becomes more complicated. We will see that in some kinds of communities the retail merchants as a group get a substantially larger part of total tourists' expenditures than do the lodging businesses. Often they are unaware of this fact, because they do not know the home location of most of their customers, and because they usually make more sales to local residents than to tourists.

The following classification helps to clarify the several relationships and dependencies (Ballman, 1982).

Tourism sales dependent firms. These are businesses that make half or more of their sales to tourists. That is, they depend upon tourists for the largest part of their business, and tourists are thus their primary market. Almost every community has some such firms; hotels, motels and campgrounds are the most ubiquitous of this class. In addition to lodging operations, those businesses that provide recreational services for people away from home also usually make at least half of their sales to tourists. These include outfitters, guide services, recreational specialty areas, theme parks, resorts, and group camps. In communities that are heavily impacted by tourists, other firm types that ordinarily fall into the next classification below will also make half of their sales to tourists; among these are sporting goods shops, restaurants, theaters and musical entertainment, and automobile services.

The proportion of the community's total tourism income that is received through firms in this class may be as high as 60, 70, or even 80 percent. Usually such a high proportion will occur in relatively smaller communities, where the tourist industry is *a* mainstay, if not *the* mainstay, of the local economy. In other communities less than 10 percent of the total tourists' expenditures may be made with firms in this class. The latter is the case in some large metropolitan centers. The difference between these communities is important to those interested in developing the tourism industry; in the former case the overall community will be well aware of the place of tourism in their community— although all may not view it positively. In the latter case community leaders, businessmen, and citizens may not even recognize tourism as a significant part of their local economy.

Tourism profit dependent firms. These businesses make 20 percent to 50 percent of their sales to tourists. While residents make up half or more of their market, most could not exist without the revenue and profits derived from tourists' sales, or could not maintain their present level of services to citizens of the local community.

Food services are the most common type of operation falling within this class. In many states food services are found to make 25 to 40 percent of

their sales to tourists. Food services are also usually a significant part of the local and state economy, often amounting to five percent or more of the gross state product.

In communities having a relatively large tourism industry, other businesses that will be found in this profit dependent class include grocery stores, gasoline and other automobile services, sporting goods, and recreational services.

Resident sales dependent firms. These are firms making some sales directly to tourists, but in an amount less than 20 percent of their total sales. They are thus not directly dependent upon tourists' sales for volume. While profits derived from tourists' sales may contribute importantly to total profits, most of these firms could operate in about their present form if they served only residents.

Included in this classification are all retail operations not noted above, whether they provide goods or services. General merchandise, clothing, drugs, hardware, building materials, health care, and legal services are among them. In many communities where tourism sales are not a large percentage of total retail sales—the case with many metropolitan areas—all retail operations except lodging and sometimes food services are in this classification.

Firms making indirect sales to tourists—the multiplier. We have noted that all operations offering goods and services at retail make direct sales to tourists. Nearly every economic activity in the community is partly augmented by tourism whether or not they make direct sales to tourists. This is through the mechanism of roundabout purchases. For example: the owner of a restaurant and its employees will purchase clothing and groceries from local stores; they will live in homes upon which they pay taxes, and that are often built by local carpenters, who are supplied from local lumber yards. This is called the "multiplier" effect.

The multiplier mechanism is discussed in detail in Chapter 6. At this stage it is sufficient to note that all community components are influenced by the tourism industry, and that the overall impact upon the community's economy is greater than the sum of direct sales to tourists.

Questions for review and further study

1. Why should we not make a Census of Business classification for tourism firms?

2. Why should a business traveler be classed as a tourist?

3. Explain why the purposes for travel to different cities vary so much from one city to the next.

4. What do you understand to be meant by saying that the tourist product is produced as it is consumed?

5. What are the possible non-tourist outputs of a lodging firm?

6. During the 1950 to 1980 period visits to elements of the National Park System increased rapidly. At the same time the number of units in the system were increased. Discuss this in terms of "supply" and "demand". (Hint: See Chapter 9, Say's Law).

7. Would it be desirable to a) increase tourism, or b) decrease tourism, in the United States and Canada? Explain your answer.

SUGGESTIONS FOR FURTHER READING

Clawson, M., & J. Knetsch. (1966). *Economics of Outdoor Recreation Resources for the Future.* Baltimore, MD: The Johns Hopkins Press.

McIntosh, R., & C. Goeldner. (1984). *Tourism Principles, Practices and Philosophies* (4th ed). New York and Toronto: John Wiley and Sons.

Murphy, P. (1985). *Tourism, a Community Approach.* New York: Methune, Inc.

Rosenow, J., & G. Pulsipher. (1979). *Tourism, the Good, the Bad, and the Ugly.* Lincoln, NE: Century Three Press.

Walsh, R. (1986). *Recreation Economic Decisions: Comparing Benefits and Costs.* State College, PA: Venture Publishing Co.

Weaver, G. (1986). *Tourism USA.* U.S. Department of Commerce.

TEXTUAL REFERENCES

Ballman, G., & U. Blank. (1982). *Impact! Ely Tourism.* Ely, MN: Ely Area Development Council.

Blank, U., & M. Petkovich. (1979). *Minneapolis-St. Paul's Travel-Tourism.* St. Paul, MN: University of Minnesota.

Blank, U. (1982). *Life Style-Tourism Interrelationships of Minneapolis-St. Paul Residents* (Staff Paper P82-9). St. Paul, MN: University of Minnesota, Department of Agricultural and Applied Economics.

Blank, U. & T. Knopp. (1984). *The North Shore's Travel-Tourism Industry and Its Market Segments.* (Sea Grant Research Report No. 7). St. Paul, MN: University of Minnesota.

Clawson, M., & J. Knetsch. (1966). *Economics of Outdoor Recreation Resources for the Future.* Baltimore, MD: The Johns Hopkins Press.

Fedler, A. (1987). Are leisure, recreation and tourism interrelated? *Annals of Tourism Research, 14*(3). Elmsford, NY: Pergamon Press.

Kaplan, M. (1975). *Leisure Theory and Policy.* New York: John Wiley and Sons Inc.

Kent, W., P. Shock, & R. Snow (1983). Shopping: Tourism's unsung hero(ine). *Journal of Travel Research, 21*(4).

Laventhol & Horwath (1986). *1985 Convention Income.* Champaign IL : IACVB.

MacCannell, D. (1976). The Tourist: A New Theory of the Leisure Class. New York: Schocken Books.

McNulty, R., et al. (1985). *The Economics of Amenity: Community Futures and Quality of Life.* Washington, DC: Partners for Livable Places.

Rosenow, J., & G. Pulsipher. (1979). *Tourism, the Good, the Bad, and the Ugly.* Lincoln, NE: Century Three Press.

Tourism Canada (1986). *U.S. Pleasure Travel Market.* Ottawa: Department of Regional Industrial Expansion.

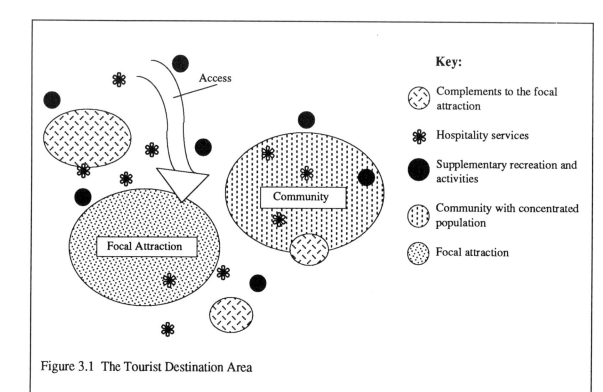

Figure 3.1 The Tourist Destination Area

THREE

The Community As a Tourist Destination Area

This chapter continues with an analytical and definitional treatment of the essential parts of a tourism system.

THE COMMUNITY AS A TOURIST DESTINATION AREA

We have previously used the term "destination"; what is a tourist destination area (TDA)? This concept deserves detailed discussion.

Perhaps the best approach toward understanding a TDA is to think of some places that you may have visited that stand out in your memory. If you have been there, you remember vividly: Washington, D.C.; the Hawaiian Islands; Plymouth, Massachusetts.

Why do you recall these places so distinctly? Each has an appeal to travelers that is widespread and powerful. And the appeal of each is distinctive:

— Washington, D.C. is the seat of the government of the most powerful nation on earth. The trappings of its power and culture are displayed in numerous ways.

— The Hawaiian Islands offer an idyllic setting with waving palm trees, warm seas, beautiful beaches and a delightful climate.

— Plymouth, Massachusetts is the landing site of the Pilgrim Colony, and includes the fabled Plymouth Rock. Nearly all U.S. citizens have known about Plymouth since their early school years. Also there is realistically developed Plimouth Plantation that skillfully interprets the life and individuals of the early Pilgrim Colony.

Travelers' recollections of each of these places make up their *tourist destination area image* for each site. This is the appeal that each site exerts upon travelers to visit that specific area. The appeal may be widespread and powerful, as is the case for the three examples given. Such destinations will draw large numbers of travelers. The appeal may be specialized, so that only certain segments of the traveling market are attracted; for example, ski enthusiasts are mainly the ones attracted to ski resorts. Many factors, such as travel costs and time requirements, may operate to modify the appeal.

As a working definition, the following is suggested for a *tourist destination area*. A TDA has: 1) a recognized, definable appeal to travelers; 2) a tourism industry of sufficient scale to deserve treatment as a factor in the local economy; 3) coherence in its geography and among its tourist-related features; and 4) political integrity, so that effective communications can take place and viable decisions can be made.

The reader may easily understand how the three examples given above fit the definition of a TDA. "But," you may ask, "what about the Corn Belt, the Great Plains or the Appalachian regions; how would one community there be distinguishable from another?" Actually, communities are as individual as are human beings, each with distinctive qualities all its own. Even in the same general region each small community differs from its neighbor community. In the Plains state of Kansas, Abilene increasingly develops its tourism character as the former home of President Dwight Eisenhower. Dodge

City, on the other hand, with its Boot Hill, projects an image of the wide-open, lawless West.

THE TOURIST DESTINATION AREA IMAGE

Tourists make travel decisions based upon their mental images of possible destinations. What they think about a location—their destination area image—is *the real reality that motivates tourists to travel.*

If a given TDA's image is in a traveler's mental foreground, beckoning, alluring and positive, that traveler will expend effort and bear significant cost to reach that particular tourist destination area (Graefe, 1987). On the other hand, a tourist will expend little effort and cost to travel to a TDA having, for him or her, a negative or weak image.

The tourist destination area image may be thought of as an average of the concepts of the area held by all travelers or would-be travelers to the area. An area's image will, however, be unique with respect to each individual traveler. Every community generates such an image—appealing or repulsive, dazzling or feeble. The creation of a compelling destination image is tourism marketing's job.

A positive image motivates travel to the given TDA by promising positive rewards from travel there (Hunt, 1975). These rewards, plus other considerations, constitute a complex package made up of: 1) experiences and rewards—derived from things seen, done and felt and people interacted with; 2) status—personal satisfaction at one's choice of a travel place, and prestige before one's associates; and 3) acceptable costs in terms of money, time, risk and effort. These factors are all assessed by the traveler in making a destination choice.

A distinctive travel destination area image makes possible differentiation in the marketplace. The greater the level of distinction that a TDA can achieve, the more this factor can be used as leverage in its advertising and promotional programs. It may also give the area a degree of monopoly control in pricing its product. Use of any such advantages requires market segmentation (discussed in Chapter 9) so that marketing effort is directed toward those tourists specifically attracted by the area, and possibly willing to pay higher prices for the privilege of going there.

Not to be overlooked is the potential for using a distinctive tourist destination area image in building community pride and *esprit de corps*. Everyone likes to feel that their community is special. This helps them to appreciate their community, and to feel good about themselves. It is an important, intangible ingredient of living quality that is sought by all. Individuals, in addition to wishing to travel to distinctive areas, increasingly also want to live in distinctive areas—and increasingly they are footloose and can do so (see discussion of Quality of Living Theory of Community Development in Chapter 6).

WHAT PRODUCES A TOURIST DESTINATION AREA IMAGE?

We have seen that tourists travel to a location where they think—have a mental image—that they will have a positive, rewarding life experience. These experiences are delivered by the things that tourists see, do and feel there. Knowing this, every community wishing to further develop its tourist industry must repeatedly ask a three-fold question: "What is our tourist destination area image? What would we like it to be? How can we influence this image?"

We have also noted that the tourism industry cross-cuts a large part of the warp and woof of most communities where tourism is a significant factor. For that reason we would expect a wide spectrum of community features to have a bearing on the production of that community's tourist destination area image. And that is true. Everything that follows in this chapter, and in much of the content of other chapters, impacts upon image.

For our purposes here, we touch on only three aspects of image production. The reader should understand that this is a broad-brush approach, intended to highlight salient factors only.

Tourists do not go places that they have not heard about. This underscores need for an ongoing, multiphased communication program—including advertising and promotion—to relevant tourism consumer groups. An immediate implication is that the destination area has determined what image it wishes to project, has a specific policy regarding its image, and has built this policy into its advertising and promotional programs.

Attractions are the first order for a tourist destination area. Tourists, we have said, go places because they think they will have a positive, rewarding experience from the things that they see and do. Virtually every community has the potential for a high-magnitude attraction. In reviewing examples of attractions, we will see that they may be as richly varied in character as all reality.

Tourists go where they are invited, and stay where they feel welcome. This calls not only for reaching out with promotion but also for genuine hospitality (Gray, 1986). An area's image can rise or fall on the basis of its hosting capability. Tourists readily sense welcome and warmth, in contrast to indifference or even disdain. Their ability to positively experience even major attractions depends partly upon the eagerness of residents to share that feature with them. Without eager sharing—hosting—only a partial experience, or possibly a negative experience, may result.

In summary, a positive tourist destination area image requires three factors:

— Tourists must have favorable information about it.
— The area must afford a positive attraction of things to see and do.
— Tourists must feel invited and welcome.

WHAT'S IN A NAME?

There is a lot in a name when it comes to its use in identifying precisely a travel destination area. It is desirable for the name to focus unambiguously upon a specific geographic area. If, in addition, the name also generates an image of the primary experience, this makes it even more appropriate.

Some high-profile tourist destination areas achieve almost universal name recognition, both for geographic and activity purposes. Disney World identifies not only Orlando, Florida but also a major family recreation experience. Las Vegas not only identifies the city by that name in Nevada, but is immediately recognized as offering a gaming experience.

Unfortunately many less prominent and/or smaller TDA's cannot hope to achieve the wide name recognition of Disney World and Las Vegas. To the extent that they have a choice of a name, they should select one that uniquely identifies them. Often nondescript names are selected. Examples include Eastern, Central, Pioneer, River, etc. These types of names, while they may apply, could also fit many other locations.

Studies of the names that tourists use to identify the area in which they vacation suggest that, for a destination area name to achieve widespread acceptance and positive site identification, there are at least four major considerations (Blank, 1975):

— The most readily identified destination area name type is that of a major physical feature. It may be that of a city, a lake, a river or a mountain.
— The name should appear on area maps, and be prominently used in advertising and promotional literature by both governmental and private entities.
— The name can be further reinforced by road signs and by other signs in the immediate vicinity.
— Activity uniquely associated with the area that is identified by the name provides further reinforcement.

Names contribute to tourist destination area images. In cases where all of the above considerations are incorporated into naming and its reinforcement, even relatively small areas have been found to achieve name recognition and identification by 95 percent or more of their visitors.

THE COMPLETE TOURIST DESTINATION AREA

Now it is useful to view an overall tourist destination area as an integrated whole. Of what does it consist? How do the several parts interrelate with each other and the area's tourism industry?

Figure 3.1 is a diagrammatic model of a tourist destination area. Shown are the essential features that must be present to support a tourism industry. Figure 3.1, and our discussion of it here, in effect expands the definition of a tourist destination area. These features are treated in detail below; in summary they include:

— The Focal Attraction
— Hospitality Services
— Complements to the Focal Attraction
— Supplementary Recreational/Activity Opportunities
— Access System
    — Transportation
    — Communications
— The Community
    — Economic System
    — Infrastructure
    — Local Citizens
— Integrating Characteristics

The Focal Attraction (or Attractions)

This is the primary tourist attracting feature. It sets the area's theme and overall thrust of its tourist appeal. Usually it provides the major "see and do" experiences. In addition, it is also the primary

factor in tourists' destination area images (Gunn, 1988).

The attractions in a community correlate with purposes for travel as discussed in Chapter 2, the section titled "Why Do Tourists Tour?" Each community will have a unique attractions' mix: for those who come to visit friends, the attraction will be specific individual residents; travelers coming to shop are attracted by the retail services; business travelers may come because of the governmental offices, or business headquarters; and so on— forming a unique mix in every community.

This discussion primarily groups the potential recreational and cultural features for development into focal attractions by the tourist destination area. It should also be recognized that shopping, business, medical and legal services operate as attractions, and may be *the* focal attractor in some communities. In the latter case recreational and cultural features may act as secondary attractions, or as complements to the focal attraction.

The cultural/recreational focal attraction(s) of any area may be based upon natural resources, man-made resources, human resources, or combinations of these. It may have only visual access—the case of a monument or scenic overlook. It may invite or require deep immersion and personal activity and involvement, as in the case of a hiking trail, a fishing area, or a significant historical site. We will review numerous examples of communities' focal attractions. The varied basis upon which they can develop will become clear from these examples.

Some may question, "My community has no outstanding natural or historical feature to serve as a major attraction. How then can we develop a tourism industry?" It is to exactly such a community that this discussion is directed. Every community has much more to build a tourism industry upon than might initially be supposed. Where there are major obvious features, seldom is local initiative required. The communities at Niagara, Ontario, and Niagara, New York have experienced large tourism development efforts, most of it from outside the original communities, and of both a governmental and private nature. This development at Niagara has been good if one views all tourism industry development as good. Such development also has undesirable features, since much of what happens is beyond the control of the local community.

Often the development around a major feature is initiated outside the community. An unfortunate result is that while there is development *in the community*, development *of the community* itself may be neglected (Fitzgerald, 1986). An important purpose here is to provide avenues whereby communities may realize healthy growth, with a viable tourism industry contributing to that healthy growth.

Some Directions in Focal Attraction Development

For communities investigating ways, means and factors for developing an effective focal attraction, guideline principles are suggested. Some of these are in the form of questions to be raised. These, along with the numerous examples given in this and other chapters, illustrate what has happened in many communities and can happen in many more.

All tourism attractions are the result of human development. This is true even though every tourist attraction has a resource and environmental base. It is also the case for "whole cloth" features such as an amusement park. Even those attractions that appear to be mainly a God-given resource require that they be set apart and designated. They also require conservation, access (both information and physical), and all of the other elements that are discussed throughout this chapter in order for tourists to receive a rewarding experience.

Asking certain key questions by the community will assist the investigation for attractions. These include:

What are our outstanding indigenous community features? Those things that are part of the community offer the best opportunity for showing off that community, providing an attraction that not only resonates with the community ambiance, but one that many others cannot duplicate easily. This allows the community to have a differentiated tourism product. In addition, such a feature lends itself best to management and control by the community. Look first at the main community characteristics. If it is an agricultural community, can the agriculture be showcased and interpreted? If it is a logging community, can natural history and logging management be featured? What is prominent or unusual about the community's history, culture, geology, economy, ecology?

Is it appropriate and fitting for our community? This is another way of saying, avoid the ersatz. Tourists expect both attractions and services to be congruent with the community's character. As a naive example, a sea shell exchange is hardly appropriate in the middle of a cornfield, or forest, or desert; sea shells should be sold by the seashore! Italian cuisine will sell best in an Italian community. An Indian pageant will usually attract markets better if it is in an area made famous by Indian use. Complementing features can best enhance and expand the focal attraction's experience when that attraction meshes with the community's makeup.

Can the attraction be developed and managed so as to offer a visitor experience of outstanding quality? If what is done is second or third rate, it may be wasted effort and a lost community investment.

There is a place and need for "whole cloth" developments. The nation's 600 theme and amusement parks, along with many sports arenas, prove the place of non-site-specific recreational facilities. These may be the focal attraction, or they may be complements/supplements.

Chapters 10, 11, and 12 discuss the principles of achieving positive results in community effort toward tourism industry development.

Some Classes and Examples of Focal Attractions

The listing that follows is intended to further assist in the definition of a focal attraction and to help show the varied base upon which it may develop. The classification and the listing is far from being fully inclusive.

Natural resources or a natural feature are usually thought of first, and they serve as the focal feature of many TDA's. As noted both in this chapter and in Chapter 7, however, the natural endowment is by no means the sole or limiting factor in tourism industry development.

— Jackson Hole, Wyoming has at its core the Grand Teton National Park, including spectacular mountains and rivers. These would appear to be powerful attractors. But its real popularity derives from the hospitality and recreational services of Jackson Hole community, the area's dude ranches, ski facilities, and river rafting services. It must also be noted that interest of members of the Rockefeller family in Jackson Hole served as a powerful assist to facility development in that community.

— Communities situated near major natural features that are designated as elements of national or state parks have the opportunity to use the otherwise *unpurchasable publicity of the public feature.* They can offer complementing recreational attractions and support visits to the park with hospitality services.

— Many communities situated on lesser water features, such as rivers and lakes, underutilize the *powerful attraction of water recreation.* There can not only be provision for water activity (power boating, fishing, swimming, and canoeing) but special water-related events.

— The local terrain may offer opportunity for special activities such as sightseeing, nature interpretation, and various kinds of trail uses.

— Local ecology and geology are fascinating to many visitors, and seldom interpreted. Cass County, Minnesota has excellent fishing lakes. In addition, in the 1970s the county commissioners established the 3600-acre Grand Portage Nature Preserve. It has a statewide support group which has developed facilities and interpretive services. It is available to all area visitors, helping them to understand and appreciate the area's soils, water, fauna, flora, and climate.

— Some communities have spectacular phenomena of widespread interest. The great tides of the Bay of Fundy and the tidal bore at Moncton, New Brunswick are outstanding examples.

Economic activity. Most travelers are interested in how people live and work in the area where they are traveling. But seldom is the local economy interpreted to visitors. Typically, local residents see themselves as producers of widgets, wheat, or woolens; often they disdain tourism as unproductive. Properly approached, interpretation of economic activity, present or past, can not only serve as a major visitor attractor, but also add much to residents' appreciation of who and what they are.

— The former mill town of Lowell, Massachusetts offers a fascinating look into that community's former economy. Much of the town has been restored and is now interpreted by the community and the National Park Service. Without this initiative, it would remain just another obscure has-been community.

— Although agriculture occupies a large part of the U.S. landscape, only about two percent of the work force can be classed as farmers. Recognizing the need for appreciation and understanding of agriculture, the Agricultural Hall of Fame and National Center has been set up at Bonner Springs, Kansas. One of the more comprehensive interpretations of past and present agriculture is provided at Living History Farms, Des Moines, Iowa.

— Lumbering, particularly in the north-woods, has always enjoyed an aura of swashbuckling romance. A State Historical Society Logging Museum and Interpretive Center tells the story at Grand Rapids, Michigan. At Hayward, Wisconsin, logging traditions and meals can be enjoyed in the private hospitality services.

— Not many people engage in mining. For that reason most are unfamiliar with the industry and are fascinated by the huge piles of mining waste, from the copper mines of Butte, Montana, to the phosphate mines of central Florida. In relatively few places is access provided for visitors to mining operations and mining communities. Positive examples include the opportunity to watch iron-ore loading docks at Marquette, Michigan; the Iron Range Interpretive Center, Chisholm, Minnesota; and interpretation of a lead mining community at Galena, Illinois. The Lavender Pit Mine, Queen Mine, and the Copper Queen Hotel give the visitor to Bisbee, Arizona an experience of the days when copper mining boomed there; and Durango, Colorado combines the mystique of gold and silver mining in the San Juan Mountains with authentic steam train rides, nearby Indian ruins, and recreational activities of rafting, skiing and trail riding.

— Industrial plant tours serve a number of communities well as major tourism attractions. This is particularly true for unusual processes, or where the product is consumed directly by the general public (Farlow, 1979). A Minnesota study found many plant tours in metropolitan centers, but, significantly, it also found 16 major tours offered in smaller communities (Simonson, 1974). Among the many U.S. plant tours, we highlight two below.

— Nearly all North American citizens are familiar with Kellogg's breakfast products. This widespread knowledge makes a visit to the Kellogg plant at Battle Creek, Michigan especially appealing.

— Hershey products are as well-known as Kellogg's. At Hershey, Pennsylvania, the Hershey Chocolate Company provides a center that interprets the entire story of cocoa from its production as a bean through the processing into consumer products. Other attractions, including an amusement park, are also available at the site.

The community's ethnic/cultural make-up is as fascinating to travelers as is the economy. People never tire of learning about other people (Tighe, 1985). Along with community history, unique features of the culture may be the most widely available factor upon which to develop a focal attraction. As is the case with the economy, showcasing the community culture can not only attract visitors but also play a major role in teaching community residents to appreciate and have pride in their community. Examples of ethnic/cultural attractions include the following:

— Stratford, Ontario brings a bit of English culture to the North American continent. It features formal English gardens and a repertoire of Shakespearean drama productions.

— The historic community of Bardstown, Kentucky presents a Stephen Foster festival that plays to a million and a half spectators in its three-month summer session. Virtually the entire community is involved in production of the festival.

— In Lancaster County, Pennsylvania, the Amish and Mennonite cultures and folkways attract millions of visitors annually. To help avoid personal intrusions and interference, they now provide museums, tours, and other points where visitors may concentrate and also spend money while admiring these unique communities.

— From Appalachia to the Ozarks there are numerous communities offering interpretations of the hill people's folklore, music and crafts. Among the many communities where there are opportunities to see and practice crafts and learn about folk ways are Berea, Kentucky, and Mountain View, Arkansas.

— German culture is interpreted in many smaller communities including New Ulm, Minnesota; Herman, Missouri; and Fredericksburg, Texas.

— Parts of metropolitan areas specialize in providing an ethnic ambience such as in the French Quarter, known as the Vieux Carre, of New Orleans; in Germantown in Columbus, Ohio; and in Old City, Albuquerque, New Mexico.

— Amana Colonies, Iowa offer superb food, quality locally made products, and a cultural/ historical experience in a productive agricultural setting.

Historic features abound. Every community has its own unique romance of human sweat, toil, tears, blood, failures, hopes and triumphs. These combine to weave together the story of every home, school, church, industry and indeed, every community. The appeal of history is attested by the estimated 76 million visits made to historic sites in 1985 (Makens, 1987). The richness and variety of the human tale is apparent in even a handful of examples:

— The little village of Grand Pre, Nova Scotia had a 150-year history of development by the French before the English arrived. It is best known as the site immortalized by Longfellow in *Evangeline* in which Evangeline is separated from her lover Gabriel.

— Hannibal, Missouri showcases its Mark Twain heritage, showing such features as the Becky Thatcher House and the cave in which Tom Sawyer and Becky were lost.

— The John Dillinger Historical Museum, Nashville, Indiana, interprets a colorful if tragic part of U.S. history.

— Connoisseurs of western novels might regard the Zane Grey Museum at Norwich, Ohio a "must see" attraction.

— Cherokee, North Carolina interprets the story of the Cherokee Indians in the Blue Ridge Mountains with a museum, Indian Village and an outstanding pageant, *Unto These Hills.*

Climatic attractions draw many people to enjoy and experience conditions different from that in their home area. One such type is the fun-in-the-sun attraction of the southern United States, Caribbean Islands, and South Seas Islands, which draw many tourists. At the opposite extreme, northern climates such as the snow and winter vacation areas of Canada, the Northern United States and mountain areas also attract visitors. In all of these cases, provision for access and facilities for activities are needed.

Religious attractions induce travel not only on the part of adherents to a specific belief, but for a wide spectrum of tourists. Illustrating the range are the following:

— The Mormon interpretation at Navoo, Illinois.

— The Billy Graham Center, adjacent to the campus of Wheaton College, Wheaton, Illinois.

— The Mother Christian Science Church, Boston, Massachusetts.

— Passion Plays, performed at a number of locations including South Dakota and Arkansas. In both of these locations the Passion Play is part of a larger recreational complex.

Specialty tourism attractions are, like the religious attractions noted above, mostly manmade. These include stadiums for major league and college sports. Among others are race tracks for dogs, horses and cars, and the horse-shoe pitching coliseum at Genola, Minnesota. Presidential memorials could be included in this class, or as cultural attractions. Examples include Johnson City, Texas, memorializing Lyndon Johnson and the "Texas Hill Folks"; and West Branch, Iowa, memorializing Herbert Hoover.

Outdoor recreational activities rank among the top tourism attractions in many small communities. Opportunities for fishing and hunting are among the top such activity attractions. There are, in addition, many others:

— The Sparta-Elroy hiking/biking trail was one of the first established in the United States along an abandoned railroad bed. It is in central Wisconsin, and brings tens of thousands of tourists to the small communities along its 33-mile route.

— Canoeing and river-floating recreational opportunities are now available along many scenic rivers in the nation.

— Campgrounds attract many to unique locations such as the harbor-side campground in the picturesque fishing village of Grand Marias, Minnesota.

Events can act as the focal attraction in their own right. It is also noted below that events often operate as complementing features to the focal attraction. Among the many kinds of attracting events are sports contests, fairs, expositions and celebrations.

— The Rose Bowl Game in Pasadena, California provides an outstanding example. Others are: State Fairs; the Veiled Prophet Celebration, St. Louis, Missouri; Aquetennial, Minneapolis, Minnesota; Mardi Gras, New Orleans, Louisiana; Stampede, Calgary, Alberta; Winter Carnival, St. Paul, Minnesota; American Royal, Kansas City, Missouri and the Presidential Inauguration, Washington, D.C.

Multiple or secondary attractors. In only a few situations does the pristine concept of a single focal attraction, around which all of the community's tourism revolves, apply. In northern Arizona the Grand Canyon of the Colorado River approaches the concept, but even it does not fully stand alone. The nearby American Indian communities, other area communities and lesser natural features also attract travelers.

Many communities have a multi-faceted attractions complex. This is particularly the case with metropolitan areas. In large cities the population, shopping opportunities, cultural features, medical services, governmental offices and many other attractions interract to attract travel.

As noted in the case of the Grand Canyon, immediately above, there may be a dominant focal attraction. But in nearly all communities there will also be secondary attractions that are independent of the focal attraction and that generate travel in their own right. Many of these do not relate to the focal attraction, and thus are not complementing features.

These multiple attractions, whether of equal or unequal magnitude in their appeal, operate to expand the community's tourism industry. The mechanism whereby they accomplish this end is discussed in the section titled "Multi-Purpose Travel; Multi-Faceted Travel Attractors."

Hospitality Services of Food and Lodging

These make it possible for tourists to live in the area, away from home. Without hospitality services, the focal attractor and its supporting elements could only be enjoyed by people living nearby, by passers-through, or by those willing to "rough it."

Hospitality services are usually a primary means whereby the community derives income from tourists. They are thus as essential as the focal attraction(s) in determining an area's tourism industry. Adequate hospitality services are a part of the development necessary to avoid the condition of the "worst of all worlds" with regard to tourism resource use, which is discussed in detail in Chapter 7. In such a situation resources are consumed or lessened in quality without compensating income to the community.

Often hospitality services may operate in such close conjunction with the focal feature as to be inseparable from it, such as the chalet at a ski run or the club-house at a golf course. In some cases the hospitality facility may become the focal feature, as in the case of famous resorts and inns, outstanding restaurants, and metropolitan hotels selling weekend packages (O'Dwyer, 1988).

The quality of hospitality facilities and services can be a major factor in whether an area's tourism industry declines, lags or expands. Hospitality businesses require constant updating to maintain current market appeal. We will see in a later section of this chapter ("The Problem of Obsolescence") that an area can easily find itself with costs sunk in an obsolescent tourism plant, along with inadequate management. A tourist destination area that is thus encumbered will usually suffer losses in destination area image and in market position.

Complementing Features and Services

Complementing features operate to expand and extend the experience, image, impact and influence of the focal attraction. They do this by providing added experiences—things to see and do that are directly related to the experience provided by the focal attraction. They may provide added access, either physical, interpretive or informational. Sometimes complementing features greatly deepen the experience of the focal attraction. In cases akin to the latter, the complementing feature may become an alternative focal attraction. Two communities demonstrate the key role of complementing features and services.

Pipestone, Minnesota, a community of 5,000 population, is sited in the thinly populated region of southwestern Minnesota. Adjacent are deposits of Catlinite, the soft red rock used by Indians to fashion peace pipes. The quarry site is sacred to Indian tribes, and is designated as a National

Monument. A visit to the Monument gives one a feel for the reverence held for the locality by Indians. Two complementing features add powerfully to the experience.

Only Indians are permitted to mine and work the Catlinite. This they continue to do, fashioning pipes and other items. It adds much to observe this work in process. Purchase of a genuine peace pipe as a memento perpetuates the experience over the years.

In the late 1940s a Pipestone resident had the inspiration of a major addition: an interpretive enactment of Longfellow's poem, *The Song of Hiawatha*. The initiator persevered and the idea caught fire in Pipestone. Today a professionally rendered soundtrack narrates *The Song of Hiawatha* as it is enacted on three weekends a year before an audience of thousands. The cast consists of Pipestone residents. Outstanding lighting effects are produced on the outdoor, life-size stage by a reported 15 miles of electrical wiring.

On-site peace pipe production and *The Song of Hiawatha* greatly expand the experience of a visit to the Pipestone National Monument.

The Black Hills of South Dakota exude the aura of the 1874 gold rush in a 5,000 square mile area. The Gold Rush era is interpreted in the towns of Deadwood, Hill City, and Lead, where active gold mining continues. A secondary image of the prairie West along with unusual geology includes the Badlands National Park. This expands the destination area to 10,000 square miles, a true western-scale, and one of the largest TDA's. The Black Hills' image was greatly enhanced by the Mt. Rushmore monument begun in 1927 by Gutzon Borglum.

Complementing the gold rush era are Indian and wild western country experiences. The statue of Chief Crazy Horse takes form on Crazy Horse Mountain, initiated in 1948 by Korczak Ziolkowski. Old Fort Meade was an Indian peace-keeping outpost. Bear Butte, now a state park, was a sacred mountain to the Indians. Prairie Homestead

Historic Site shows prairie life in a sod dugout. The area's fauna, flora and geology are made accessible in many ways: A private, drive-through park provides viewing of bear, elk and big horn sheep; Custer State Park has the world's largest herd of buffalo; Badlands National Park preserves access to western badland topography, and aeons-old fossilized animal remains; and Mammoth Site yields new Mammoth bones only 26,000 years old.

Many other features serve to supplement the experiences available: Wall Drug, Black Hills Passion Play, hot springs baths, and western-style hospitality services.

Other Supplementary Recreational Activities

Many tourists wish to go to an unusual or different place for vacation. Oddly, while there, many of the things that they wish to do and will participate in are things that they could have done as well had they stayed at home. This forms part of their linkage to things familiar.

A familiar game appears especially rewarding when played in a new, different, and exotic ambience. For that reason golfing devotees will take a "golfing vacation" in which they try out the links in distant communities. Travel magazines often assist them in their quest for a new golfing experience (McCallen, 1985). Enthusiasts of other types of sports such as tennis may also take "sports vacations." Often specialized sporting magazines assist in indicating where the sport can be enjoyed (Socolow, 1988; Lichtenstein, 1985).

Such travel behavior suggests that communities seeking to develop their tourism industries are well advised to make adequate provision for everyday recreational activities: Golf, tennis, swimming, shopping, movies, bowling, bars, dancing and other activities. These facilities make it possible for visitors to participate in a familiar, enjoyable activity, and for people to meet people and at the same time enjoy an exotic ambience. These supplementary facilities and services act to broaden the area's tourism market appeal, extend the experiences available, expand the area's sales package, and its opportunity to generate income through the tourism industry.

The Community

From the viewpoint of the travel-recreation industry, the community consists of three parts:

The local economic system provides the livelihood for resident citizens. It includes the tourism industry along with other economic activities. A balanced, diversified economy usually serves the end of economic health and viability better over the long run, in contrast to concentration in a single economic activity. The tourism industry serves best in contributing to balance, expansion, economic health and stability rather than as the major or sole economic generator.

The local residents are people who give the community its human content. They also operate the services and facilities necessary for tourists' experiences. Local residents figure prominently in the community's delivery of a hosting experience.

Community infrastructure and services make it possible for the community to operate and for residents to live there. Roads, power utilities, telephone, water and waste disposal, and police and fire protection are among the items of infrastructure. These facilities and services are as essential to the tourism industry as they are for living by residents. In communities that are tourist-impacted, such as where population doubles or triples in the travel season, the infrastructure may need expansion in order to accommodate these temporary residents.

It is almost a rule that the essential role of the community in the area's delivery of tourism and recreational services will be underestimated if not

largely ignored by non-residents (Blank, 1980).
Such oversights commonly occur when "outside"
interests attempt new developments in a given
community. When proper community contact is not
established, the residents resist, and a confrontation
develops. This situation is discussed in detail in
Chapter 5.

The Access System

The access system includes both the transportation
and the information networks. People do not go to
places that they do not know about and/or that they
cannot get to by means that are reasonable to them.
The access/linkage system is treated in greater
detail in Chapter 8. In summary it includes the
following:

*The communications/information access
system* includes two-way communication from the
TDA to its market, and from the market to the TDA.
Information access includes all means by which
tourists gain destination area images except on-site
visits.

Transportation/physical/visual access. The
nature and quality of transportation affects both the
number and types of traveler/vacationers. Good air
travel access and improved highway access may
greatly expand the market possibilities for a
destination area. For many features, access must
not only be physical, but also visual. In cases where
sightseeing is an important part of the experience,
the provision of visual access may be a priority
item. Visual access may, in turn, involve both
transportation and information systems. Transportation within the given area not only includes
provision for access, but may be a major part of the
area experience.

Integrating Characteristics

Ambience, integrity and scale operate as integrating
factors. They are less tangible than the six features
treated immediately above. Together with those six
features, ambience, integrity and scale produce a
Tourist Destination Area, an area having a special
mystique and aura for the traveler, plus both
positive market definition and critical mass.

Ambience is the overall aura or mystique. It can
sometimes be almost palpably felt: On the Atlantic
Coast in Maine; in the majestic giant Sequoias of
California; deep within the northwoods of Ontario;
surrounded by the open big-sky country of Montana; enveloped in the clubby, antique intimacy of
an old and famous inn; and while caught up in the
frantic, varied activity of a large city. Each TDA
has its own unique ambience which is variously
constituted from ingredients including the environment, the facilities, the hosts and the fellow visitors.

Integrity suggests the manner in which the
TDA's several parts function together to reinforce
the focal attractor and the area's overall appeal as a
travel destination. Prominent factors contributing to
integrity are internal communication and cooperation, and *esprit de corps*.

Scale ensures that the TDA is of a size sufficient to have critical mass large enough to support
the essential components and to have sufficient
attracting power. At the same time it must be small
enough to communicate and function internally.
Scale may be as narrowly circumscribed as Gettysburg National Battlefield plus the immediately
adjacent Gettysburg, Pennsylvania community. It
may be as large as the combined communities
around Kentucky and Barkeley Lakes in Kentucky
and Tennessee, including the two lakes plus the
Land Between the Lakes.

MULTI-PURPOSE TRAVEL: MULTI-FACETED TRAVEL ATTRACTORS

Much travel is multi-purpose in nature. That is, travel is undertaken because travelers find that the total appeal of two or more travel attractions in the same area is sufficient to induce them to make a trip that they would not undertake for either attraction singly. This observation builds the case for multiple attractors, as well as for well developed complementing features and supplementary activity attractions.

Figure 3.2 illustrates the case implied by much of the discussion in this chapter, where the appeal of one major focal feature succeeds in generating travel. Line 'S' is the perceived schedule of costs required for experiences supplied. Line 'D' is the schedule of willingness to pay for experiences gained by a given traveler to a given destination area. Since lines S and D intersect, travel will take place, assuming there is no other more attractive destination area. The price 'P' may, in addition to money, include time, effort and other cost factors. The quantity 'Q' includes the total of all travel experiences consumed.

The reader will note that a tourism supply curve may be thought of from more than one viewpoint. In this example we are considering the supply curve offered by a community as perceived by the prospective traveler. This supply curve will be unique to each traveler. In other analyses, the aggregate supply curve for tourism services offered by the community to all tourists may be appropriate.

Figure 3.3 illustrates a situation in which travel will not occur. It might be the case of an individual wishing to confer with an agency official in the state capitol. The supply 's_1' and demand 'd_1' lines do not intersect; the individual will use the telephone, mail, or simply forgo conferring.

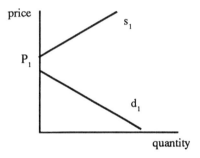

Figure 3.3 Non-Travel

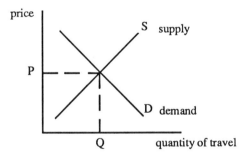

Figure 3.2 Supply-Demand Equilibrium in Community Tourism

Figure 3.4 also illustrates a non-travel situation. It might be the case of a major sports event which of itself lacks sufficient appeal to attract the given individual to travel. In both Figures 3.3 and 3.4, 'p_1', the intercept of the supply curve on the price axis, represents the cost of travel to the given area.

Now assume that the situations illustrated in Figures 3.3 and 3.4 occur in the same destination, and are faced by the same potential traveler. Figure 3.5 shows what may happen. The supply lines 's_1' and 's_2' can be summed. The resulting total supply curve, 's_T', still intersects the price axis at 'P_1', since cost of travel does not change, but the curve is more horizontal. The total demand curve 'D_T'

which is the summation of 'd$_1$' and 'd$_2$' has now shifted up and to the right. The result is that 'S$_T$' and 'D$_T$' now intersect, and barring more attractive travel possibilities, the traveler will undertake/ consume travel experiences in the quantity 'Q' at a cost of 'P$_2$'.

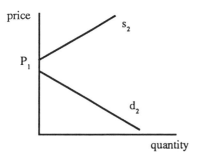

Figure 3.4 Non-Travel

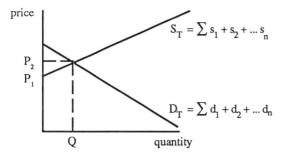

Figure 3.5 Multiple Supply and Demand:
Travel Occurs

The idea of multi-purpose travel might appear to do violence to the pristine concept of travel generated by a destination image derived from a single powerful focal feature. But every community has more than one travel attractor. The larger and more complex the community, the more multi-faceted its travel attracting capabilities. We have noted that tourists to metropolitan areas frequently have secondary travel purposes, such as shopping, cultural events and sports events. The mix of the appeal of each of these attractions will differ for each traveler; indeed the mix will probably be different for each traveler on each different trip. Thus the destination area image consists in one case of a major sports event and a satisfying restaurant meal; in another case it consists of shopping facilities and an evening's theater entertainment; and many other variations and combinations may occur.

A CLASSIFICATION OF TOURISM DESTINATION AREAS

In this preliminary discussion of the what, how, who and where of tourism, we now look at one approach to classifying destination areas. This approach is intended to assist the individual or group concerned with tourism development in thinking further about the basis for the local tourism industry and the most appropriate steps for its further advancement.

High-Amenity Recreational Areas

Some communities are endowed with high-amenity resources such as major unique geology, high quality water, mountains, or winter sun. They have a well-recognized tourism industry from the viewpoint of both tourists and local residents. Examples include larger cities such as San Diego, California and Phoenix, Arizona or they may be smaller such as Ely, Minnesota or West Conway, New Hampshire. Such communities usually have a set of well-established, definable, tourist-serving firms.

Specialty Tourism Communities

Specialty tourism communities have a special attraction for travelers; often it is a major man-made entertainment feature. Examples as Las Vegas, Nevada, and Orlando, Florida. The nature of the income from tourists will be unique in each case. In the case of Las Vegas, it concentrates in the gaming places. In Orlando, entertainment places such as Disney World are important direct beneficiaries of tourists' expenditures. In each case hospitality services complement the major feature.

Hinterland Metropolitan Area

Inland metropolitan areas, such as Indianapolis, Indiana, Cincinnati, Ohio, and Omaha, Nebraska appear to lack the travel appeal of cities situated on or near high-profile or natural amenities or man-made attractions such as those noted in the above two community classes. But every community has tourism, and this is as definitely true of inland/hinterland cities as it is of other, apparently more favorably sited communities. In the first place it should be recognized that all cities have location advantages relative to transportation routes and/or markets and/or resources. These advantages are responsible for the city's attaining its current stature. They are attributes that are all-too-frequently underestimated when the tourism of such inland/hinterland metropolitan areas is being considered.

Hinterland metropolitan areas have a surprisingly large tourism industry. It is usually based upon the areas' functioning as centers of trade, commerce, manufacturing, culture, human services and population. Because of the prominence of their trade center functions, a high proportion of their dollars received from tourists are from purchases made through retail stores and services. This in no way minimizes the role of hospitality services; they are essential. But, in addition to hospitality service

sales, the income from tourism is spread throughout a range of retail firm types (see Figure 2.4). Because of its more dispersed nature, the tourism industry of these communities may have a low profile that is easily underestimated.

Smaller Hinterland Communities

Smaller hinterland communities also have a tourism industry potential. They may initially lack spectacular natural endowments or the broad appeal of a large metropolitan area. But potential for expansion is limited only by the vision and initiative of their people.

The major thrust of this book is directed toward the last two destination area classes. These are the areas for which the "natural" tourism advantages are less obvious. Advantage is a relative term; tourism advantage can be developed. The benefits of a viable tourism industry are available to nearly all communities.

OBSOLESCENCE OF TOURISM DESTINATION AREAS

It has been noted by many students of tourism that tourism destination areas tend to come into strong market favor, and that many then experience a relative decline in popularity. Coney Island, New York is noted as a one-time immensely popular place that has long since lost its strong appeal. Resort vacationing in upstate New York and in the Upper Great Lakes area are other tourist destination areas that have experienced boom and bust in use, at least in relative terms.

What produces such cyclical market behavior? Many areas started as upscale areas, appealing to the wealthy. But there is a strong tendency for mass to follow class. Area quality and appeal often deteriorate as increasing volumes are served. Adding to the effect are technological developments in travel and in travel marketing; technological and marketing innovations almost always have differential effects upon different TDA's. Cyclical change is also produced by competing areas, coupled with failure of the given destination area to renew adequately.

Upper Great Lakes area resorting may be taken as an example. It began in the latter 19th century when vacation travel was the province mainly of the relatively well-to-do. It experienced its period of most rapid growth coinciding with the first mass family automobile travel in the 1930s, and continuing for a decade following World War II. It had the exotic appeal of pristine waters and semi-boreal forests; it had a natural air-conditioned climate; it almost had a monopoly on inland lakes fishing; and it was accessible to the majority of the United States population from the Middle Atlantic to the Midwestern states.

Then, dependable artificial air-conditioning became available; large artificial lake complexes were developed in other areas of the nation; and the fun-in-the-sun areas developed facilities and marketing. There were also major developments in demand and transport: Family incomes grew and with them, their travel aspirations; along with demand change was the introduction of mass travel by air. These developments not only made remote locations within the United States accessible, but put virtually all travel destination areas in the world in competition with all others. Throughout the progress of these developments, most communities of the Upper Great Lakes continued with business as usual, selling the northwoods as a fishing experience and mostly failing to tap into the newly developing marketing and travel systems.

These communities continue to offer an excellent vacation experience, but they failed badly to maintain relative market share, and are now caught with sunk costs in an obsolescent tourism plant. A part of their plight can be attributed to the normal processes of technological, social and economic development. But a major part was due to a myopia of what they were about. *Most appeared to think*

that they were selling a fishing experience. In reality they were in the vacation/fun business. As the market shifted, good tourism business operation required that they update facilities, activities offering and marketing procedures.

The problem of obsolescence in a destination area's tourism industry closely parallels the problem of maintaining market viability on the part of other industries. Why were the managers of the U.S. automobile industry apparently unable to foresee the strong market swing to smaller, fuel-efficient automobiles, that almost caused the demise of U.S. industry which continued to emphasize size and horsepower? Could the U.S. steel industry along with its labor unions have foreseen the near-fatal competition from overseas, and taken adequate corrective measures at an earlier stage before the United States suffered severe setbacks in its mining and ore processing operations?

The tourism industry in a given destination may have similar problems. It may become caught with sunk costs in an obsolescent plant. Its managers may fail to read the new marketing trends, and ignore new travel and other technologies. Not every area can nor should be *avant-garde*, but much can be accomplished with maintaining marketing methods and physical plant so that it remains abreast of current trends in the society and economy.

Questions for review and further study

1. Explain why the TDA's image is a crucial factor in its ability to successfully attract travelers.

2. In what sense can every part of a TDA be called a travel attraction?

3. Under what conditions (kind of tourist; purposes for travel; etc.) may an entire state be a TDA?

4. What distinctions do you make between "complementing features" and "other recreational features" of a TDA?

5. How closely related are the community's ambience and its focal attraction?

6. Identify two TDA's and explain how their characteristics fit the TDA definition.

7. Show ways in which the community can complement and expand upon tourists' experiences of its focal attraction.

SUGGESTION FOR FURTHER READING

Gunn, C. (1988). *Vacationscape, Designing Tourist Regions.* New York: Van Nostrand Reinhold. (Chapters 4 and 5).

Simonson, L., B. Koth, & G. Kreag. (1988). *So Your Community Wants Travel / Tourism? Guidelines for Attraction and Serving Visitors* CD-BU-3443, St. Paul, MN: Minnesota Extension Service, University of Minnesota.

Weaver, G. (1986). *Tourism USA.* U.S. Department of Commerce. (Chapter 5).

TEXTUAL REFERENCES

Blank, U. (1975). Tourists Define Area by Lakes, Communities. *Minnesota Travel Tourist Notes, 13*(2). St. Paul, MN: University of Minnesota.

Blank, U., L. Simonson, & G. Ballman. (1980). *A Needs Assessment of Tourism Firms Serving the Boundary Waters Canoe Area Wilderness Vicinity.* St. Paul, MN: Agricultural Extension Service, University of Minnesota.

Farlow, S. (1979). *Made in America: A Guide to Tours of Workshops, Farms, Mines and Industries.* New York: Hastings House Publications Inc.

Fitzgerald, J., & P. Meyer. (1986). Recognizing Constraints in Local Economic Development. *Journal of the Community Development Society, 17*(2). Athens, GA: University of Georgia.

Graefe, A., & J. Vaske. (1987). A Framework for Managing Quality in the Tourism Experience. *Annals of Tourism Research, 14*(3). Elmsford, NY: Pergamon Press.

Gray, J. (1986). *Marketing to Tourists.* Speech to Northeast Missouri Travel and Conference, Hannibal, MO.

Hunt, J. (1975). Image as a Factor in Tourism Development. *Journal of Travel Research, 13*(3).

Lichtenstein, G. (1985). Desert Delights. *World Tennis, 32*(9). New York: World Tennis Magazine.

Makens, J. (1987). Importance of U. S. Historic Sites as Visitor Attractions. *Journal of Travel Research, 25*(3). Boudler, CO: Business Research Division, University of Colorado.

McCallen, B. (1985). Legendary Links, A Golfer's Half-Dozen. *Travel Holiday, 164*(2). New York: Travel Magazine Inc.

O'Dwyer, J. (1988). Elegant Southern Inns. *Americana, 15*(6). New York: American Magazine.

Socolow, B., & E. Schmidt, Jr. (1988). Coastal Gateways. *World Tennis, 35(10).* New York: U.S. Tennis Association.

Simonson, L. (1974). *Plant tours.* Unpublished doctoral dissertation. Texas A & M University, College Station, TX.

Tighe, A. (1985). Cultural Tourism in the USA. *Tourism Management, 6*(4). New York: Expediaters of the Printed Word, Ltd.

Every community has resources that can be developed to improve its comparative advantage in the tourism industry. Toadstool Park, Nebraska Badlands, Nebraska. Photo credit: Nebraska Department of Economic Development

FOUR

The Economic Limits To Tourism

This chapter views tourism in the context of the overall economic and social system. It examines the way in which people live, work and play, asking how the system's several constituent parts operate together. The following four chapters continue this holistic analysis of the community and its tourism industry component.

Specifically, this chapter treats the question "What, if anything, really sets limits upon the tourism industry?" Such a question requires an answer before embarking upon a program of tourism industry development. We will not be able to tell what the tourism industry should be, but we will be able to understand whether or not there are principles operating to limit tourism's potential in a given community. In the chapter that follows immediately, we will see that other factors usually operate in most communities to stunt the development of the tourism industry at far below its real economic potential.

The discussion in this chapter considers the limits to tourism in two separate contexts:

The context of a large economic system such as the United States. Two basic principles apply in the case of a large system: The shape and size of the production possibility frontier, and the relative preference of consumers for travel and recreation compared to their preference for other goods and services.

The context of a single community, or travel destination area. Two basic principles are emphasized in this latter case: The principle of comparative advantage, and that of carrying capacity. We will examine each of these contexts separately.

A LARGE ECONOMIC SYSTEM

By a "large system" is meant one that is self-sufficient within itself, and that does not depend upon other outside markets or sources of supply. Actually, in the present highly interdependent world, there is no one nation-state fitting this description. To be fully faithful to the idea, it would be necessary for us to use the entire world when talking about such a system. However, it is sufficiently easier conceptually to deal with the United States alone, Canada plus the United States, or a system of similar scale. The reader is encouraged to think in those concrete terms in the discussion that follows in this chapter. No great violence is done by simplifying to a single large economic sector of the world.

The alert reader may, at this point, question the apparent omission of international tourism. It is not omitted. Consideration of the international tourism scene is an integral part of the market and competition in the case of every tourism destination area. Treatment is accorded it at relevant points through the text. However, in this chapter subsection, we are assuming a self-sufficient system for purposes of illustrating key principles.

National Production Possibility Frontiers

Why can't all of us travel and recreate all of the time?

Most of us know intuitively that this isn't possible. The reasons are four-fold: (1) some of us must spend some of our time producing the other things that we want and need—food, clothing and shelter plus many related items in our advanced economic system; (2) some of us must also produce the goods and services needed to make travel and recreation possible; (3) we each have different tastes; even if it were possible, not everyone wants to recreate all of the time; indeed, given the strongly-ingrained work ethic in some of our population, many feel uncomfortable when they are confronted with a large block of unobligated time; (4) the physical resources for travel are limited.

Line abcd in Figure 4.1 represents the production possibility frontier of an economic system. *This frontier is the total amount of goods and services that the system is capable of producing at its given stage of technological, social, political and economic development.* Travel and tourism production is represented on its horizontal axis. The production of all other goods and services is represented on the vertical axis. Line abcd traces the possible trade-offs between the production of travel and tourism and the production of all other goods and services.

Depending upon society's preferences, it may choose to produce a large amount, g_1, of other goods and services, along with a relatively small amount, t_1, of tourism and travel. Alternatively, it may choose to produce a smaller amount of other goods and services, g_2, along with a larger amount of tourism and travel, t_2.

Note that line abcd is convex upward and to the right. This reflects the operation of the law of diminishing returns. The system can shift from point a, where only other goods and services are produced, to point b on its production possibility

frontier curve. In doing so it adds a reasonable amount of travel and tourism, at the low cost of giving up only a relatively small amount of production of other goods and services. In moving from point b to point c, more travel and tourism are produced, but the cost in terms of other goods and services that must be given up is relatively higher. Finally, should the system elect to shift from point c to point d, it would gain only a little more travel and tourism while giving up a relatively large amount of ability to produce other goods and services. The reader should verify that moving in the opposite direction—from point d to c, from c to b, and from b to a—produces exactly the opposite effects.

If we were portraying a really self-sufficient, large economic system, points a and d would not be

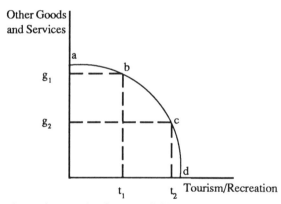

Figure 4.1 Production Possibility Frontier

possible. That is, no system could operate with only travel and tourism. Figure 4.2 extends the production possibility frontier curve, and has a new set of points a, b, c, and d. In segment a-b of the production possibility frontier curve of Figure 4.2, added travel and tourism is actually complementary to the production of other good and services. This situation can be hypothesized as one in which, at point a, there is not sufficient travel to service the productive activities of the system, for example, insufficient information interchange, inadequate supply systems, etc. As more travel is added, a higher level of production of other goods and services is possible.

At the d end of the production possibility frontier, shown in Figure 4.2, there is not sufficient physical productivity to sustain tourism. The

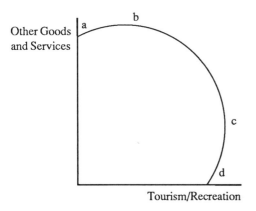

Figure 4.2 Production Possibility Frontier— showing section with tourism and other goods and services as complements

system can elect to add production of other goods and services while at the same time increasing its travel and tourism. In such a setting there are not enough automobiles, roads, fuel supplies, etc., produced to allow the travel and tourism that the system wants to have produced. We will see that not all systems necessarily operate on their production possibility curve, and that there actually appears complementarity between tourism and many other forms of production in some communities or subparts of a larger system. However, under most circumstances a large system would be expected to operate in the b-c segment of the curve shown in Figure 4.2, where travel and

tourism production is competitive with the production of other goods and services.

As has already been partially discussed, the shape and size of any country's production possibility frontier curve depends upon the stage of development of its technological, economic, political and social systems. Figure 4.3 compares production possibility frontier curves of two nations having similar population numbers but with each at different stages of development, hence having different levels of per capita wealth production. Curve p is the production possibility frontier curve of a poor or economically underdeveloped nation. It has limited ability to produce other goods and services, and produces relatively even less travel and tourism. Most of its productive effort must be devoted to those things needed for survival. Curve p contrasts with curve r, which is the production possibility frontier curve for a rich or economically developed country. The latter country can produce a much larger amount of other goods and services. Its ability to produce travel and tourism is, relatively, even larger, since it has the wealth to allow a larger freedom of choice between tangible goods and travel, tourism, recreation and related services.

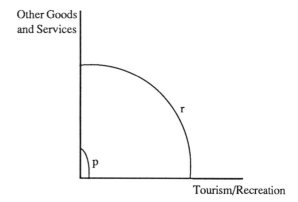

Figure 4.3 Production Possibility Frontiers— rich (r) and poor (p) countries

National Preferences Determine Relative Amounts of Tourism

What determines at what point on the production possibility frontier a society will actually operate? Selection of this point is the *function of the tastes and preferences of the society's consumers*. Prices and relative production levels reflect at any time the relative preference of the society for "other" goods and services, compared with travel and recreation. This is shown in Figure 4.4.

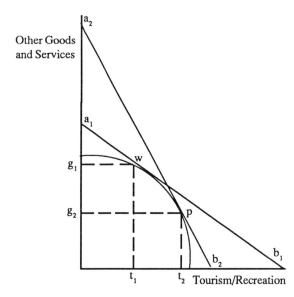

Figure 4.4 Production Possibility Frontier—
preference determination

In Figure 4.4, price line a_1-b_1 intersects the vertical or goods axis at a point that is just one-half as far from zero, as the point at which it intersects the horizontal or travel and tourism axis. This represents the taste-preferences of a society that is willing to give up two units of travel and tourism

for only one of other goods and services. In other words, it places a relatively low value on travel and recreation, and we might think of it as a society oriented toward the work ethic, and the consumption of tangible things. Line a_1-b_1 touches the production possibility curve at 'w' and hence this system will produce g_1 of other goods and services, and t_1 of travel and tourism.

The price line for a relatively more travel-and-tourism oriented society is represented by line a_2-b_2. This society is willing to exchange two units of other goods and services for one unit of travel and tourism. In other words, it values travel and tourism relatively highly. This price line touches the production possibility curve at 'p'. A society having this preference pattern will produce a smaller amount of other goods, g_2, and a larger amount of travel and tourism, t_2, than the society illustrated in the paragraph immediately above.

Note that both society 'w' (work) and society 'p' (pleasure) operate at the same production possibility level per capita. They can each produce total goods and services of equivalent value. However, the mix of their productive output is different since one society values travel and tourism relatively much more than the other.

The production possibility frontier is only a *possibility*. There are many instances in which a country might be operating at below its potential output. Such a situation is illustrated in Figure 4.5 by a country having the indicated production possibility frontier, but that is deficient in output and only produces at d (deficient). This might be the case of a country that made poor use of or left undeveloped many of its travel and tourism resources. Its citizens thus receive less in living satisfactions than might otherwise be the case. In Chapters 5, 6 and 7 we will see that local communities sometimes penalize themselves because they limit tourism industry development to a level well below its full potential.

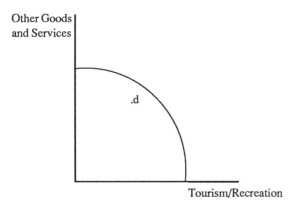

Figure 4.5   Production Possibility Frontier—
case of deficient production system

LIMITS TO TOURISM INDUSTRY DEVELOPMENT AT THE COMMUNITY LEVEL

In a community, state or region that is an integral part of a larger system or nation, the limits imposed by the overall system's production possibility frontier also apply. The influence of the overall system's technological, political, economic and social development extends to each of its constituent communities, first by limiting their productive capabilities, and secondly through the mechanism of overall demand for tourism and all other goods and services. In addition, for a community, the principles of comparative economic advantage and of carrying capacity act to define the limits to its possible tourism industry.

The Community's Comparative Advantage in Tourism

A community that is part of an intra-dependent system strives for efficient production of export goods and services—those things that it may sell to other communities in order to get money. This purchasing power, in turn, is used to buy the goods and services that other communities can produce more efficiently. As part of a larger system it does not need to be concerned about an internally balanced production of all goods and services. So long as it is productive, what it lacks it may get by exchange. If, by development of its tourism industry it can get better return from its human and natural resource inputs than by developing some other economic activity, it should do this. If, on the other hand, some other activity can produce income more efficiently, that is the activity to expand. This is the meaning of comparative advantage to the individual community, state, or region (Perloff, 1960; Fitzgerald, 1986).

A community may have a comparative advantage in the tourism industry in two ways. The first situation is fairly obvious. It is the case in which a community has features that have a high capacity to attract travelers, it is accessible to market areas, has the necessary infrastructure, and a work force that is skilled in serving tourists, or that can adapt readily to this employment. Hence it has an advantage over other tourist destination areas in the tourist industry.

Williamsburg, Virginia illustrates a community having a large comparative advantage in tourism. Restored colonial Williamsburg acts as a powerful travel attractor. Williamsburg is sited near the heavily-populated East Coast travel markets.

Cape Cod, Massachusetts is another illustration of this kind of comparative advantage in tourism. The sea coast ambience attracts travelers, and nearby are the large populations of New York, Boston and other parts of New England and Middle Atlantic states.

The two destination areas differ markedly in the character of their major attractions. That of Williamsburg is manmade and based upon human history, while that of Cape Cod is the "natural" Atlantic Ocean. Both, however, have undergone extensive development to bring them to their

Whatever the underlying resources, and processes by which they reached the present state of their tourism industries, it is clear that both Williamsburg and Cape Cod enjoy a large comparative advantage in the tourism industry, when contrasted with, for example, northwestern Kansas. The former two attract and serve a large volume of travelers. Because of their comparative advantage in the tourism industry, Williamsburg and Cape Cod are better off, the traveling public is enriched from the experiences there, and the entire U.S. economy— which includes the value of tourism services—has a higher productive output in terms of living quality for its citizens. Higher, that is, than if these two communities devoted most of their productive resources to agriculture, cotton milling, or some other economic activity. In these cases the well-being of everyone is improved because they are producing tourism services and can do so better than most other areas.

A second case of comparative advantage may be more difficult to understand, and also difficult to justify in terms of long-term national welfare. It is nevertheless a real comparative advantage. It occurs in the case of communities that have an absolute disadvantage in the production of any given product or service, including tourism. That is, other communities can produce anything that these communities can produce at lower cost to the consumer, and/or with higher returns to the pro- ducer. This might be the case of tourism-producing communities in relatively isolated areas that are high cost tourism producers because of the travel costs for getting there. It might also be the case of smaller communities nearer large population centers but lacking both a suitable manufacturing industry and good travel attractors. *These kinds of communities are still better off to develop their tourism industry, if it yields the best return that they can realize from their human and natural resources among the several economic activity choices available to them.*

A number of observations may be applied to the second case of comparative advantage. If indeed the returns to human labor are lower in the areas that have high travel costs, or where the presently available recreational experiences are of low magnitude, then the overall economy and the lot of the individuals involved could be improved by moving people from these areas. Dollar returns are, however, not the only measure of reward to people. Some prefer to live in given areas because it is their ancestral home, or because they like its living features, and part of their reward comes from living where they choose. Thus many parts of a community's population are resistant to being moved. In addition, there are uptrends as well as downtrends in the fortunes of local economies. Rather than simplistically shifting populations during a down cycle, it is often wiser to carefully reassess the local options, and mount efforts to regenerate the economic health of the community.

Limitations Imposed by Carrying Capacity

Carrying capacity may limit the expansion of tourism in a given community (Rosenow, 1979; Murphy, 1985). The idea of carrying capacity is quite simple. It was first used by ecologists who were concerned that overuse of fragile ecological sites might damage them, hence they developed measures of the number of visitors that a given ecology could tolerate over time and still maintain the quality of the resource.

Specifying the tourism carrying capacity of a community becomes complex in its application. It is fixed in terms of numbers of tourists only for specific levels of facility development and resource management, and for specified kinds of recreational uses.

Carrying capacity interrelates a number of factors:

Numbers of users and their experiences gained. It is often overlooked that each user has individual specifications for the intensity and kind of experience sought. Some choose only to "dip their toe" into the experience, preferring to remain on familiar turf and to avoid risks or surprises. Others strive for total immersion in a new, different, or challenging experience. The impact upon resources and facilities and upon the experiences of other tourists may be sharply different in the case of each different kind of user.

Resource management, facility development and maintenance of resource quality. The capacity of most areas to handle tourists is limited mainly by human ingenuity in its management (Hardin, 1977). For example, carrying capacity can be changed by altering the degree of direct access to the resource that is permitted. The resulting experience may be different for many tourists, but not necessarily less rewarding.

Provision for quality of living for residents, and for the proper operation of other-than-tourism economic activities. If it requires two hours to move from one side of the downtown to the other during the peak of the tourist season, this can seriously hamper the living quality of residents and the operation of other economic activities. Such a problem is subject to management—it may simply indicate an inadequate infrastructure of local roads and highways. Tourists can also put pressure upon facilities and resources that residents use, causing unacceptable crowding in fishing, boating and swimming waters, on the golf course and similar amenity features.

We might examine the carrying capacity of a tourist destination area having a major lake as its focal attraction. This will allow us to illustrate how different uses and facility development can produce large differences in carrying capacity.

If fishing is the major recreational activity in the TDA, there will be predictable limits to carrying capacity. Under heavy angling pressure, the quality of fishing may deteriorate rapidly and only use restrictions can maintain the experience.

With power boating as the major use the quality of the experience does not deteriorate from one time to the next. But at any given time there can be competition for the surface of the water and a safety problem that will make the experience less rewarding to many users.

The greatest use made of water is to look at it. Ordinarily, many more can "use" the lake visually than can fish or boat on it. Limitations in this case might be roads, picnic places and overlooks, as well as places to eat and sleep. But the impact upon the water resource itself would be quite different than in the case of direct use.

Even more user numbers and more tourist dollar spending might be achieved by taking advantage of the lake area ambience. Development of amusement parks, theaters and shopping areas could provide for many and varied activities in an area having a special ambience.

The reader will understand how, under different development and management systems of a given attraction resource, the number of tourists and dollars of income can vary widely. *The many ways for expanding carrying capacity act to transform a given limit under one form of use into a social, design, technological and economic problem of how to appropriately expand use while providing rewarding experiences and maintaining the resource base.*

Questions for review and further study

1. Will a change in tastes between tourism and all other goods and services cause a national economy to produce at a different level of

2. Why does an unproductive large system (a poor nation) produce less tourism and travel as a proportion of its total output, compared to a more productive (richer) system?

3. What alternatives does a community have, if it has an absolute disadvantage in the production of all items that it is able to produce?

4. What factors usually operate to prevent a TDA from having a totally tourism-based economy?

5. Explain why carrying capacity is highly flexible.

6. What causes the production possibility frontier of a nation to expand? To contract?

7. Describe the factors that you think act to give one community a relative advantage over another in the tourism industry.

SUGGESTIONS FOR FURTHER READING

Samuelson, P. (1980). *Economics.* (11th Edition). New York: McGraw-Hill, Inc. (Parts one and five, Chapter 34).

Shelby, B., & T. Heberlein. (1986). *Carrying Capacity in Recreational Settings.* Corvallis, OR: Oregon State University Press.

TEXTUAL REFERENCES

Fitzgerald, J., & P. Meyer. (1986). Recognizing Constraints in Local Economic Development. *Journal of the Community Development Society,* 17(2). Athens, GA: University of Georgia.

Hardin, G., & J. Baden (Eds). (1977). *Managing the Commons.* San Francisco: W.H. Freeman.

Murphy, P. (1985). *Tourism, A Community Approach.* New York: Methuen.

Perloff, H., et al. (1960). *Regions, Resources and Economic Growth.* Resources for the Future. Baltimore, MD: Johns Hopkins Press.

Rosenow, J., & G. Pulsipher. (1979). *Tourism, the Good, the Bad, and the Ugly.* Lincoln, NB: Century Three Press.

Well appointed hospitality facilities serve not only recreational travelers; they are necessary to the operation of most kinds of economic activity. Oceanside, California. Photo credit: Motel 6

FIVE

The Social-Political Operating Limits To Tourism Industry Development

This chapter continues the view of how societies live, work, and play together, with emphasis upon the individual community's tourism industry.

In the preceding chapter, we have seen that the economic limits to tourism industry development for the individual tourist destination area or individual community are partially set by the larger system of which it is a part. Within that framework, comparative advantage and carrying capacity operate as major, economic, limit-determining factors. Both of these factors are flexible and subject to management. In other words, in an advanced economy, the extent of the tourism industry's expansion in a given community is often limited primarily by the management capability, imagination, and ingenuity of its citizens. This flexibility in tourism development for the individual community is in contrast to that of a whole system, where specific theoretical limits to the tourism industry exist for any given state of the society and its technology.

Few communities approach even remotely their potential in a viable tourism industry. Real world observation suggests that lack of hard and fast limits to a community's tourism industry operates as only one factor. Many communities apparently could develop their tourism industry, yet they fail to do so (Murphy, 1985). Some of these lack the economic balance and vitality that tourism could help provide. Some communities may operate well below their production possibility frontier.

This chapter's purpose, then, is to examine aspects of why so many communities flounder in the process of tourism industry development. While specific communities are not named, the examples are composites from observation of real communities. The problems illustrated are widely encountered, thus it is expected that many communities will be able to identify aspects of their own situation in the vignettes presented.

We will examine several classes of social and political situations that act to limit tourism industry development as follows:

Inappropriate Developmental Philosophies
— A developmental philosophy for the 19th century.
— The status quo: A recalcitrant power structure.

Fear of Competition by Existing Industries
— The one-industry town.
— Existing hospitality businesses: Will added tourism industry be harmful?

How, By and For Whom Shall Resources be Managed?
— Tourists get in our way.
— Environmentalists—plus and minus.
— Public Resource-Managing Agencies.

Inappropriate Developmental Approaches:
— Worse than none!

THE ECONOMICALLY HEALTHY COMMUNITY

Before examining negative cases, where tourism industry growth falters, we first accentuate the positive. Under what conditions is there good opportunity for tourism industry growth, as well as opportunity for development of the community's total economy (Lackey, 1987)?

An economically healthy community is not necessarily one in which all resident families are millionaires. Rather, it is one that looks to the future with hope, and that manages prudently and creatively those resources it has for living and making a living. Community economic health largely depends upon the community mindset just as human health often has a major psychological content. There is community pride. The economic base is stable or growing; this makes it possible for leaders and entrepreneurs to plan with confidence. Diversity in the economic base adds to stability, and makes community leaders more willing to accept new forms of economic activity. Finally, community leadership is heterogeneous, that is, it is drawn from a number of different power bases.

This vignette of an economically healthy community is far from comprehensive. It especially concentrates upon qualities of a non-depressed community where tourism industry growth is possible (Richards, 1984).

An up-spiral operates in the case of an economically healthy community, giving it momentum. Businessmen and investors are optimistic and seek out new opportunities for enterprise. New investment adds jobs, creating added opportunity for new investment. Added jobs attract workers who need schools, churches, housing, streets and other services. These services in turn add to the community's appeal, create more jobs, and further support the up-spiral of the growth momentum. This is the opposite of what often occurs under conditions of economic stagnation or depression where there is often withdrawal from aggressive action (Stokes, 1980; Murphy, 1985).

Two other observations often help in understanding tourism industry growth in many communities:

— Frequently a major triggering event adds impetus to the tourism industry. It may be a major new private investment. It may be a new public investment such as that or a park of a reservoir. It may be an internal community event such as loss or change in a local industry. Such an event brings to light new opportunities, or causes a reassessment of currently available opportunities.

— Major new projects, developments and/or investments can often be traced to the vision and entrepreneurial leadership of one person, or a small group of persons. At the same time we will see that while specific leadership is important, implementation usually requires widespread involvement.

New Glarus: A Community That Could!

New Glarus, Wisconsin is a community of about 1,500 population, lying about 30 miles southwest of Madison. It provides us with an example of a smaller community that thrives upon the tourism industry.

Settled in 1845 by immigrants from Glarus, Switzerland, New Glarus developed a typical Wisconsin-Swiss economy: dairy farming and cheese manufacturing. Fortunately, the community retained pride in its Swiss heritage. In 1938 it began a William Tell observance on the Labor Day weekend; in 1942 a Pioneer Village, featuring the early primitive buildings and crafts of the mid-19th century, was started.

About 1960 a triggering event occurred: The cheese plant closed. Faced with loss of its major employer, as well as ready markets for its dairy farm production, New Glarus could easily have become a bedroom community to Madison. Instead the community leadership decided that their Swiss ethnic heritage offered opportunity for building their tourism industry.

Many new features now give a Swiss ambience to the community and impart to the visitor the experience of being in a special place. Most of the downtown and many other buildings are now in Alpine architecture; even the bank drive-through has a Glockenspiel. The centerpiece of the Pioneer Village is an interpretive building in modern Swiss architecture. Now six special events provide incentive for multiple visits to the community including a Winter Festival, Heidi Drama, and Swiss Independence Day Celebration. Outdoor activities are available, highlighted by the 23-mile Sugar River hiking-biking trail with its trailhead at New Glarus. Combined with these and many other things to see and do is an offering of Swiss food and lodging in well-appointed, Swiss-motif motels.

There is diversity to the community's economy. Agriculture continues. A Swiss Lace Factory not only provides employment, but its retail outlet is a major attraction. New Glarus also attracts people to live there to enjoy its clean, thrifty, Swiss ambiance, and private retirement facilities have located there.

New Glarus is a community accomplishment. As in many such cases, however, there have been special leaders. Among them is the late president of the Bank of New Glarus. Not only did he provide organizational leadership to development, but he backed many efforts financially.

INAPPROPRIATE DEVELOPMENTAL PHILOSOPHIES: A DEVELOPMENTAL PHILOSOPHY FOR THE 19TH CENTURY

The 19th century work ethic philosophy, already noted in Chapter 1, continues to be strongly held by many individuals in today's society. This view of the world causes problems in adapting to a number of aspects of the current society, and especially to the tourism industry (Napier, 1980). At the same time, the work ethic philosophy has made and continues to make constructive contributions to our society. It dominated the thinking during the period of rapid in-gathering of immigrants, and expansion westward into the vast North American frontier. There was urgency to gain control of nature, and an infinity of things to be built and accomplished: tree clearing, dwellings, farm development, swamp drainage, roads, schools, churches, railroads, bridges, and many others. The future of the society rested on its zeal to undertake and overcome physical difficulties. Work was, and is, good!

Despite the continuing need for members of the society to understand and value the place of work, the work ethic philosophy has two elements that have doubtful value in the present setting. The first is the view of "production" as consisting only of the creation of tangible, physical items. The production of services, such as tourism, is sneered at. We can easily understand how, in a day when there was urgent need for food, shoes, housing, and roads, that physical production became highly valued.

Oddly in our current society, most tangible items have a still larger intangible component. This is the case with such items as autos, housing, and clothing. An auto, for example, provides transportation, but so does a bicycle. If use of a bicycle is too strenuous, there are motorcycles. If motorcycles are too exposed to weather, there are $7,000 automobiles. But many buy $15,000 to $30,000 automobiles. Why? The answer is that the high-priced auto yields pleasure and status. These are similar to the psychic rewards that we get from tourism.

Extending from this view is the second problem aspect of the work ethic philosophy: the idea that effort devoted to intangibles or services, because it does not yield a physical product, "produces nothing." This philosophy applies particularly to the production of pleasurable, intangible experiences. Since it is a waste of time to produce nothing, time devoted to this purpose is sinful.

One closely related, humorous definition of the work ethic…"the haunting, lurking fear that someone, somewhere, might be having a good time!"

Somehow negative aspects of the work ethic philosophy persist regarding tourism, despite the fact that a majority of our households now take recreational trips more or less regularly and also that the overwhelming portion of our current work force is devoted to service production. Currently 73 percent of United States work effort is engaged in non-tangible, service work; this has expanded from 43 percent in 1929.

The attitude produces hostile expression toward tourism, travel, recreation and leisure pursuit in numerous ways. During the energy shortage of the late 1970s it particularly came to the fore. A county commissioner in a midwestern state said, "Every time I see a large boat being pulled down the highway behind a car, I see red!" The county where this individual served as commissioner derived more income from the manufacture of boats than from any other economic activity. A high-level, presidential economic adviser said, "We can cut out pleasure travel." The idea apparently was that the United States could thereby save petroleum. But not only was the statement reflective of an outdated philosophy, it made dubious economic sense. At the time four million people were employed in tourism nationwide, and well over half of them depended upon pleasure tourism travel for their livelihood. What was the nation to do with these more than two million workers?

The understanding limitation extends to the highest national policy levels and with damaging consequences. Within the U.S. Department of Commerce is the U.S. Travel and Tourism Administration (USTTA), the job of which is to sell tourism in the United States to people in other nations. The United States particularly needs international tourists because of massive international trade deficits, mounting to nearly $200 billion annually, that plagued the United States during the 1980s. Tourism is a means for gaining added foreign exchange. But despite the critical need for export sales, it has been difficult to maintain funding for the USTTA. In a recent year the United States' international tourism sales effort was forced to operate with only 12 percent of the resources that Greece expended for tourism. The gross domestic product (GDP) of Greece is just over one percent that of the United States.

Fortunately progress toward reducing resistances to tourism industry development has been made. In many communities, favorable attitudes are encountered (Napier, 1980). Pragmatism appears to play a role. In reaching for new revenues, states appear to now turn toward tourism; in just the 1984 to 1987 period the combined total of state tourism promotional budgets grew by 52 percent.

INAPPROPRIATE DEVELOPMENTAL PHILOSOPHIES: MAINTAINING THE STATUS QUO

An "Established Power Structure Factor" operates in some communities to reduce the chances for further industry diversification. It arises from the fact that positions of power on the bank board, school board, and the chamber of commerce are mostly held by people who already "have it made." In communities that are economically stagnant, many of these leaders do not feel need for added income or wealth. A new industry, whether tourism or some other major added economic activity, would bring a new set of leadership that could potentially challenge them for their positions of power and prestige. Perhaps without fully realizing why, these community leaders either resist or are passive toward new industry. This attitude tends to either bring on or perpetuate economic stagnation.

Small town chambers of commerce appear particularly susceptible to this disease. They are predominantly controlled by the merchants on what is often an economically status quo "main" street. This explains the often-observed discussion by chambers of commerce about need for tourism and other new industry in the community, and the seldom-observed active participation in really helping it happen. Tourism, which requires sharing the community with strangers, is seen as particularly repulsive.

The "dominant power structure disease" appears to become more virile and to develop complications in the case of communities that have suffered economic reverses. In the face of adversity most people become more conservative, and unwilling to risk further losses. Any kind of new proposal now appears riskier than before, both in economic terms and in terms of threats to leaders' prestige. Further, economic reverses and risk aversion often lead to intracommunity jealousies and suspicions; increasingly the world is seen as zero-sum: what my neighbors or fellow businessmen win, I will lose. Thus, not only does each person shrink from new ventures himself; ventures by anyone else in the community are also opposed.

What then occurs is a downward spiral of economic and social institutions in the community. The old power structure holds on determinedly. Sometimes community institutions must reach an advanced stage of decay before new leaders with a different vision can emerge from the rubble and begin the rebuilding process.

THE ONE-INDUSTRY TOWN

Dominance by the principal economic base makes it difficult for many communities to move aggressively into tourism industry development. This difficulty is more likely to infect a small to moderate-sized community, such as one under 50,000 in population. It occurs where a single industry is dominant, such as mining, forestry and wood processing, agriculture, or a single processing or manufacturing plant.

One-industry communities often suffer economically because of lack of diversification in their economy. They are buffeted by the vicissitudes of

the given industry, which are often exaggerated if the decisions about the local operation are made at a corporate headquarters located in a distant city. Many local citizens are aware of these hazards, but they appear helpless in breaking out of the strait-jacket imposed upon them by their dominant economic base activity. Why?

In the first place, dominance by one economic activity limits many local citizens in what they can recognize as legitimate productive activity. Alternatively, even if individuals do have a wider vision of economic activity possibilities, they feel an obligatory loyalty to the dominant economic activity because "that's where our bread is buttered." If the local activity is concentrated in producing widgets (or sawmilling, or mining, or dairy production, or fabric milling) this orients the local mindset to widget production plus all of its supporting activities. Employee training is needed for widget production; marketing and supply activities are needed to augment widget production; there is general knowledge about corporations involved in widget production; and local bankers and real estate firms must pay heed to decisions about widgets, their production and marketing. Not only is less attention paid to economic activities that do not produce widgets, but disinterest grows into disdain: widget production is not just an activity, it is *the* activity and we are anointed to do it!

For the sake of emphasis, this sketch of mindsets is over-drawn, but the evolution of a mining, or forestry, or widget-producing psychology clearly influences the thinking of many citizens in such a community. They then experience difficulty in recognizing the tourism industry, or any other endeavor not related to their principal economic base activity, as an appropriate generator of income for their community. If tourism is suggested it is viewed as getting in the way of, and competing for, workers, space and attention in the production of widgets.

The power structure of many small communities is controlled by spokespersons for the dominant industry; this reinforces the community's mindset. Not only do citizens tend to "think, eat, and sleep" the dominant economic activity, so do all of the community's principal institutions. This occurs because leaders in the plant or industry often also perform community leadership roles. Consider: The bank will be dominated by directors who work for or are connected to the dominant industry, and the bank will make most of its loans to the industry, and to the people who are associated with it. Directors of the school board will be employed by the industry. Officers of the most prestigious churches will be the dominant industry's employees or officials. The city council will make many of its decisions in support of the dominant industry, as will the chamber of commerce. All of these factors reinforce the mindset regarding what is legitimate industry. They tend to crowd out tourism development as well as pursuit of other economic opportunities.

EXISTING HOSPITALITY BUSINESSES RARELY SUPPORT TOURISM DEVELOPMENT

Existing hospitality businesses and other tourism-related operations may be among the more resistant of community elements toward tourism industry expansion, upgrading, or development. This, at first glance, appears irrational, but their fear of competition provides a simple explanation. However altruistic toward the community a motel operator might be, he still sees the occupancy and profit level of his own operation as a primary obligation. Added overnight capacity in any form is, at least initially, bad since it will reduce profit possibilities for the business that he currently operates. Here again is seen the operation of a zero-sum mentality: any new added business will mean less for me. Thus the existing tourism industry emphasizes only the need for promotional activities by the community, city, or chamber of commerce. It is in their

interest to have their existing businesses operate at full capacity. They may, however, support the development of complementing activities, such as attractions, events and conventions.

Unfortunately, many local as well as state tourism councils are composed exclusively, or nearly so, of hospitality and recreational industry representatives. This is an important reason why such groups devote nearly all their energies to advertising. Tourism councils so constituted are not interested in developing the community's or state's tourism industry; they are interested in filling existing facilities in which the group's representatives have sunk costs.

In contrast to the sometimes narrow view on the part of the owners of current hospitality businesses, broadly oriented community leadership often seeks the more general welfare of the community. They are more objective in their view of the community's tourism industry. Thus, they can more readily understand and support the need for both diversification of the community's economic base, and expansion of industries in which the community has a comparative economic advantage.

HOW, BY, AND FOR WHOM SHALL RESOURCES BE MANAGED?

Squabbles over who will do what, with what, to what and for whom, at a distance sometimes appear humorous or unnecessary. Controversies over the use of tourism/recreational resources occur almost as a regular part of American life. But they are far from unnecessary. They are, instead, an integral part of the workings of a democracy. They represent the struggles of different value systems seeking adequate expression in policy decisions, as well as the claims of different interests upon the rights to resource use. Only in a dictatorship can such arguments be eliminated, hence few of us would opt to eliminate them. But protracted struggles over resource management and development appear, at least in the short run, to limit the tourism industry of many communities (Blank, 1982). Briefly discussed here are a few of the manifestations of value systems in conflict.

Tourists Get In Our Way, Proclaim Many Local Residents

To a community resident, who sees no value in tourism, the tourists are an aggravation. They "catch our fish," "take our parking places," and "make our highways unsafe." Then tourists add insult to injury; they start demanding specific services and attempting to dictate how resources will be managed: water quality standards, where outboard motors may be used, and what the building regulations will be. Local residents resent this intrusion into their home turf.

Even though the attitude may have provincial qualities, local resentment of non-residents' claims upon the local community is not without justification. The right to first claim upon any area belongs to citizens of that area. Anyone contesting this concept should give thought to what their own attitude might be should there be a serious threat to control of their own back yard. Suppose it were proposed for use as a park, factory, nature preserve, or building a road? At the same time, any citizen resenting tourists in the home community should also examine his own situation. Nearly all U.S. citizens travel outside their home communities. During this travel they hope to be received with courtesy and treated well. Their right to good treatment while in other communities has a cost: that they be good hosts to visitors who are in their own home communities. Citizens' rights to enjoy amenities of lakes, cities and facilities away from home carry with them the responsibility to also share local amenities with travelers from elsewhere.

Environmentalists Make Up a Part of the Contesting Melee

Environmentalists' unifying feature is a professed regard for the quality of the environment, but their specific interests and methods may vary widely. The society owes much to the vision and persistence of some members of this group in establishing preserves, and recreational areas. But environmentalists may also be a part of the problem.

Their approach is sometimes elitist: it assumes that resource uses as proposed by them are "best for everyone." In reality their proposals may incorporate mainly the values and wants of a limited few, but require payment of costs by all through public revenue. Further, many proposals to establish resource management involve restrictions upon local residents, contributing to the problem noted immediately above.

Environmentalists are also often guilty of inadequately considering the welfare of the local community. Residents of small communities often view the economic struggle for jobs and income as paramount. Reservation of a large tract of land for environmental or recreational purposes may remove it from its current production role and either reduce or cause change in the local community's economic base. Further, this reservation action is usually initiated outside the community, and seldom involves the local community to more than a token extent. This causes the community to view the action as loss of control over "their" own resources.

Often the local community functions as an essential, complementing factor in use of a tourism/recreational resource by the public. Usually facilities are needed both for tourists to stay in the area, and to access the recreational opportunities (Blank, 1980). Seldom do environmentalists fully understand or appreciate this relationship. Because of this oversight they fail to gain the support and cooperation of local communities that are situated near a major natural resource. Inadequate tourism facility development often results, which may limit enjoyment of the recreational resource by the general public.

When the local community has not properly "bought in," it may attempt to circumvent management rules and divert development into channels that are not compatible with the management of the natural resource. This suggests need for full partnership with the local community in any environmental and land reservation effort. Rather than a win-lose confrontation, a win-win result can be achieved in which both the community and the larger society gain.

Public Resource-Managing Agencies May Hurt as Well as Help

Public agencies have been established to help with management and development of resources, but these agencies can only carry out policies established by the public decision-making process, and may in the process create new problems. Included in public agencies are national agencies such as the National Park Service, U.S. Forest Service, U.S. Army Corps of Engineers, Bureau of Land Management, and many others; state agencies include Departments of Natural Resources, Parks, Transportation and Highways, among others; at the local levels there are county commissions, zoning boards, and park and recreation departments.

Fortunately these agencies have many genuinely dedicated staff members. They represent a vast depth of expertise in many kinds of resource management from fish to flowers.

These agencies may also be a part of the problem, sometimes in circumstances beyond the individual agency's control. A too-frequent occurrence is the case of overlapping jurisdictions. An example is Crane Lake, Minnesota, where at least 15 different agencies, representing all levels of government, claim jurisdiction over the affairs of the 100 inhabitants. Crane Lake is near the Canadian boundary, and on the edge of both the Voyageur's National Park and Superior National Forest. Many decisions profoundly affecting managers of recreational businesses in Crane Lake are made at a distant bureaucrat's office with little opportunity for direct feedback on how those decisions impact on the community's individuals and businesses (Blank, 1977).

Governmental agencies are established to carry out specific tasks. But, because an agency must be governed by legislative rules, and is not charged with the general welfare, its operation can cause considerable friction. This can happen when an agency, often at the promptings of a special interest citizen's group, seeks and obtains laws mandating a specific management approach to a given area or resource. The law is then enforced with the use of quasi-police power. The result for the local community may be less than optimum.

Less than optimum social results can also occur in cases in which agency personnel persist in management of a recreational resource for uses that are partly out of date. Examples include the exclusive management of a stream for fish production, when canoeing is a major, emergent use; or management of a forest solely for timber production when hiking, cross-country skiing, and nature interpretation can be accommodated and represent uses of growing importance.

Frictions of the type illustrated here can persist for long periods. Certain resource management struggles have been underway throughout the entire 20th century. We have noted that these are a part of the democratic process through which conflicts in value systems are resolved. They occur because we have a wealth of resources, and the range of use alternatives is wide. Thus, in a sense, they represent "Insurmountable Opportunities." Needed are procedures to reduce unnecessary frictions. Some of these are suggested in Chapters 11 and 12.

INAPPROPRIATE DEVELOPMENT— WORSE THAN NONE!

Tourism industry development may sometimes be ill-timed, inappropriate, or over-done. Cases of failure to recognize that the tourism industry can have a substantial potential beyond its present scale are common. But there are also examples of over-optimistic tourism facility development that have had an effect exactly the opposite of what was intended or expected. Unfortunately, this effort often involves prime recreational and tourism resources having strong market potential (Richards, 1984). While local entrepreneurs may be involved, such efforts often also have large inputs from investors and/or developers who are not residents. Seeing the quality resources and sensing their market potential, the investor/developer reasons, "If it worked in the Rocky Mountains, or in Hawaii, why not here?" This reasoning is not necessarily in error, but there may be a failure to adequately adapt to the site, the management capabilities and financing strength of the entrepreneurs, and to the rate at which the market for this new site can be developed.

Faulty analysis based on inadequate information often bears much of the blame for these failed developments. Such developments quickly go through a series of financial "wringers." This process illustrates another case of loss of control by the local community. Even if local investors were initially involved, the "wringing out" process usually eliminates them. Both private investors seeking profit and capital appreciation, and governmental agencies helping to develop the local resources and economy, may be caught in this kind of operation (Rosenow, 1979).

Sometimes advice of "experts" compounds the problem. The developers realize that they need good advice, and hence seek out consulting and/or design firms having considerable stature. These latter have had experience with large-scale developments, and their advice often is to scale up the operation in size and appointments. Such advice apparently is given in all sincerity, although there is a lingering room for suspicion that some firms hope to construct monuments to themselves—using the client's funds! At any rate, there is an alarmingly high initial failure rate by large recreational/tourism developments done from scratch by groups who are relatively inexperienced in the given geographic area. Overbuilding commonly occurs in many such cases. This observation in no way negates the value of expert consultative assistance with tourism project development, but it suggests care in its choice and use.

Most tourism/recreation related hospitality operations require relatively large capital inputs. This presents another hazard: that of predicting economic cycles. Many otherwise well-conceived projects were forced into untimely bankruptcy because of unfortunate business cycle timing. An unforeseen business cycle downturn can restrict capital and force interest rates to ruinous levels. As a consequence the original investors may be forced into bankruptcy and lose control of the project.

Added to the genuinely sincere efforts at development, and most apparently are sincere, are the operations of "Quick Buck Artists." The latter's sales efforts may exhibit a strong presence of "booze, broads and brawn," with the intention of turning investment quickly or executing a "successful bankruptcy." A result is poor quality or incompleted development, a partial rape of resources, and serious disillusionment with the tourism industry on the part of the involved community and its citizens (Fitzgerald, 1986).

The influence of project failure often extends beyond the individual project. The effects may extend over an entire region—even, in some cases, nationwide. A summer resort or ski lodge in an economically depressed area that has received financial support from either private or governmental sources, but that has failed, will influence availability of funding for succeeding projects. An uncompleted second home project by an unreliable developer has been observed to sharply curtail the sale of second homes elsewhere in the region, even that of homes offered by a fully responsible developer. Observations of such failures reinforce the image of tourism as a risky type of development. They cause many investors, entrepreneurs and communities to adopt a cautious approach. A cautious approach is warranted, but if overdone, can cause the community to seriously underuse its resources.

Fortunately most non-resident, as well as local, investors and developers are well-intended and honest. But any development can be less than optimum unless community leadership complements the action in a fully informed, responsible way.

Questions for review and further study

1. Describe an up-spiral in a growing, economically healthy community.

2. Describe a down-spiral in a depressed community.

3. What are the needs in our present society for the work ethic philosophy?

4. Why do those who are relatively well-off in some communities lack motivation to support further development of the community's economy?

5. What kinds of tourism industry growth will be beneficial to the presently operating hospitality businesses?

6. What are likely to be differences between the economy of a community that depends upon only one industry for its economic base and that of a community with a diversified economic base?

7. Describe instances of misguided or improper approaches to development of tourism facilities.

8. How would you structure a tourism board or committee that would pursue tourism development vigorously, and that would also avoid serious problems of vested interests on the part of the board membership?

SUGGESTIONS FOR FURTHER READING

Dillman, D., & D. Hobbs. (1982). *Rural Society in the U.S., Issues for the 1980s*. Boulder, CO: Westview Press, (Part 5, The Community).

TEXTUAL REFERENCES

Blank, U., D. Larsen, & L. Simonson. (1977). *The Crane Lake Connection*. Staff Paper P77-3, St. Paul, MN: Department of Agricultural and Applied Economics, University of Minnesota.

Blank, U., L. Simonson, & G. Ballman. (1980). *A Needs Assessment of Tourism Firms Serving the Boundary Waters Canoe Area Wilderness Vicinity*. St. Paul, MN: Agricultural Extension Service, University of Minnesota.

Blank, U. (1982). Insurmountable Opportunities. *Minnesota Travel-Tourist Notes, 19*. St. Paul, MN: University Extension Service, University of Minnesota.

Fitzgerald, J., & P. Meyer. (1986). Recognizing Constraints in Local Economic Development. *Journal of the Community Development Society, 17*(2). Athens, GA: University of Georgia.

Lackey, A., R. Burke, & M. Peterson. (1987). Healthy Communities; The Goal of CD. *Journal of the Community Development Society, 18*(2). Athens, GA: University of Georgia.

Murphy, P. (1985). *Tourism, A Community Approach*. New York: Methuen.

Napier, T., & E. Bryant. (1980). Attitudes Toward Recreation Development: An Application of Social Exchange Theory. *Leisure Sciences, 3*(2). New York: Crane Russak and Co., Inc.

Richards, R. (1984). When Even Bad News is Not So Bad; Local Control over Outside Forces in CD. *Journal of the Community Development Society, 15*(1). Athens, GA: University of Georgia.

Rosenow, J., & G. Pulsipher. (1979). *Tourism the Good, the Bad, and the Ugly*. Lincoln, NB: Century Three Press.

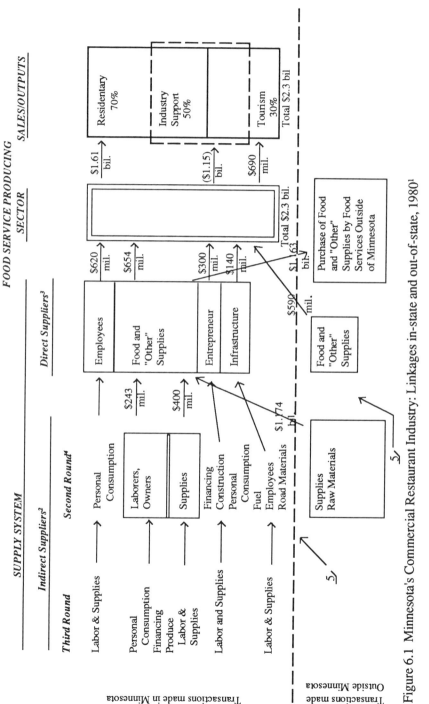

Figure 6.1 Minnesota's Commercial Restaurant Industry: Linkages in-state and out-of-state, 1980[1]

Note: Vertical length of each component is proportional to its dollar value.

Source: Blank, U. & R. Olson. *Food Services: A Major Minnesota Economic Component, Staff Paper*, p 83-11, Dept. of Agriculture & Applied Economics University of Minnesota, St. Paul 1983.

(1)— Arrows show the direction of input and output movement. Labeling on arrows give the dollar values, where available. Quantitative estimates of "Second Round" suppliers are available only for the "Food and Supplies" segment. (2)— The supply system is often referred to as the "Backward Linkage," meaning that it is the means for food operations to link backward into the economy for labor, supplies, equipment, management and financing in order to operate. In doing this, food services generate economic activity in the community. (3)— The percentage of total inputs purchased by Minnesota food services are Labor (payroll), 27; Food and Other 54 (Food = 40, Operating supplies and service = 14); Entrepreneurial, 13; Infrastructure, 6; for a total of 100%. (4)— Names of second and third round inputs are symbolic only. The mix of inputs is much more complex than shown. (5)—Out-of-state purchases are made by the "Employees," "Entrepreneurial" and "Infrastructure" components as part of second round supplies. Quantitative estimates are not available for these purchases and they are only illustrated symbolically. There will also be out-of-state purchases as part of the third round inputs by all elements of the second round linkages.

SIX

Interrelationships:
The Tourism Industry and the Local Economy

Tourism, more than any other industry, relates to the total community. This wide range of interrelationships derives first from the necessity of tourists to be physically present in the community in order to consume its tourism offering. Tourists come because of a community feature, or combination of features, that attract them. This attraction puts emphasis upon things to see and do, economic activities, and the overall character of the community's resources and ambience.

While in the community, tourists require everything of the community needed to recreate, live there and travel. They actually need everything that they would have needed had they been in their home community, but in very different proportions. In fulfilling their needs, tourists contact almost the full range of local citizens, facilities and services.

The tourism industry yields employment, profits, rents and taxes to the community, just as do other economic activities. It does this through the sale of goods and services to tourists who are present in the community. Even though the money changes hands locally, tourism sales are export sales. That is, they are, by definition, sales to non-residents and thus bring in "outside" money. The income thus generated has a beneficial economic effect upon the community's economy similar to that produced by income from sales outside the community of minerals, the output of a manufacturing plant or agricultural production.

This chapter begins treatment of the complex tourism-community interrelationships. It discusses in detail the mechanisms of community income production from the tourism industry. Employees, tourism firm entrepreneurs and local supplying firms have a role in this process and they are also discussed. Finally, the seldom-treated role of the tourist industry in community economic development theory is explained. Misunderstanding of these relationships creates much of the confusion and mythology surrounding tourism.

TOURISM'S FORWARD AND BACKWARD LINKAGES TO THE COMMUNITY: AN IN-DEPTH EXAMINATION

The manner in which the tourism industry contributes its output and forms part of the community's economic base is illustrated in detail here, using the Minnesota food service industry as an example. Minnesota, appropriately, represents an average state. It has about one-fiftieth of the U.S. population, distributed well among metropolitan and nonmetropolitan areas, and its tourism offering ranges from a primitive wilderness experience to a sophisticated urban setting.

A food service example is used for a number of reasons: In the first place, detailed information is available for Minnesota food services, enabling an in-depth understanding of the income-generating process (Blank, 1983). Further, this look at a single industry type allows study of interrelationships that would be incomprehensible in attempting to treat all of the multifaceted tourism industry at once. Food service is the largest SIC industry class that is centrally involved in tourism. It has 67 percent of the total number of employees of the major, tourism-involved industry classes (USTDC, 1984). Also, virtually every community has food services and can identify with this type of tourism firm.

Included in the illustration are not only those operations providing prepared food, but also aspects of the specialized food service supplying system. Inclusion of the food service supplying system expands the range of insights into economic interrelationships. Sales of food away from home are estimated at between 11 and 12 percent of all retail sales in Minnesota. In addition, the Minnesota food service supply system makes more than one billion dollars of export sales to food services outside of Minnesota. Together, the food service industry plus the food service supply system make up a significant part of Minnesota's economy.

The economic relationships discussed here for food services are illustrative, in a general way, of such relationships for all tourism-related types of firms. Each type of firm has an output to tourists, and the inputs to the firms have the same kinds of components: Employees, suppliers, entrepreneurs, and community infrastructure. Details of these relationships may be quite different for each firm type.

Economic interrelationships of the food service industry are explained in terms of "forward" and "backward" linkages. The *forward linkage* consists of the productive output of the industry to the community and the society, and the *backward linkage* is made up of those things that the industry requires in order to produce its output. The latter is the mechanism by which income is generated in the community. Income is both direct and indirect, and the combination of these two income sources

produces the *multiplier*. This is the process whereby one dollar spent to purchase the industry's output "turns over"—is respent in the community—to generate more than one dollar of community sales. Forward and backward linkages are portrayed graphically in Figure 6.1.

Outputs, or "Forward Linkages," of Food Services

In 1980 Minnesota food services' sales were estimated at $2.3 billion. A full understanding of this output requires looking at more than simply the dollar value. In the first place, a restaurant provides not only physical sustenance, but also a set of services that the customer either cannot perform for him/herself or that the customer purchases them as contributions to his/her desired lifestyle. Secondly, sales are made to different classes of customers who buy for different reasons.

The obvious services provided are preparation of food, its serving, and auxiliary services. But the output to food service patrons is much more than food. A major part of this additional type of output may be called "lifestyle enhancement."

We might look briefly at the last half-century's pattern of eating out. The 1930/1940s era marked a period of rapid changes in lifestyle which included increases in the consumption of food away from the home. In 1930 the U.S. population spent only 3.7 percent of its disposable income for eating out. Between 1935 and 1940, U.S. disposable personal income increased by 29 percent, the population also became more mobile as automobiles came into wider usage, and purchases of food away from home increased sharply. By 1945, 6.3 percent of disposable income was spent for food and beverage away from home. Disposable income has continued to grow since 1945, but the proportion spent for eating out has shown a tendency to stabilize at about 5 percent. Combined in this eating out lifestyle are time-saving, convenience, social experience, entertainment, adventure, variety and status. Examples include:

—The ready availability of food services makes possible an "at will" choice of when one will or must undertake food preparation at home.

—Food and drink consumed in pleasant surroundings with one's friends may be among the most valued of social experiences.

—Experiencing another culture through the ethnic ambience and cuisine of a theme restaurant offers adventure and variety.

—Restaurants provide the setting to see the "notables" or be seen by others.

Thus the food service system of a community operates to meld and mold many of the ingredients and forces that make up that community's self-perception as held by residents, and its image as held by non-residents. The quality and variety of food services occupy a continuing, prominent role in the process. The bottom line consists of the community's success as a fulfilling place to live, as well as to visit.

One approach to an analysis of food service users divides clients into two major types, each of which is further subdivided. In addition, a subclass cross-cuts both of these two major classes. The discussion below adds details to the classes as illustrated in Figure 6.1:

Residentary, or sales to local residents. In 1980, 70 percent of all Minnesota's commercial restaurant sales, or $1.6 billion, were to residents of the local community. Four complexly interrelated types, by purpose for purchase of food away from home by residents, are identified:

For convenience.
Under conditions of necessity.
Related to business or institutional activities.
The quest for life experience enrichment.

A separate study of Minneapolis/St. Paul households provides further insights into the "enrichment" component of residentary sales (Blank, 1982). It was found that there were, per family, an annual average of 69 person-occasions of "eating out for fun." This average includes all households. (A person-occasion counts each person one time for each activity, e.g., two people from the same household eating out together would count as two person-occasions).

Tourism, or sales to non-residents not regularly commuting to work or school in the given community. Restaurant sales to tourists totaled $700 million in 1980 or 30 percent of all Minnesota restaurant sales. When selling to non-residents, restaurants are exporters, generating new income for the local economy. Food service sales to tourists vary greatly, percentage wise, by community. They are dependent first upon the traveler-attracting capability of the community, hence its general tourist trade; secondly, tourist sales depend upon the quality of the food services themselves. Some of these interrelationships between tourists, their travel purposes, and the community's food service industry are illustrated by the following:

Some tourists travel for recreational and cultural purposes: To attend a sports event, theater, celebration, etc. They may or may not also purchase food in the destination community. They may choose to eat at home or along the way. If they are not staying overnight, but can be induced to eat in the community having the recreational attraction, the economic impact of their visit increases. Dining out can be an integral part of the overall experience of travel. Twenty-nine percent of Minneapolis-St. Paul tourists reported "dining out" as an activity during a visit there, although a much higher proportion reported some expenditures for restaurant food (Blank, 1979).

Eating out on the occasion of visits by friends and relatives is an important "hosting" activity. This activity also depends in part on both the host's and visitor's image of the local food services. Sixty percent of Minneapolis-St. Paul households reported that they act as hosts to out-of-the area visitors, and "usually" take them out to eat (Blank, 1982).

In destinations having a relatively large tourism industry compared to the rest of the economy, food services may represent a substantial part of the community income. For example in Minnesota's North Shore area (the 150 miles of Minnesota bordering Lake Superior, from Duluth to the Ontario border), tourists' expenditures amount to 35 percent of the total of all retail, plus selected services sales. Thirty-seven percent of tourists' expenditures in the area are for food and food services. This means that food service sales to tourists alone are equal to about 13 percent of all the area's retail and selected services sales (Blank, 1984).

Those traveling on business might, at first thought, appear stuck with food services in the given community. This is only partly true. Business travelers have considerable flexibility to adjust where they will be at mealtimes and for overnight lodging. They can arrange to be in places that attract them and avoid areas with poor services.

The food service industry at certain travel nodes exhibits dramatic growth. Hinckley, Minnesota, illustrates such a situation, and adds detail to the travel node discussion in Chapter 2. In 1982 one food service operation at Hinckley had more than 100 on its payroll and was the largest private employer in Pine County. In addition, there are a number of other food services at this same location. Taken all together, the food services of Pine County are among its largest for-profit industries. How did rural Pine County with an otherwise limited economic base develop such a relatively large food service industry? Hinckley has a population of less than 1,000, but it has a major location advantage for food services: It is directly on Interstate 35, almost exactly halfway along the 165-mile route from Minneapolis-St. Paul to Duluth. It thus has an ideal location as a "travel break." Fortunately for the community, entrepreneurship recognizing this opportunity came along. Capitalizing upon the destination image that has been created, this entrepreneurship is now expanding the tourism sales package by developing a major theme park, Mission Creek.

Industry support consists of food sales to those who must be away from home temporarily for vocational purposes. Our economy requires travel on the part of many people, and food services are essential in order for this travel to take place. Food services and other hospitality businesses thus support, in part, most of the operations of our economy and society. The input that they make to the overall economy is as essential as is that of raw materials, parts supplies, and energy. Without the services needed by people to live away from home, modern industry could not operate.

Industry support is estimated to make up about 50 percent each of *residentary* and of *tourism* food sales components, totaling $1.15 billion in 1980 in Minnesota. Interrelated subparts include:

— *Business travelers*—modern business, social and governmental institutions require travel for sales, management, education and technical consultation. Most of this travel can be classified as tourism.

— *Meeting/conferencing*—face to face interaction is required by nearly all aspects of private and public life. Food services often provide the setting, in addition to meals. Food sales resulting may be classified as residentary or tourism, or parts of both, depending upon home location of participants.

— *Worker convenience*—many employed people find going home for meals impractical. Food services at or near the workplace provide convenience and save time and travel. Most such sales are to local residents.

Food Services as Community Economic Base: Backward Linkages and the Multiplier Effect

We have noted that food services, in common with other tourism-related firms, generate jobs, profits, rents and taxes, thus forming part of the community's economic base (economic base is discussed later in this chapter). Food services have beneficial community economic effects because of the purchases—backward linkages—that these operations make in the community in order to produce their output. Each tourism-related firm type differs in its backward linkage pattern. The pattern also depends upon the community itself—its size and its complex of resources and services. Thus the local economic impact of tourism may vary considerably.

Two characteristics of food services deserve special attention in consideration of economic base:

— *Food services are geographically dispersed, as noted earlier.* This means that they have a widespread impact, since nearly all communities in the United States now have food services. Only travel fuel services, another type of travel/tourism firm, are so thoroughly dispersed.

— *The food service multiplier is relatively large.* The food service system transactions multiplier has been estimated at 2.3 for the United States—not to be confused with the $2.3 billion of Minnesota food service industry sales (Maki, 1977). This means that for every dollar spent for food in restaurants, another $1.3 of sales activity is generated. Usually the multiplier will be larger for a large community than one that is smaller. This is because the larger community can supply from within itself more of the inputs needed by the food service firm, and also by many other kinds of firms.

A large food service multiplier occurs because a high proportion of the money received for food sales is re-spent in the local economy. Figure 6.1 shows what happened to the $2.3 billion of 1980 Minnesota food service sales. Seventy-four percent of $1.71 billion of these purchases are made from Minnesota-based "direct suppliers" or "first round suppliers." Each of these who receive money in the first round must, in turn, re-spend this money to create a second round of spending. Employees spend for personal needs; businesses spend to pay their own employees, for energy or supplies. This creates a third round. In each round of spending, money is "lost" out of the community or state economy. The re-spending continues in succeeding rounds until all of the original money is dissipated from the local economy. This local re-spending causes the multiplier effect, and re-spending outside the local economy (losses) limits its size.

"Food and other supplies" illustrate the way in which losses occur. Just under half—$590 million—of food and other supplies is purchased from firms located outside Minnesota.

In Figure 6.1 it is assumed that all direct (first round) purchases made by food services, except "food and other supplies," are made within Minnesota. This is generally true, although exceptions are known: Some employees commute across the state line; some restaurants are managed, franchised and/or financed by out-of-state owners (entrepreneurship); energy generated in other states is used in parts of Minnesota (infrastructure). Note that the purchases and sales out of state of "food and other supplies" are specifically quantified for the first and second rounds. Data for other out-of-state transactions are not available; hence they can only be illustrated symbolically.

The First Round Inputs

Further insights into the backwards linkage process can be gained by more detailed examination of the four major subparts making up the direct inputs or first round linkage of the supply system.

Employees include hired labor only. The 1980 Minnesota food service payroll was $640 million, or 27 percent of all inputs. It is estimated that 400,000 different individuals were involved in this payroll, including all full-time, part-time, and seasonal employees; these employees use their income for living purposes: to purchase food and clothing, buy automobiles, support their church, pay taxes, etc. This is the second round. In turn, each from whom employees buy must re-spend the money. The clothing merchant, for example, pays the clothing manufacturer/wholesaler, his own employees, rent and utilities on the store building and uses the profit for his own personal consumption. This creates the third round of inputs.

Food and other supplies include both food and items such as food raw materials, table service, specialized restaurant services and restaurant equipment. Over half, 54 percent, of all 1980 Minnesota restaurant purchases were for supplies—totalling $1.24 billion. But, as noted above, only slightly more that half, $654 million, was supplied

by Minnesota-based specialized supply firms. The specialized food service supply system is well developed in Minnesota and sells (exports) about twice as much to out-of-state food services as is bought from out-of-state by Minnesota restaurants—$1.16 billion vs. $590 million. Figure 6.2 shows the Minnesota specialized food service supply system diagrammatically.

Because of its scale, the specialized food service supplying system purchased, within Minnesota, inputs for its own operation having a value almost equal to its sales to Minnesota restaurants—$643 million of input vs. $654 million in sales. This means that, in its own right, the system was contributing substantially to Minnesota's economy. Many of the system's suppliers—second round for the food service industry, first round for the specialized food service supplying system— were agricultural processors and wholesalers. Farm producers were a part of this supply system. Truck farmers selling directly to local restaurants would be first round suppliers. Other farm producers may be as far back as the fifth round.

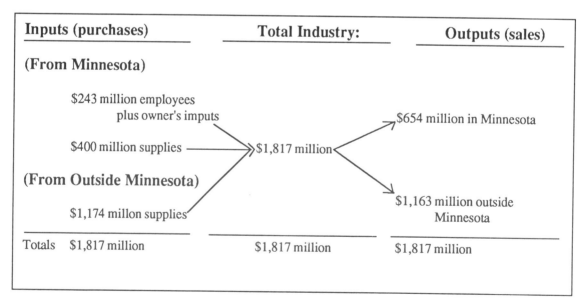

Inputs (purchases)	Total Industry:	Outputs (sales)
(From Minnesota)		
$243 million employees plus owner's imputs		$654 million in Minnesota
$400 million supplies ⟶	$1,817 million	
(From Outside Minnesota)		
$1,174 millon supplies		$1,163 million outside Minnesota
Totals $1,817 million	$1,817 million	$1,817 million

Figure 6.2 Minnesota Food Service Supply System

There were, in 1980, a total of 463 firms in the Minneapolis-St. Paul Metropolitan area that operated as part of the specialized food service supplying system. The kinds of supplying interests and the number in each group are as follows:

Food Suppliers	Number
Wholesale Grocers	33
Fruit and Vegetable	46
Meat Purveyors	69
Poultry	12
Fish and Shellfish	11
Frozen Food and Specialties	59
Dairy Products	31
Bakery	36
Wholesale Liquors	16
Non-Alcoholic Beverages	21

Operating Supply Firms	
Cleaning and Sanitation	25
Menus	5
Equipment and Design	42
Linen Suppliers	8
Paper	25
	463

Entrepreneurship includes the functions of investment, risk, financing, and management (management supplied by owners, not hired). Using slightly different terminology, it includes profits, return to owner-managers, return to unpaid family labor, and all interests and rents whether actually paid or imputed. Its second round backward linkage includes living expenditures by owners, financing costs, and capital development costs such as construction. The input amounted to $300 million, or 13 percent of all food service inputs in 1980.

Community infrastructure consists of facilities and services that are necessary for the community to operate, and that are available to serve all citizens and businesses. This input required 6 percent of all sales and totalled $140 million. Payments for infrastructure include items such as utilities, insurance, and real estate taxes. Sales taxes are not included in infrastructure nor in the total food services industry figure of $2.3 billion. In its second round, real estate tax money may be spent for roads, street lighting, police protection, and in some cases to improve community aesthetics, such as for parks and landscaping. Other second round expenditures include fuel and employee payrolls to operate energy-supplying plants, and the purchase and operation of telephone equipment.

The discussion in this subsection has shown definitively how food services as a part of the tourism industry produce employment, profits, rents and taxes. They thus function as part of the economic base of the local community.

LINKAGES AND MULTIPLIERS OF OTHER TOURISM-RELATED FIRM TYPES

Other tourism-related firms also produce an output in the form of a specific product or a service that contributes to the tourists' experience. Since they must also have inputs, they also generate local community income. The details for each one differ considerably from those of other firm types.

For example, *gasoline service stations* ordinarily have a much lower sales multiplier than food services, since a high proportion of their sales income goes immediately outside the local community for petroleum supplies. Differently located gasoline service stations may vary drastically in their degree of tourism involvement. Those stations located on an interstate freeway may make most of their sales to tourists, while those located in the inner community may make almost all sales to residents.

A *resort* will usually make almost all of its sales to tourists. Its input structure differs greatly from that of food services and gasoline service stations. Most resorts have a large real estate investment relative to cash flow. This means that expenditures for construction, rents, interest and real estate taxes will ordinarily be proportionately larger than those of the other two types.

A SIMPLE INPUT-OUTPUT EXAMPLE OF MULTIPLIER CALCULATION

Transactions multipliers of the type that we have been discussing thus far are usually calculated by the use of input-output analysis. The actual process is quite laborious. However, an understanding of the principles involved can be achieved relatively easily. Since multipliers are commonly discussed, it is important that those interested in tourism and other industry development have basic insights into multipliers, the data required for their calculation, and the computation process. For that reason a simple example is given here as a complement to the preceding discussion of Figure 6.1, and that of income multipliers that follows this section.

The first step in determination of a transactions multiplier requires that the community's total economy be classified by types of producing and consuming segments. Each is then systematically sampled to determine from whom and how much each purchases, and to whom and how much each sells. The findings are then arranged in a transactions matrix, that in exceedingly simplified form would look like Table 6.1.

Notice that in Table 6.1 we have an economy that consists of only two producing sectors: manufacturing and services. The production, or sales, of each sector is shown in the rows (horizontally); the consumption, or purchases, of each sector is shown in the columns (vertically). For example, the manufacturing sector shows sales as follows: 30 units to services and 20 units to final demand, for a total output of 50 units. The services sector sells 40 units to manufacturing and 50 units to final demand, for a total output of 90 units.

Not only have we simplified the example by having only two producing sectors, but no internal sales within the manufacturing or services sectors are shown. In addition, there is no household producing sector; households are represented only in the final demand. In the real world these simplifications would not occur.

In this example the manufacturing sector must purchase 40 units from services in order to produce its total output of 50 units. At the same time the service sector purchases 30 units of manufacturing output in order to produce its total output of 90 units.

Table 6.1
Transactions Matrix

| | | *Consuming Sectors* | | | |
		Manufacturing	*Services*	*Final Demand*	*Total*
Producing	Manufacturing	—	30	20	50
Sectors	Services	40	—	50	90

Now we are ready to prepare a general equation, written as follows:

$$x_{11} + x_{12} + Y_1 = X_1$$

$$x_{21} + x_{22} + Y_2 = X$$

Figure 6.3 Generalized Formula

In the equation x_{11} represents the output of industry 1, manufacturing, used by industry 1; in Table 6.1 this value is 0. x_{12} represents the output of industry 1, manufacturing, used by industry 2, services; in Table 6.1 this value is 30. Y_1 represents the final demand for industry 1, manufacturing. X_1 represents the total output of industry 1, manufacturing. Similarly, the second row in Figure 6.3 represents the respective outputs or sales of the service sector to manufacturing, services, final demand, and total output of services.

Since x_{11} and x_{22} are both 0, we may rewrite the equation omitting them:

$$x_{12} + Y_1 = X_1$$

$$x_{21} + Y_2 = X_2$$

Figure 6.4 Simplification of Generalized Formula

In order to permit mathematical manipulations, we now calculate "technical coefficients" as follows:

$$A_{12} = \frac{x_{12}}{X_2} = \frac{30}{90} = \frac{1}{3}$$

$$A_{21} = \frac{x_{21}}{X_1} = \frac{40}{50} = \frac{4}{5}$$

Figure 6.5 Technical Coefficients

These technical coefficients have specific meaning, and add insights into the internal workings of the economy that we are illustrating. In computer terms, technical coefficients are referred to as "coefficients of the inverse matrix." A_{12} gives the ratio of the output of sector 1, manufacturing, required for the production of each unit of total output of sector 2, services. We have determined that this is 1/3 by substituting the appropriate data from Table 6.1. Similarly, A_{21} gives the ratio of the output of sector 2, services, required for the production of each unit of total output of sector 1, manufacturing. This we determine to be 4/5.

Now we can rewrite the equations so they can be solved in terms of final demand. We do this by multiplying through by X_2 in the top line of Figure 6.5, to get a new symbol for x_{12}: $A_{12}X_2$. We multiply the lower line Figure 6.5 by X_1 to get a new symbol for x_{21}: $A_{21}X_1$. Then substituting for x_{12} and x_{21} in Figure 6.4 we get:

$$A_{12}X_2 + Y_1 = X_1$$

$$A_{21}X_1 + Y_2 = X_2$$

Figure 6.6 Generalized Equation for Solution in Terms of Final Demand

Now, substituting values for technical coefficients from Figure 6.5, and data from Table 6.1, we have two simultaneous equations in two unknowns.

$$X_1 - 1/3\ X_2 = 20$$

$$-4/5\ X_1 + X_2 = 50$$

Figure 6.7 Equation for Solution (Simultaneous Equations)

If we solve the set of simultaneous equations in Figure 6.7, we will get $X_1 = 50$, and $X_2 = 90$. This we already had in Table 6.1. But there are other valuable insights that we can gain from Figure 6.7. Suppose, for example, we wanted to see what happened to the outputs of the economic sectors if the final demand for sector 1, manufacturing, increases by 50 percent from 20 units to 30 units. We can substitute 30 in place of 20 in the equations of Figure 6.7, and then solve for X_1 and X_2. We find that all sectors of the economy change (except final demand for sector 2, services). Instead of the values in Table 6.1, we get an input-output transactions table with the values in Table 6.2.

Note that the total input of sector 1, manufacturing, went up by more than the increase of 10 units in final demand. This is because services are used by manufacturing to produce its output, and service sector output had to increase by 10.9 units. But manufacturing is also an input into services; hence when the final demand of manufacturing increased, manufacturing's output had to expand not only to take care of the extra final demand, but also to provide needed additional inputs into services. Services, in turn, had to increase to provide added inputs into manufacturing. Also note that the increase in total output of manufacturing is 13.6 units while the total output of services increased by 10.9 units. This latter is 4/5 of the manufacturing output increase, which is exactly what the technical coefficient A_{21} in Figure 6.5 told us it should be. Technical coefficient A_{12} is 1/3, and this equals 3.6 units of manufacturing (total manufacturing output increase of 13.6 minus 10—the increase in final

demand) divided by the total increase in services output of 10.6. Thus the input-output technique allows us to gain insights into the dynamics of an economy's inner workings.

Had we used more that just a two-sector model, for example 20 sectors, we could have gained some added valuable understanding of how economies work. For example, we might have found that sector 5, a tourism-related class of operations, made direct purchases only from sectors 2, 8, 9, and 14. Then let us determine what happens when we assume that the output of sector 5 increases by 20 units.

After completing calculations such as illustrated by Table 6.2, we might find that in addition to output increases in the four sectors from which direct purchases were made by sector 5, the output of an additional 10 sectors also increased as the result of an increase in the output of sector 5. What happened? The increase in sectors 2, 8, 9, and 14, from which direct purchases are made, we call the "direct multiplier" effect. As output of each of these four sectors increases, they must make added purchases to support this production. They make purchases from a diverse range of economic sectors in second and succeeding rounds, thus generating an "indirect multiplier" effect. The direct plus the indirect multipliers are summed to determine the total transactions, or sales multiplier.

What we have observed about tourism's impact upon the economy is somewhat like that of the operation of an ecological chain. Every part of the

Table 6.2
Computed Data for Transactions Matrix

		Consuming Sectors			
		Manufacturing	*Services*	*Final Demand*	*Total*
Producing	Manufacturing	—	33.6	30	63.6
Sectors	Services	50.9	—	50	100.9

system depends, directly or indirectly, upon every other part. A purchase by tourists from any firm tends to have repercussions throughout the entire community. As is said of an ecological system, "When one part of the world is moved, everything else rattles!"

THE INCOME MULTIPLIER

How much of the money that tourists spend becomes income for people in the community? We have reported an estimate of 2.3 for the food service sales/transactions multiplier. This means that for every dollar spent by tourists, an added $1.30 of sales is generated. This figure, however, is deceptive; most of the money leaks out of the community and is not available as income for residents.

An income multiplier indicates the ratio of tourism sales to actual personal income that is available to spend for consumption by community residents. We will use the data from Figure 6.1 to do a crude calculation illustrating an income multiplier.

We have already noted that 74 cents of each dollar of tourists' expenditures for food are converted into local community transactions in the first round. Twenty-seven cents of this goes to employees as direct personal income. We assume, in addition, that half of the 14 cents going to entrepreneurial purposes goes directly into personal income. This means that 34 cents goes into personal income in the first round.

In the second round, we note that there is a substantial employee/owner income for the food and other supplying sector. This amounts to 10.6 cents per dollar of food service sales ($243/$2300), and only 36 percent—the Minnesota proportion—can be used ($654/$1817). This means that the personal income to food supplier personnel in this second round is 3.8 cents (10.6 cents x 36 percent).

As an allowance for all succeeding rounds, we add an additional one-third of the above amounts. We also add 3 cents as a probably more than generous allowance for personal income that may accrue to the community residents from the six percent of sales that is expended for infrastructure.

Table 6.3
The Income Multiplier, Minnesota Food Services, 1980

	Cents per Dollar of Sales	
First Round		
Employee Income	27.0¢	
One-half of Entrepreneurship	7.0	
Total First Round		34.0¢
Second and Succeeding Rounds		
Employees and Managers of Food Supply Systems	3.8¢	
One-third of 34 cents	11.3	
One-third of Food Supply, First Round (3.8¢)	1.3	
Infrastructure, Second and Succeeding Rounds	3.0	
Total Second and Succeeding Rounds		19.4¢
Income Multiplier		53.4¢

Our thus crudely computed income multiplier for each dollar spent for food away from home in Minnesota is 53.4 cents. According to this calculation, barely a little more than half of each dollar spent becomes income in the pockets of local citizens. Table 6.3 summarizes the computations.

At first glance, this income multiplier may appear low. But that of many other industries is still lower. Food services and most other tourism-related industries have as an ingredient a relatively large proportion of personal services. For that reason, income multipliers of many other industries, such as manufacturing and agriculture, are still lower as a proportion of sales.

TOURISM INDUSTRY MULTIPLIERS: THEIR USE AND ABUSE

Overall tourism industry multipliers have been determined by researchers. These represent aggregates including the different firm types that make up the tourism industry. Because they represent the total tourism industry they are of considerable interest to communities (Archer, 1977). We have used single firm type examples in the forepart of the chapter in order to avoid the complications of dealing simultaneously with multiple types of firms as we attempted to gain an in-depth understanding of the economic interaction process. But an overall figure is the most relevant in viewing tourism's impact upon the community.

Tourism industry multipliers have been computed by Liu and Var for metropolitan Victoria, British Columbia, as follows (Liu, 1983):

— Transactions or sales multiplier 1.50
— Income multiplier .65
— Government revenue (taxes) .21.

Harmston has calculated aggregate multipliers for out-of-state travelers to the state of Missouri (Harmston, 1984):

— Transactions or sales multiplier 2.06
— Income multiplier .78
— Government revenue (state and local taxes) 20.

The multipliers for an entire state are seen here to be larger than those for a single city. This supports our previous observation that a larger community should have larger multipliers because it should be able to provide proportionately more of the needed inputs.

The multiplier has its greatest value first in understanding the economic interrelationships of the tourism industry with the community. We can see how the internal economic mechanisms operate to affect the entire community. The multiplier values show the ultimate impact upon the community's economy. Secondly, we can construct economic models of the community, if transactions data have been gathered such as those illustrated in Table 6.1. With such a model we can determine the possible impact of alternative strategies that might result from developing different economic components of the community.

Unfortunately, the multiplier concept has been often misused in connection with tourism. In their zeal to promote tourism industry development, individuals related to hospitality businesses and community betterment have sometimes used preposterous multiplier values—some claiming glibly that "the tourist dollar turns over (as much as) 12 times before it leaves the community." A cursory look at the real world would easily convince the strongest believer in such a relationship level that it could not in reality be true. Many states and communities have direct tourism sales amounting to at least 5 percent of their gross product. With a multiplier of 12, 60 percent of the economy would be dependent upon tourism as the economic base generator. This leaves unrealistically small shares for the balance of the other components of economic base such as manufacturing, mining, agriculture, etc. (see the section on Community Development Theories in the last part of this chapter).

An unhappy result of overblown claims for tourism and tourism multipliers has been the creation of widespread skepticism about the tourism industry's benefits to the community. Objective listeners simply dismiss, out of hand, what they hear. The detailed treatment to economic interrelationships that is given here attempts to dispell myths and reduce misuse of the concepts.

What effect should multiplier figures have upon attempts by a community to develop its economy? Its greatest use may be in improving understanding by leaders and citizens generally that tourism sales by a local firm benefit the entire community (Milne, 1987). Rather than overemphasis upon the multiplier, the most important considerations for tourism industry development deal with questions of comparative advantage. These include: What are our tourism resources? How well do these resources adapt to effective demand? How do we strengthen and support existing industries? What kinds of diversification will provide the best balance for our economy? And most importantly: What is possible and feasible?

TOURISM AS THE STIMULATOR OF ECONOMIC GROWTH

Are there, in fact, empirical examples of economic health and growth resulting from the tourism industry? There are indeed. Scholars tend to favor input-output analysis, which employs the precise mathematical manipulations involving matrix algebra. Matrix algebra, in turn, requires the use of computers, since on a practical basis only the high speed of computers makes it possible to solve large matrices. On the other hand, for many practitioners as well as students, the historical-analytic comparisons that follow may be equally or more helpful.

Missouri Examples of Community Economic Growth Through Tourism

The Ozark Mountain region of the central United States has long been considered economically disadvantaged. The tourism industry is altering this pattern. Here we will compare economic growth and development in two Ozark communities with what has been commonly considered as a better-endowed, advantaged northeastern Missouri community. We will see that economic patterns now operate to reverse the fortunes of these communities.

Figure 6.8 shows the long sweep of population change throughout the 20th century (1900 to 1984) for:

—*The United States.*
—*The state of Missouri.*
—*Branson/Table Rock area.* This three-county (Barry, Stone, and Taney) Missouri area is rugged and remote from large population centers. It was originally settled mainly by mountaineers migrating from Kentucky and nearby states. Their major income was timber harvest and subsistence agriculture. Harold Bell Wright's *Shepherd of the Hills* brought it notoriety early in the 20th Century. In 1912 a water reservoir, Lake Taneycomo, was completed as a private power source. These events brought tourism on a limited scale. In 1959 an even larger water reservoir, Table Rock, was constructed by the U.S. Army Corps of Engineers. Major private tourism industry investment and development followed: a large theme park, more than a dozen well-appointed facilities featuring Ozark music, drama and other entertainment, and supporting hospitality services. A result has been rapid growth of the tourism industry.

—*Lake of the Ozarks*, a four-county Missouri area including the counties of Benton, Camden, Miller and Morgan. Its major first settlers also came to log and practice subsistence farming. In 1931, Union Electric Company completed the

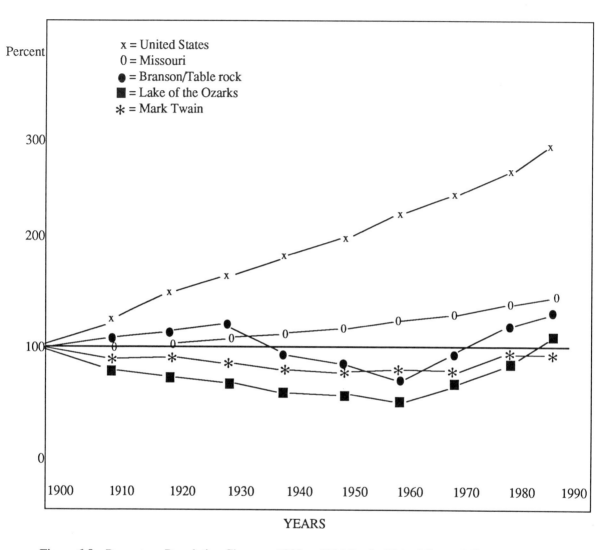

Figure 6.8   Percentage Population Changes, 1900 to 1984 for the United States, Missouri, and Selected Missouri Recreational Areas

Source: U.S. Census of Population

Counties composing the lake recreation areas:
    Mark Twain—Audrain, Marion, Monroe, Pike, Ralls and Shelby
    Lake of the Ozarks—Benton, Camden, Miller and Morgan
    Branson/Table Rock—Barry, Stone and Taney

50,000 acre Lake of the Ozarks. It serves as a supplemental power source for the St. Louis area. This lake was then the only major recreational water available south of the Great Lakes in the central United States. There followed what, in greatly oversimplified form, may be described as a four-stage tourism industry development:

1. Emphasis mainly upon fishing in the lake. Primitive resort cabins—mainly a "roof and a path"—were developed. Private lake cottages, mostly minimal in scale and appointments, were constructed.
2. Upgrading began shortly after World War II. This development included better appointed chain motels and improved food services; and main roads were surfaced.
3. Large-scale convention/resorting facilities offering golf courses and swimming pools were developed.
4. Expansion in the activities' attractions including shopping malls and entertainment features. For many of these, water added only ambience. Upgrading in private homes, both for residents, second homes, and retirement. Major improvement in roads to accommodate traffic.

*—Mark Twain Lake/Hannibal—*a six-county northeast Missouri area including the counties of Audrian, Marion, Monroe, Pike, Ralls and Shelby. This area was and continues to be predominantly agricultural. Hannibal was a major 19th Century river port, but has experienced little development throughout the 20th century. Recently there has been expansion of manufacturing plants. The area does have considerable resources that could support development of the tourism industry. The famous American author, Mark Twain, was born and grew up here, and many sites in the Hannibal vicinity were made famous by his books. Potential for tourism industry development was recently added with the creation of the 20,000 acre Mark Twain

Lake in 1983 by the U.S. Army Corps of Engineers (Blank, 1986).

Population growth in the state of Missouri did not keep pace with that in the United States. But it did grow by 61 percent over the 84-year period. Population in the Mark Twain Lake/Hannibal area declined 19 percent, having fallen throughout the entire period except for stabilization in the 1970-1984 period. The pattern in Branson/Table Rock and Lake of the Ozarks was very different. During the 40-year period 1920-1960, their populations declined more precipitously than that of the Mark Twain Lake/Hannibal area. But in the most recent 24-year (1960-1984) period, populations in the two tourist-impacted areas grew faster than that of even the United States.

Why the differences in population growth in these three sub-areas of Missouri?

The Mark Twain Lake/Hannibal area has primarily an agricultural economy that, up until now, has not developed substantial other means of economic base. Agriculture is a raw materials supplying industry, along with forestry, mining and fishing. Throughout the past century raw materials supplying industries have suffered from two kinds of economic pressures:

—As technical advances have occurred, the production of raw materials has become more efficient in terms of direct man-power needs. This has made it possible for human resources to shift out of agricultural and other raw materials production.

—Raw materials product prices are subject to severe boom and bust cycles. These create periodic mini-depressions that are often not fully shared with the overall economy. Evidence for these bust cycles is seen in the agricultural depression of the 1980s, the oil-patch problems in Texas and Oklahoma, and depressions in many metals-mining communities in the late 1970s and 1980s.

Communities suffering depression in the midst of a generally prosperous economy lose population. Under conditions of falling population numbers, a community's institutions and people services erode: it becomes increasingly difficult to support churches, schools, and retail services. Shortages of employment opportunities cause many of the most talented youth to go elsewhere—a serious community loss. The downward-spiralling cycle, particularly during economic busts, feeds upon itself. Reduced services may make the community less desirable as a place to live, further encouraging not only young people but others who are footloose—out of a job or bankrupt—to leave.

Both Branson/Table Rock and Lake of the Ozarks were initially involved in raw materials production: timber and subsistence agriculture. As noted above, their population numbers fell even more rapidly in the 1920-1960 period than even that of Mark Twain Lake/Hannibal. About 1960 there was a "take-off" point for the tourism industry of the two southern areas, after which their populations grew at a rate more than twice that of the United States. Population increases for the 1960 to 1984 period were 77 percent and 71 percent, repectively, vs. 32 percent for the United States.

Why did this shift in population growth trends occur in these Southern Missouri areas? We noted the major public and quasi-public investments in large water impoundments there. Water has long been and continues to be a major travel attractor. The water developments were followed by private investment in recreational, living, and service systems. This process is ongoing. Original investments have now experienced several generations of redevelopment and upgrading of the package of attractions, infrastructure and services offered to residents and tourists. As a consequence they attracted an increasing flow of tourists. With the tourists came a growing number of residents, both to enjoy the lake ambience and to take advantage of opportunities offered by the expanding tourism industry.

Industry trend comparisons illustrate the growth of tourism in the Branson/Table Rock and Lake of the Ozarks areas. In Figure 6.9, percentage growth in retail sales of the five areas under comparison are charted for the 1967-1982 period. During this 15-year period, retail sales grew at a faster rate in both tourism areas than in either the state of Missouri or the United States, while that of the Mark Twain area lagged. Comparisons of eating and drinking sales show similar patterns.

Now we make a comparison of other industries in these several geographic areas, using Figure 6.10. This comparison provides us with a highly significant finding: Namely, that *manufacturing industry payrolls in dollars went up at a much faster rate in the Branson/Table Rock and Lake of the Ozarks areas than in any of the others under comparison.* This refutes the common misconception that tourism and manufacturing are primarily competitive. In this case they are not only compatible but appear to be complementary.

It may be hypothesized that at least three factors are operating to stimulate this rapid growth in manufacturing payrolls in the two tourism producing areas. In the first place, manufacturing was at a low level at the start of the period under comparison, in the two tourism areas. Secondly, rapid growth in resident population, retail services generally and hospitality services specifically generated a need for locally manufactured items. Finally, the influx of new residents and of tourists brings people of many new talents to the area; they perceive opportunities and needs, both local and for export, that they act upon. These findings do not guarantee that every area having tourism industry growth will also have rapid growth in manufacturing industry payrolls. But they do demonstrate that such a tourism-manufacturing relationship can, and does, happen.

A related comparison finds that, in the Branson/Table Rock and Lake of the Ozarks areas, *growth in the tourism industry appears in no way to have occurred at the expense of the agricultural industry.* In fact, the sales of farm products held its own in

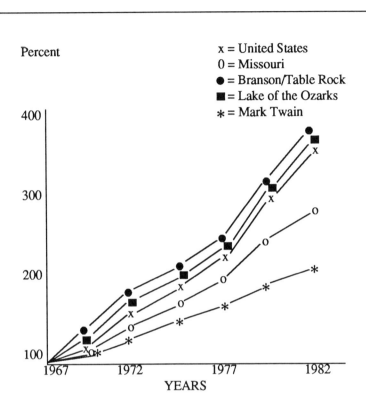

Figure 6.9   Percentage Changes in Total Retail Sales, 1967
              to 1982, for the United States, Missouri, and
              Selected Missouri Recreational Areas

Source: U.S. Census of Business

Counties composing the lake recreation areas:
    Mark Twain—Audrain, Marion, Monroe, Pike, Ralls and Shelby
    Lake of the Ozarks—Benton, Camden, Miller and Morgan
    Branson/Table Rock—Barry, Stone and Taney

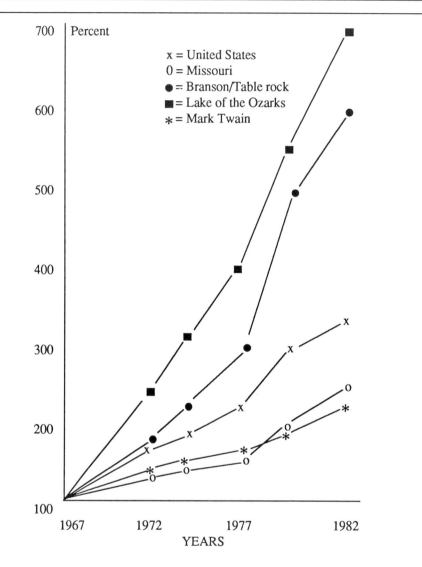

Figure 6.10 Percentage Changes in Manufacturing Industry Payroll
           Dollars 1967 to1982, for the United States, Missouri, and
           Selected Missouri Recreational Areas

Source: U.S. Census of Business

Counties composing the lake recreation areas:
   Mark Twain—Audrain, Marion, Monroe, Pike, Ralls and Shelby
   Lake of the Ozarks—Benton, Camden, Miller and Morgan
   Branson/Table Rock—Barry, Stone and Taney

comparison with Missouri areas. Changes in the 1969 to 1982 period observed were:

— Mark Twain Lake/Hannibal—up 172 percent
— Missouri—up 156 percent
— United States—up 196 percent
— Branson/Table Rock—up 170 percent
— Lake of the Ozarks—up 172 percent

As with manufacturing, there may be some complementarity between tourism, population growth and agriculture, e.g., truck crop production for local consumption and/or roadside sale. What is certainly demonstrated is that there is not a necessarily negative relationship between tourism industry growth and agricultural production.

This analysis of areas where there has been recent growth in the tourism industry, and its empirical comparison with other areas, suggests the following relationships between the tourism industry and the local economy:

— Growth in the tourism industry can not only stem the tide of net out-migration, but stimulate renewed population growth.
— Concomitant with tourism industry growth is expansion in the hospitality firm sales and retail sales generally. (This is somewhat axiomatic, since tourism can only grow if sales of retail goods and services increase.)
— Growth of tourism may be compatible with, and even complementary to, the manufacturing and agricultural industries.

An Example From a Mining and Timber-Producing Area— Northeastern Minnesota

An example of the tourism industry's role in providing economic stability and growth in an area otherwise wracked with severe economic crises, comes from northeastern Minnesota. Examined is the 14-year economic history for the period 1970-1984 of the six-county Minnesota area including Aitkin, Carlton, Cook, Itasca, Koochiching, Lake and St. Louis Counties. Cook County stands out from the other five, and is compared with them and with the state of Minnesota.

This six-county area lies in extreme Northeastern Minnesota and is known as the iron mining region. Within it are the famous Mesabi and two other iron ore ranges. It also has timber harvest and spectacular tourist attractions, including the semi-boreal north woods and waters; Duluth, one of the most spectacularly-sited cities in the world; crystal-clear Lake Superior; the million-acre Boundary Waters Canoe Area (BWCA); and Voyageurs National Park. In addition, the iron mining operations have potential as major tourist attractions in their own right.

The tourism industry has been largely rejected—relegated to a decided second-place status, except in the periphery, which includes Cook County. This is typical of an economy having a major blue-collar job base. During the 1970s, however, growing competition from international iron mining operations severely impacted the area. Mining was sharply curtailed with resulting unemployment and other economic dislocations.

Cook is the only county in the area without mining or major wood processing operations. It has timber production, commercial fishing (largely gone), an early agriculture (now completely gone), and tourism. Its tourism industry, like that in other parts of northern Minnesota, began a relative decline in the 1960s. Unlike that of most other northwoods areas, Cook County's tourism is now resurgent, thanks to an influx of young, vigorous entrepreneurs, to a climate and terrain lending itself to winter sports, and to new, but not overwhelming outside funding. Now a summer and a winter tourism industry has developed that is economically viable and growing.

During the 1970 to 1984 period total employment in the five counties of the region, excluding Cook, grew by seven percent. The state of

Minnesota's employment increased by 38 percent, from 1.66 million to 2.29 million. By comparison employment in Cook County grew by 66 percent.

Figures 6.11 and 6.12 show the economic structure of Cook County compared with the other five counties. In 1970, services and retail trade employment were already relatively large in Cook County, at 41 percent. By 1984 these employment sources made up nearly half of the total—48 percent. These proportions compare with 32 percent and 42 percent in services and retail trade

employment for the five-county area in the same years. Cook County's manufacturing, construction and "other" employment was almost stable percentage-wise—28 percent and 26 percent—and governmental employment actually declined in relative terms. At the same time manufacturing, mining, construction, and other employment fell significantly in the five-county area, from 46 to 37 percent.

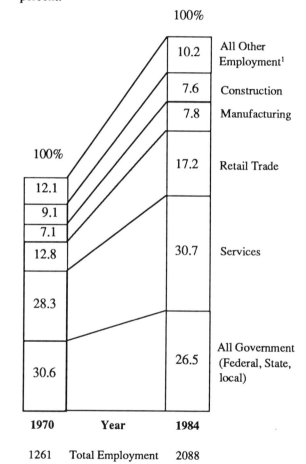

Figure 6.11 Industry Segment Shares of Total
           Employment, Region 3, MN,
           Less Cook County, 1970-84

Figure 6.12 Industry Segment Shares of Total
           Employment, Cook County, MN, 1970-84

[1] "All other employment" includes industry segments: Agriculture, Forestry, Fisheries, Transportation, Public Utilities, Whole-Sale Trade, Finance and Industries.

Source: Maki, W. *Minnesota Simlab*, special tabulations from unpublished data of Regional Economic Information System, U.S. Department of Commerce, Bureau of Economic Analysis, Washington, D.C., 1987.

The reader will note that Cook County's manufacturing employment rose both in absolute terms and also in relative terms. These data support the observed growth of manufacturing employment in the presence of tourism industry growth also seen in the Ozarks areas examples.

This Cook County example offers an antidote to the problem of obsolescence discussed in Chapter 3. It also demonstrates that tourism can support a growing employment base in an otherwise depressed economic area.

TOURISM AND THE COMMUNITY: EMPLOYMENT AND THE WORK FORCE

Tourism Industry Employment: Part of the Rapidly Rising United States Service Industry Work Force

Table 6.4 shows the striking macro-trend in expansion of U.S. service industry's employment compared with employment in goods-producing

industries. In the 58-year period from 1929 to 1987, employment in the service industries grew from 43 percent of total U.S. employed people to 73 percent. By contrast, employment in goods-producing industries —including agriculture, mining and manufacturing—decreased relatively from 57 percent to 27 percent of total employment. For the first 20 years of the period, until 1950, this adjustment proceeded slowly. Since the 1950s it has progressed much more rapidly.

A more specific measure of tourism industry employment is shown in Table 6.5. Payroll employment for selected travel industry sectors is compared with total U.S. payroll employment for the 10-year period from 1976 to 1986. In that decade, travel industry payrolls increased by 57 percent, compared with an expansion of 26 percent in total U.S. payroll employment (USTDC, 1984). Judging by current economic and employment reports (in 1988), the rapid expansion of service industry employment continues. This employment expansion in tourism and other service industries is largely responsible for total U.S. unemployment dropping below the six percent rate in the latter part

Table 6.4
Employment Trends in Goods-Producing Industries and Service Industries, 1929-1987

Industry Sector	1929 %	1941 %	1950 %	1970 %	1987 %
Agriculture	25	20	14	5	3
Other Goods-Producing Sectors (mining, manufacturing)	32	35	35	35	24
Services	43	45	51	63	73
Total Percent	100%	100%	100%	100%	100%
Employment (in millions)	41.8	45.7	52.4	74.4	105.0

Source: Bureau of Labor Statistics, U.S. Department of Labor, Washington, DC

Table 6.5
Payroll Employment Trends, Travel Industry and Total U.S. Employment, 1976-1986

Industry	1976	1979	1982	1986	Percent Change 1976-1986
		(Payroll employment in thousands)			
Travel Industry	5,592	6,716	7,211	8,755	plus 57%
Total U.S.	79,382	89,805	89,580	100,099	plus 26%

Travel industry payroll employment are totals for intercity highway passenger transportation, air transportation, eating and drinking places, hotels, motels and tourist courts, amusement and recreation services.

Source: U.S. Travel Data Center and U.S. Department of Labor

of the 1980s. The much-sought-after manufacturing employment accounted for only 18 percent of the total employed work force in 1987, and is more likely to contract, at least in relative terms, rather than to expand.

Many Aspects of Tourism Industry Employment Compare Favorably with High-Tech Industry Employment

A revealing example, comparing high-tech industry employment with that of food services, comes from Minnesota. High technology industries are an important employer in Minnesota, and recently (1979) accounted for 148,000 jobs there. Employment by four large high technology corporations—3M, Honeywell, Univac, and Control Data—totalled 50,000. The balance was distributed among smaller firms that also comprised this dynamically growing industry, most of them concentrated in the Minneapolis-St. Paul metropolitan area. Many positive factors attend this situation and a

comparable industry might be coveted by many other states (Drake, 1982).

Interestingly, employment by the Minnesota food service industries has many characteristics that compare favorably with employment in high-technology industries. Among the comparisons that we might make are the following:

— In overall employment numbers, food services compare favorably with high technology firms. The 1979 estimate of Minnesota employment by high technology firms was 148,000 compared to a 1982 estimate of 125,000 full-time equivalents in food service.

— Both forms of employment have a history of rapid growth. Minnesota food services employment grew at a compound annual rate of 7.6 percent over the 1967-1977 period, compared to 4.1 percent for high technology industry jobs over the 1959-1979 period.

— The geographic distribution of food service and many other tourism-related industry jobs is superior. Every community has some tourism-related jobs, whereas most high technology jobs are in the larger cities.

—While high-tech sounds glamorous, many such jobs are assembly-line jobs. When high-technology firms locate in outlying communities, the higher-paid positions commonly go to imported personnel rather than local residents (Samuels, 1983).

While this comparison is not fully comprehensive, it does highlight the fact that jobs in food services—one type of tourism industry firm—compare favorably in numbers and in many other respects with highly sought-after employment in other industries.

Characteristics of Tourism-Related Jobs

The growth potential in tourism industry jobs makes them desirable. Like the industry itself, its employment needs wider understanding. We now examine aspects of tourism employment.

— Tourism jobs are not sought after and recognized because many tourism-generated jobs are invisible. The difficulty partly arises from the fact that the industry is, in fact, a varying proportion of a number of different firm types. This difficult-to-see, tourism-related employment situation compares with the high visibility of most manufacturing employment. Manufacturing is usually concentrated in one large building, or building complex, with a large parking lot filled with employees' vehicles.

— Many tourism-related jobs are relatively low paid, seasonal, and part-time. Concomitant with high tech, many tourism jobs require only low or entry-level skills.

— There are substantial community gains from the ready availability of tourism-related jobs (Davidson, 1987). We might ask, "If only high-skill-level, high-wage jobs are available, what happens to the young, unskilled, and other poorly qualified job seekers?" Tourism services can

employ many of these who would otherwise fall through the employment slats. Among these are many second income earners who do not want a full-time job, or one that employs only during regular hours; and many who need jobs close at home. In addition tourism-related firms have been able to adapt widely to handicapped people. Handicapped, unskilled, and those with only part-time availability are thus productively employed, whereas many other types of employment cannot adapt to them.

— In thirteen states tourism is now the largest employer (Ronkainen, 1987).

— The tourism industry is a significant employer of younger workers. Many older high school and college youth find employment in theme parks, resort areas, campgrounds, and other operations of that nature. Food services, particularly, employ youth. A Minnesota study found that at any one time 11 percent of employment-age teenagers were employed there (Blank, 1983). It is estimated that during the 1970s, 25 to 40 percent of Minnesota youth received their first major work experience in a food service. Hospitality services thus help to shape the work habits, discipline, and work attitudes of a high proportion of young people.

— Increasingly, tourism-related jobs are well paid. Many operators have discovered that skilled employees who do their work well, and who can "host" visitors properly, deserve and are well worth a substantial wage. Good hospitality business operators can often boast that they are able to hire some of the community's most capable people, because theirs is the best wage available. In addition, managers and individual proprietors also may be well remunerated. Statistics showing the better remuneration of these groups are masked by the large number of low-paid jobs in the industry.

The fact that tourism-related firms are able to employ many who would not fit into other employment situations, may be a major plus to many communities. It also suggests that the industry may be inappropriately maligned for low pay levels.

When factors such as experience, skill levels, part-time employment, and worker convenience are fully taken into account, tourism industry wage levels probably compare favorably with those of many other employing industries.

UNITED STATES INDUSTRY DYNAMICS

In contrast to many industries, there are a large number of small businesses in the firm types making up the tourism industry. The Small Business Administration classifies 98.8 percent of the tourism-related business types in Table 6.5 as small businesses (USTDC, 1984). Thus the tourism industry offers an important route by which individuals may become business owners and managers. This is the dynamic part of U.S.'s industry. These small operator-managers are free to succeed or fail, grow or stagnate. Many fail; the Small Business Administration estimates that four out of five small businesses do not survive the first ten years. Further, by some of the author's observations of hospitality firms, as few as one out of 15 develop beyond the "ma and pa" stage. But there are also some that win, and win big. These winners help to regenerate and revitalize, not only in the tourism industry, but the U.S. economy.

Dynamic growth in the tourism industry's employment and sales has been noted. Tourism firms' employment growth, Table 6.5, is over two times that of U.S. employment generally. Travel industry sales increased 153 percent in the 1976 to 1986 period compared to 137 percent for the U.S. gross national product (USTTA, 1988). Few other segments of the economy have expanded at the rate of tourism industry sales.

While a high proportion of tourism-related firms are small, there are also large firms. These organizations handle a substantial share of total sales and also contribute importantly to U.S. economic dynamics. They are highly competitive, and face a constantly shifting market demand. This demands

that they be creative in their product offering and in their marketing programs.

McDonald's, the fast food operation, illustrates some of these competitive dynamics. In 1987 McDonald's spent a total of $3 billion for marketing. Their product dynamics are even more instructive. McDonald's started in the 1950s with gaudy golden arches as their visual trademark. By the 1960s their management realized that U.S. incomes had grown substantially, and tastes were being upgraded. Accordingly they toned down the size and gaudy nature of their arches and their buildings were converted to earth-tones having a solid middle class appearance. They instituted rigorous operating standards and management training. Nor was the baby boom lost on them; they added playgrounds with elaborate equipment. Recognizing the value of time to many of their customers, they were among the pioneers of drive-throughs. Throughout all of this they continually experimented with menus, adding breakfast, fish sandwiches, and many other offerings. This cursory sketch illustrates the manner in which this one firm has continuously adapted to dynamics of the marketplace.

SOME LIMITATIONS OF SMALL PROPRIETORSHIPS

Not all aspects of smallness of firms represent economic dynamics. We note here three conditions often prevailing in small tourism-related firms, as well as in other small businesses, that have positive attributes, but that may also have serious limitations.

Often small businesses result from an owner having "purchased a job" for himself and his family. These firms provide opportunity for the family to work together gainfully, in the manner of families operating subsistence farms. This aspect of small hospitality firms emphasizes human values and lifestyle. Emphasis on family values to the exclusion of business management may weaken the community's service-supplying system.

Closely related is the fact that many operators of small tourism proprietorships enter the business with both inadequate management skills and financial backing. Many such operators lack a concept of the industry of which they are a part and have no ambitions to expand beyond a "ma and pa" operation. Often they exist for a time by living up their capital and property depreciation, without realizing fully what they are doing. Lacking capital, the manager may even find it necessary to work part-time elsewhere—thus giving inadequate time and attention to management, marketing, and operation of the business.

In cases where a high proportion of a community's tourism industry is made up of small and/or part-time proprietorships, this structure could operate as a serious impediment to optimum tourism industry development. Negative aspects of the syndrome might include a failure to recognize and/or take advantage of new market opportunities; a failure to make new investment because the entrepreneurs lack both the financing power and vision; tourists feeling that they have not received adequate treatment; and effort often wasted with intraregional market struggles among the small operators, instead of expending it on an adequate regional marketing program. Thus, managers of small firms may do an excellent job—but they may not.

A BALANCED ECONOMY: THE GOAL

Throughout, this book stresses need for the local community to give heed especially to two aspects of the economy: first the need for a diversified, balanced economic base, and secondly that the community realize the full extent of its comparative advantage in the use of its resources and pursuit of economic activities. Since many communities have an underdeveloped tourism industry, the advantages of its expansion have often been argued. At the same time, unrealized comparative advantages should be investigated and any economic activity pursued.

A brief treatment is given to four common industry types. In many communities these form the major economic base. But, like the tourism industry, they have negative as well as positive features. Along with positive aspects, some of these negative features are noted. This is not to suggest that these industries are inappropriate, but rather to assist communities in asking relevant questions in the face of any proposed industry addition or expansion.

Agricultural Production

Agriculture appears to be "the natural" economic activity where adequate conditions of soil and climate occur. In its food and fiber producing role, agriculture's necessity is undisputed. But as we have seen in the Mark Twain Area example, some communities that have relied mainly upon their agricultural economy have, by degrees, been reduced almost to ghost communities bereft of services and many human living amenities. The boom-bust nature of agricultural economies hastens the process. Because local residents are familiar with agriculture, there is rarely recognition or so much as a whimper of the negative role of the agricultural industry in this demise. Modern agriculture adds another hazard. It relies upon new technologies that involve the use of pesticides and herbicides. These contribute to crop yields, but may also be hazardous to farmers using them, as well as to the overall natural environment including foods and water.

A number of non-traditional agricultural-related opportunities are available, including truck farming, nurseries, and the raising of other specialty crops and livestock. Unfortunately, traditional agricultural communities resist moving into these endeavors, much in the same way that they are reluctant to support the introduction of non-agricultural economic activities.

Agricultural Supply Systems

Agricultural suppliers follow the trends of the local agricultural economy. When agriculture prospers, farm suppliers prosper, and they "bust" when agriculture "busts." When agricultural depression is widespread, as occurred in the 1980s, the malaise reaches back into communities producing agricultural equipment and other supplies. These suffered widespread unemployment and sometimes permanent loss of the supplying industry, as corporations consolidated operations to improve efficiency.

Mining Communities

Mineral resources are often envied by other communities. Exploitable mineral deposits often pay for exceptional public facilities and services during the life of the mineral extraction. But the boom/bust nature of economies based on this type of raw material raises questions concerning its value to the local community. Minerals often distort the real meaning of wealth production, producing unstable, abnormal societies, and abnormal impacts upon many of the society's members. Perspective and economic balance is lost in the quest to extract all that is possible from the mineral windfall. Mining also has other problems; it may produce spoil dumps and runoff that pollutes streams. The United States suffers from inadequate recognition of true mining costs: the need for helping mining-impacted communities toward stability, and need for management of the external effects upon the environment.

Manufacturing and Processing Operations

Manufacturing is among the most sought-after types of economic activities. The activity can be helpful in providing economic balance. Processing, using a locally produced raw material, is a particularly appropriate way to vertically integrate the local economy.

While manufacturing operations add economic balance, they may also contribute to instability. Most manufactured products now face the dynamic competition of a global market. Such international interdependence is a major positive factor in today's world, but can cause difficulties to producers of specific products, and to the communities dependent upon factories for employment. Among the more dramatic examples is the U.S. electronics industry that, since the 1970s, has been confronted with massive competition from abroad. Another factor producing instability at the local factory level is the absentee ownership of many such operations. This means that the local community lacks control and the operation is subject to decisions of some distant, impersonal manager.

There are still other human community problems with most manufacturing. Where an assembly line operates, those thus employed become part of a machine. Because of this reduction of their humanity, manufacturing employees often attempt to "escape" the local community on weekends and other occasions; they are thus less fully a part of the local community. Finally, air, water, and visual pollution often accompany manufacturing activities. Most can be managed, given recognition of the problem and the will to do so. Citizens often overlook or excuse environmental hazards—an acrid pall enveloping a community is described as, "It smells like money!"—rather than acting to manage the problem.

Communities able to analyze their opportunities for human living and economic activity can emphasize those economic activities that are best fitted. There are many others in addition to tourism and the four noted above. Medical, other human services and high technology industries may require a special climate of human resources, or location advantage. Trade—warehousing, wholesaling, retailing—also requires location advantages. And there are a world of others, each fitted to some specific community. The community fabric serves best that weaves together appropriate economic activities, meshing them with the community's blend of human, man-made, natural and locational resources into a rich tapestry of human society.

FUTURE TOURISM INDUSTRY EMPLOYMENT; FIRM SIZES

Will the rapid rise in tourism industry employment continue? Almost certainly not at the rate realized in the recent past. In the 1970s and early 1980s the numbers of teenagers and older youth peaked. This provided a readily available work force for the labor-intensive hospitality services. Because of this ready availability, pressure to reduce labor inputs was not strong. The U.S. is now undergoing a demographic shift toward a much lower proportion of youth (see Chapter 9). *This shift will almost certainly call forth greater creativity toward improving labor productivity* through developing labor-efficient layouts, procedures, and equipment. Low labor productivity in hospitality services results directly in low wages. It is entirely likely that employment growth will slow in the tourism industry, and that the result may be good in terms of a more productive labor force and higher wages.

A better-equipped work force will be needed. This calls for training and educational efforts by private firms and associations, and by public educational institutions. Along with proliferation in tourism and hospitality firms, there has been expansion in the public educational offering relevant to these types of operations. This offering ranges from vocational training in food preparation, housekeeping, etc., to four-year management curricula at the college level.

A trend in many industries has been toward coalescence of firms into larger entities. Coalescence has occurred in such tourism firm types as public carriers and travel agencies. There are also conglomerate corporations holding hospitality chains, while they also operate other businesses that may be only vaguely related.

While trends to larger scale operate, many factors appear to intervene to alter the process. These include cycles of regulation and deregulation; buyouts, takeovers, and splitoffs; national economic cycles of boom and recession; altered patterns of travel resulting from changes in energy availability, international instability, and travel technology; and many other adventitious factors. Further, the population and industrial system has within it a plethora of ways in which human ingenuity and the desire to strike off in new directions may assert itself. Many factors weight the scales in favor of reducing the number of small operations, but in opposition are strong biases toward proliferation of proprietorships. So long as there are only minimal barriers to entry, a high proportion of small tourism businesses can be expected. These are part of the U.S. economy's dynamics.

Tourism itself as an industry is expected to experience strong growth—see Chapter 9.

COMMUNITY DEVELOPMENT THEORIES: HOW DOES GROWTH OCCUR?

In this section we examine systematically and analytically the way in which growth and development occur in a community, and the tourism industry's role in that growth. In doing this, we will be looking further at the way in which people live, work, play, learn, produce, consume—a vast mosaic (Tiebout, 1962; Harmston, 1984; Smith, 1984).

We discuss here human needs and wants and how society is organized to meet these needs, from the most elementary subsistence to the full richness of which human life is capable (Alchin, 1965). While we will not be quantifying them in this section, implied is the flow of materials, energy, people, information and capital.

Growth has held center stage in the United States since its inception. In 1870, a little more than 100 years ago, the United States was a nation of 40 million people having a gross national product of about $4 billion. By 1987 population had increased six times to 245 million, and gross national product was up over 1000 times to $4.6 trillion. The latter contains a substantial element of inflation, but even without the inflation—in real terms—U. S. economic growth has been spectacular. About every generation—each 30 to 50 years—per capita real wealth has doubled. This means that sons and daughters could afford twice the goods and services that their parents had. Grandchildren can afford four times what grandparents had! The impact of this income expansion upon lifestyles, and especially upon travel and tourism, has been profound. It places demands upon every community to be a tourist destination as well as a place to live, and offers opportunity for communities to participate economically in this ongoing dynamic pattern.

Examined below are three theories of economic development. The reader is cautioned that these by no means represent the full range of development thought. There are, for example, investment-induced development situations, and others in which political entrepreneurship plays a lead role. These three are discussed because they apply particularly to the way in which most communities operate, and they contribute substantially toward understanding of tourism industry development.

The Export Base Theory of Economic Development

Export base theory assumes economic growth to take place due to the ability of local industry to produce enough to meet outside demand. The "multiplier" or backward linkages, as discussed earlier in this chapter, then operate to expand the benefits and extend them throughout the economic sectors of the community.

Export base theory is the major basis for most location theory. It assumes that population is attracted by and grows because of the exploitation of a resource or a goods—or service—producing activity. It is the theory of development implied when chambers of commerce and/or industrial development committees set out to attract an industry into the community. This industry may be tourism, a plant to process local raw materials or a footloose manufacturing operation.

Export base theory classifies community economic activities into two types (Perloff, 1960):

—*Basic industry or activity*—that which produces for outside demand. This generates income for the community that may be used to buy other things that it needs from the rest of the world.

— *Service, or residentary industry*—those activities that operate within the community to make it possible for people to live there. These include schools, churches, utilities, local retail stores, etc.

The community is assumed to be part of a larger economic system, and interdependent with the rest of the system through trade.

Tourism classifies as a basic industry, since it produces to sell to non-residents, thus bringing outside income into the community. This is true even though the nonresident must be physically present in the community to consume its tourism services. As the employees of tourism-related firms or of a manufacturing plant receive their pay and then re-spend it to satisfy their living needs, the backward linkages—the multiplier effects— function. Comparative advantage may also be seen as a part of the theory; ideally the community produces those things for which it is best adapted, and purchases from the rest of the world items in whose production it is relatively disadvantaged.

The Sector Theory of Community Development

Sector theory assumes growth to take place due to an internal development sequence in which relative emphasis is shifted from raw materials production to processing and manufacturing to trade, services and communications.

Sector theory emphasizes technological advance, income elasticity of demand, labor adaptability, division of labor and both internal and external trade (Perloff, 1960). It classifies activities into:

— *Primary industries*. The raw materials-producing activities: agriculture, forestry, fisheries and mining.

— *Secondary industries*. The processing and manufacturing activities that transform raw materials into more desirable products.

— *Tertiary, and sometimes also quatrinary activities*. Trade, services, communications, and government.

The theory assumes that humans need and can consume only finite amounts of the direct output of primary industries. Improved technology and division of labor makes processed products available. These are relatively more desirable, and have a higher income elasticity of demand (see Chapter 9 for a discussion of elasticity of demand); that is, as people's incomes increase due to productivity, they purchase relatively more of manufactured products

than the direct products of primary industries. Technology drives down production costs, making outputs of both primary and secondary industries relatively cheaper. This increases wealth, creating a demand for better living quality and hence for services, the tertiary activities. These have the highest income elasticity of all. That is, it is difficult to satiate demand for services and related items.

As technology renders primary and secondary production more efficient, human and other productive resources shift from the primary industries into secondary and tertiary industries. At more advanced stages, it may also be possible to shift labor out of the secondary industries of manufacturing and processing. Thus, at advanced stages, a high proportion of human resources are in the tertiary industries of trade, services and communications. In this system tourism is classed as a tertiary industry.

In the modern world, sector theory applies better to large aggregate systems or nations than to a single community. The United States illustrates sector theory, as can be noted in Table 6.4. In 1929, 25 percent of the employment was in agriculture; less than 60 years later it had fallen to only three percent. During the last 17 years of the period, 1970 to 1987, total employment in all raw materials production, processing and manufacturing was almost stable; it was 27.1 million in 1970 and 28.0 million in 1987. Throughout the 1929 to 1987 period, employment in services expanded by more than four times.

The theory explains the impact of macro economic forces upon communities. Many communities, primarily dependent upon agriculture, have lost population throughout the 20th century. Communities engaged in heavy manufacturing, such as many of those in Michigan, thrived during the 1940s and 1950s, but have since had difficulty. Those involved in communications, electronics, medicine, government, and tourism have often fared better in recent decades.

The Quality of Living Theory of Community Development

Quality of living theory turns traditional location theory (the export base theory) on its head. Instead of starting with an exploitable, productive resource, it starts with living resources and with people. It assumes that large numbers of the population are footloose, and can and do live where they wish. They seek out high amenity places to live and move there in numbers, rather than aggregating around a job source. Because of the people concentration, and because people with considerable ability are attracted, they begin enterprises. These become significant economic activities, which in turn attract added population because of the activity as well as the living amenities.

Since people move to the location to enjoy the amenities, they often further enhance those amenities by upgrading the cultural, recreational, and entertainment facilities, as well as by adding other people-serving institutions such as education and medicine. The attractiveness of the original amenities, as well as their augmentation, serves to attract both added residents and tourists. In fact, many communities illustrating this theory, were, in large measure, populated by people who originally came as tourists or as temporary residents.

Industry classification in terms of the quality of living theory is similar to that of the export base theory, except that it is more complex. Any production for sale to the outside world is clearly basic industry. On the other hand, much of what is considered residentary industry by the export base theory is also basic industry. That is, it adds to quality of living, attracting population, and also attracting tourists. Thus a "pure" residentary sector becomes difficult to isolate. Observation of communities indicates such a difficulty in many communities; many components of the residentary sector operate in a dual capacity. To the extent that this is true, the quality of living theory is partially operable in many communities.

All regions of the United States have communities where the quality of living theory operates as a major growth factor. It operates in the high amenity, water-sited communities of the Upper Great Lakes; in Colorado and many other sites in the Rocky Mountains; along the Pacific Ocean; in areas of Appalachia; the Ozarks; and throughout the Sun Belt. Phoenix, Arizona is a near-classical illustration. Many college communities are a special example. They attract populations because of their cultural amenities. With a growing "footloose" proportion of our population, the Quality of Living Theory can be expected to exert an increasing impact upon communities.

Putting Economic Growth Theory to Work in the Community

Which theory is better? Should one choose Export Base, Sector, or Quality of Living Theory? The answer: Yes! That is, it is neither possible nor necessary to choose among them. They all apply to most communities. The need is to learn the wisdom that each teaches and apply it in the most appropriate manner possible.

From one point of view, living amenities merit top priority. Much that contributes to living quality is manageable. Increasingly, industries consider living quality as a factor in location. Most factors contributing to living quality also contribute to the tourism industry. Most importantly, citizens live in the community 52 weeks of the year. They deserve a living community that they enjoy, and in which they have pride.

Comparative advantage grows, first, out of the community's location and its endowment of human, man-made and natural resources. Beyond its initial advantages, however, what a community does with its locational and resource advantages—its ingenuity in development—makes the real difference. A balanced, diversified and soundly based economic system can result. Such an economic system can be more adaptable to future opportunities, and less susceptible to economic vicissitudes.

Questions for review and further study.

1. Explain how the "backward linkages" of a tourism firm operate to produce the multiplier.

2. Why is the community income multiplier usually less than one for the tourism industry as well as for most other industries?

3. Discuss the dynamic aspects of the tourism industry and tourism employment; explain their contributions to the overall U.S. economy.

4. According to the Export Base Theory, how does economic growth occur?

5. What are the major factors operating to produce growth in the Quality of Living Theory of Community Development?

6. Show why tourism is a tertiary industry (Sector Theory).

7. Show ways in which the tourism industry is complementary to the Quality of Living Theory of Economic Development.

8. Why are there a relatively high proportion of part-time, low-wage employees in the tourism-related industries?

SUGGESTIONS FOR FURTHER READING

Harmston, F. (1983). *The Community as an Economic System.* Ames, IA: Iowa State University Press.

Perloff, H., et al. (1960). *Regions, Resources and Economic Growth.* Resources for the Future. Baltimore, MD: Johns Hopkins Press.

Samuelson, P. (1980). *Economics.* (11th ed.). New York: McGraw-Hill Book Co. (Part 2, Chapter 12; Part 6, Chapters 37 and 38).

TEXTUAL REFERENCES

Alchin, E. (1965). *A Reconnaissance Research Plan for Community Development.* (Technical Bulletin 49). East Lansing, MI: Institute for Community Development, Michigan State University.

Archer, B. (1977). *Tourism Multipliers: The State of the Art.* Cathays, Cardiff, Wales: University of Wales Press.

Blank, U., & M. Petkovich. (1979). The Metropolitan Tourist: A Comprehensive Analysis. *Proceedings, Tenth Annual Conference Travel and Tourism Research Association.* Salt Lake City, Utah: Bureau of Business and Economic Research, University of Utah.

Blank, U. (1982). *Life Style-Tourism Interrelationships of Minneapolis-St. Paul Residents.* (Staff Paper P82-9). St. Paul, MN: Department of Agricultural and Applied Economics, University of Minnesota.

Blank, U., with Missouri Cooperative Extension Service. (1986). *Northeast Missouri Tourism Industry.* Columbia, MO: University of Missouri, Columbia.

Blank, U., & R. Olson. (1983). *Food Services: A Major Minnesota Economic Component.* (Staff Paper P83-11). St. Paul, MN: Department of Agricultural and Applied Economics, University of Minnesota.

Blank, U., & T. Knopp. (1984). *The North Shore's Travel/Tourism Industry.* (Sea Grant Research Report No. 7). St. Paul, MN: University of Minnesota.

Davidson, T. (1987). The Impact of Travel and Tourism on the Local Economy: Just What Is It? *Proceeding Eighteenth Annual Conference TTRA.* Salt Lake City, Utah: Bureau of Economic and Business Research, University of Utah.

Drake, W. (1982, July 19). Back-to-Basics Jobs Creation Lesson Needed. St. Paul, MN: St. Paul Pioneer Press.

Harmston, F. (1984). *The Missouri Economy 1977.* Jefferson City, MO: Division of Manpower Planning, State of Missouri.

Liu, J., & T. Var. (1983). The Economic Impact of Tourism in Metropolitan Victoria, BC. *Journal of Travel Research, 22*(2). Boulder, CO: Business Research Division, University of Colorado.

Maki, W. (1977). *1977 Minnesota SimLab Model.* St. Paul, MN: University of Minnesota.

Milne, S. (1987). Differential Multipliers. *Annals of Tourism Research. 14*(4). Elmsford, NY: Pergammon Journals Inc.

Perloff, H., et al. (1960). *Regions, Resources and Economic Growth.* Resources for the Future. Baltimore, MD: Johns Hopkins Press.

Ronkainen, I., & R. Farano. (1987). U.S. Travel and Tourism Policy. *Journal of Travel Research. 25*(4). Boulder, CO: Business Research Division, University of Colorado.

Smith, C. (1984). Determining Economic Base—A Process of Community Study. *Journal of the Community Development Society, 15*(2). Athens, GA: University of Georgia.

Tiebout, C. (1962). *The Community Economic Base Study.* (Supplementary Paper No. 16). New York: Committee for Economic Development.

U.S. Travel and Tourism Administration and Travel and Tourism Research Association. (1988). *Proceedings of the Second Annual Travel Review Conference: The 1987 Experience—A Basis for Planning*, Washington, D.C.

A healthy tourism industry depends more upon development and management than upon the community's natural resource endowment. Lake of the Ozarks, Missouri. Photo credit: Missouri Division of Tourism

SEVEN

Interrelationships—Community Tourism Resource Management

This chapter continues the discussion of community tourism industry interrelationships. It specifically treats tourism resources and their management as these bear upon tourism industry development.

WHAT IS A TOURISM RESOURCE?

A tourism resource is any factor, natural or man-made, tangible or intangible, that is available to contribute positively to tourists' experiences of a community.

In common usage it is more usual to think of natural features as tourism resources. This discussion will proceed from the above definition. It will swing back and forth between treating natural tourism resources and man-made resources, and between tangible resources and intangible resources.

From one viewpoint, tourism resources may be classed in the same way as other community resources:

— *Natural tourism resources*—include features of terrain, climate, geology, water, fauna and flora.

— *Man-made tourism resources*—include those features in which human activity has had a major creative role: the human community with its institutions, the economy with its several parts, hospitality facilities, many recreational facilities, and historical/cultural features.

— *Human tourism resources*—include such factors as hosting capabilities, provision of human services, the ingenuity of human beings to adapt and create, and many aspects of ambient culture.

— *Community location*—with regard to physical resources and with regard to market access; location is a distinct, exploitable factor in tourism potential. It is only tangentially a tourism resource as defined above. Its role is frequently noted throughout the text, and it is treated further in Chapter 8.

This broad concept of tourism resources brings good news to many communities. It suggests, as tourism resources, many things other than natural or pre-existing features. It offers potential for any community to expand its tourism industry without limitation by its natural resource endowment.

A resource can only be defined in terms of use. This characteristic of resources is separate from the fact that physical things can be described in concrete terms. For example, the mineral pitchblende has existed throughout human history, but was it a resource of any kind until ways to use the uranium that it contained for energy were developed?

Something is a tourism resource only if it is available and contributes positively toward tourists' experiences:

— A river that is badly polluted with industrial waste may not only *not* be a tourism resource, it may constitute an aberrant detraction from the community's tourism appeal. Typically, rivers have been viewed as secular and profane and communities have "turned their backs on them." Now there dawns the realization that rivers can be major factors contributing both to living quality and to tourist appeal. Communities such as San Antonio, Texas; Savannah, Georgia; St. Louis, Missouri; Stillwater, Minnesota; and Memphis, Tennessee now treat their riverfront as a major tourism asset.

— A unique cultural heritage may operate to impart a sense of place and family background to a community's residents. But unless it is at least partially shared, it is limited in its role as a tourism resource. Amana Colonies, Iowa, and the Amish/Mennonite cultures of Lancaster County, Pennsylvania provide access in many ways—through tours, museums, and cuisine, among others—so that the visitor can experience a part of the culture.

— Plentiful game does not draw hunters if no one knows about it, if all land is posted, or hunting access is otherwise unavailable.

— A historical feature that no one knows about, and that is not physically or visually accessible, is not a tourism resource. In common with many other *potential* tourism resources, it is best characterized as one of the community's "well-kept secrets." Many such secrets repose obscurely in every community.

All components of the community act, or can act, as tourism resources. These components were discussed in Chapter 3. All of them—focal attraction, hospitality services, complementing features, supplemental activities, the community, its people and community ambiance—contribute to tourists' experiences.

Implicit in these comments is the concept of a tourism resource as a developable attribute of many features that are present in every community. This chapter primarily plays upon variations of this theme: tourism resources, and resource quality—their development, management and maintenance.

It extends beyond this theme to suggest that *tourism resources not only can be managed but can be created.*

THE RESOURCE MANAGEMENT IMPERATIVE: RESOURCE QUALITY

We have noted that tourists come to a community because it attracts them: It has something that they want to see or do. Without regard to their intended travel purpose, they come voluntarily. How long they stay, whether they return and whether they recommend the destination to others depends largely upon the satisfactions of their visit.

In order to be satisfied, tourists need to feel good about the destination that they chose: that it lived up to their expectations and beyond; that they are proud of the choice of destination and feel that it gives them stature; that the experience that was positive and fulfilling. Such feelings of satisfaction and positive reward can only be achieved from a set of quality experience-delivering factors. Among them are services, personal treatment and the set of natural and man-made features with which they interact. Thus tourist satisfactions depend upon resource quality.

Quality in resources consists of their having attributes rendering them capable of delivering positive, rewarding experiences, without seriously aberrant detractions. Such quality can be illustrated with examples:

— A scenic overlook should afford the participant the thrill of visual access to a powerful view. If it is a view of nature, it should not show exploitation or erosion unless these are the intent, and/or properly interpreted. The viewer should feel safe. Some physical exertion to reach the overlook may enhance its impact, but if it is strenuous, this factor may defeat the purpose of affording the experience to an economically viable number of tourists.

— A historic site usually requires extensive interpretation in order to deliver a powerful "reliving of the happenings" experience to the visitor. In addition to knowledge access, combinations of visual and physical access are usually necessary. The site must retain a critical quotient of original features without distracting intrusions of modern development.

— A village may exude the charm of a particular culture, ethnic group, occupational pursuit, or geographic setting. The architecture, structural types and street layout may be unique to the given site. Clutter and disorder can largely wipe out positive experiences, and, conversely, inappropriately modernized design with concrete, steel and glass can be equally ruinous to tourists' experiences.

— Hosting quality is real. Visitors readily sense genuine welcome and eagerness to serve. They stay where they feel welcome.

— An outdoor recreational experience, such as fishing, hunting, boating, hiking or bird watching, is heightened if there is evidence of good natural resource stewardship—or at least no evidence of pollution or inappropriate exploitation.

The above examples illustrate resource quality in its role of contributing to positive experiences of tourists in a community. Without quality the experience downgrades to one that will not be voluntarily sought. Accordingly, the community's tourism industry will fail to develop its potential, and may atrophy (Pilgram, 1980).

Residents of a community have an even more powerful incentive to maintain and enhance resource quality in addition to its potential in spurring tourism industry development. *This community is their home, everyone wants to be proud of their home, and residents' living quality is partly a function of local resource quality.* Interestingly, pride of residents in their home community can often be a major factor contributing to hosting and other tourism resource quality (Liu, 1987; Partners for Livable Places, 1981).

THE MAKING OF A TOURISM RESOURCE

All Tourism Resources are the Result of Human Development

We noted in Chapter 3 that focal attractions are produced by people's developmental efforts. This is equally true of all tourism resources. In addition, we have noted in this chapter that tourism resources can be created.

This important principle might, initially, appear to fly in the face of reason. "Surely," the argument might go, "natural features that yield recreational satisfactions are not manufactured by people!" True, their basic essence is not man-made. But without development they would not be a tourism resource, yielding positive experiences to the visitor.

Development is of several kinds, varying with the nature of the resource and the mix of facilities, features and services that make up the community's tourism offering:

Provision of access. This is the process whereby a facility is made available for tourists' use. In order to use a resource they need to know about it and understand it. They also need to be able to see it and/or get to it physically. Access also includes the process of designation or reservation whereby a resource is indicated as available for visitor use. Provision of access applies to all tourism resources, whether nature-and real estate-based or cultural and intangible.

Adaptation for tourist use is necessary for most existing parts of the community that serve the residents in an ongoing way. A manufacturing plant needs to be adapted so tours by visitors can be made (Simonson, 1974). Usually the infrastructure—roads, power, waste systems, etc.—must be altered to handle visitor volumes. Human beings need to be trained in specific job skills and hosting capability.

Enhancement of many resources and features upgrades their capability for delivering positive experiences. Such things as upgrading the visual aesthetics of community entrance routes, or of buildings; adding interpretation of fauna, flora, history, and geology; and expanding the activities and entertainment available are enhancing steps. Adaptation and enhancement will be seen as closely related.

Whole-cloth development involves construction from scratch. Many lodging/hospitality facilities as well as food services are developed whole-cloth. Increasingly, entertainment/recreational facilities are from whole-cloth. The most spectacular are the large theme parks and sports arenas, but also evening entertainment, shopping facilities, and kiddie parks are developed without a necessarily pre-existing base.

The reader will recognize that a large number of potential tourism resources exist in many communities. What determines which ones shall be developed, and to what extent? It is suggested that such decisions depend in a large measure upon the tourism industry goals that the community sets for itself (see Chapter 11) and the destination image that it seeks to create (see Chapters 3 and 11). Ideally a community will develop the mix of tourism experiences as a part of its tourism offering that best complements and supports the focal attraction(s) and that provides the full range of things to see and do, keeping in mind the community's specific tourism market segments.

The Natural Resource Endowment—Not Necessarily a Limiting Factor in Tourism Industry Development

The community's endowment of natural, historical and other pre-existing potential tourism resources interacts in a dynamic, synergistic manner with development activities and developed features to produce the community's destination area image and its tourist industry. Poorly endowed communities often appear fatalistic. They may feel that because they lack major pre-existing resources that they have little tourism industry potential. But we have indicated that *development* is not only a major factor; *it is often the major factor in growth of a community's tourism industry*. This fact reduces the impact of the "luck of the draw" in terms of natural resources, and places the community in control of its tourism industry.

Figure 7.1 illustrates the interaction between pre-existing and/or natural resources with developmental and investment activities in producing the community's tourism income. The two curved lines in Figure 7.1 represent different levels of community tourism income. They may be thought of as lines on a contour map rising above the plane of the paper, with their height above the paper being proportional to the numbers assigned to them. In the illustration, the community with a level "a" of natural tourism endowment attains a tourism income of $5 million with a developmental level of "u" (underdeveloped). But with the same level of natural or pre-existing resources, $10 million in tourism income can be generated with a "d" (developed) level of its tourism industry. Development, in such a case, might include all of the processes discussed above—access, adaptation, enhancement, and whole cloth—in generating a more adequate tourism industry income.

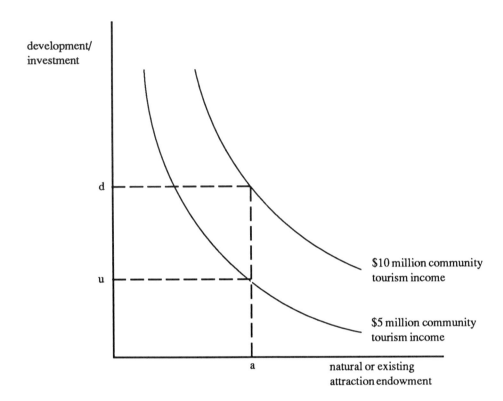

Figure 7.1 Relationship of Community Tourism Income to Natural Attraction's Endowment and to
        Tourism Industry Development

Adapted from: Blank, Uel. "Interrelationship of the Food Service Industry and the Community," A.
                Pizam, R.C. Lewis and P. Manning, (Eds.) *The Practice of Hospitality Management*,
                AVI Publishing Co., Inc. Westport, CT, 1982.

Two case examples may be helpful:

Frankenmuth, Michigan, a town of 4000 population, generates the bulk of its community income from tourism. It only has in addition a small manufacturing operation, a brewery and an agricultural service industry. Oddly, unlike most communities having a major tourism industry, Frankenmuth is situated in the midst of agricultural land in Michigan's almost featureless "thumb" area. It

does not even have one of the state's many lakes, although it is on a small stream, the Cass River.

Two entrepreneur families sparked Frankenmuth's tourism industry. Zehnders were a local farm family that began by serving Sunday chicken dinners. This business has now grown into two large, multifaceted food service facilities where excellent food is served amid German *gemutlichkeit*. The Zehnders also support other related operations. Bonners, begun about 1950, now claims the distinction of the largest Christmas supply store in the world.

These two operations taught the community that tourists would be attracted by excellent services and products, and that money could be made from serving tourists.

Other things followed as the community caught a vision of the possibilities: The local grist mill was restored. A unique Italian village display was designed, developed, and put on display. A second brewery has been started. There are craft shops, many other food and drink places, and special events. The downtown area has taken on the architectural look of a Bavarian village. To accommodate visitors, the large St. Lucas Lutheran church even has a full-time tour guide. Because of the appealing ambience of the community, it attracts an increasing number of people who simply want to live there—the quality of living theory in operation.

Frankenmuth originally had little of what is commonly considered a Bavarian ambience. Its population does have a mostly German-ethnic background, and there was the one brewery. But there was not the rugged terrain, nor the German-style architecture in the downtown, or residential area so characteristic of many such communities. It has something more important than natural or historical resources: It had the natural resourcefulness of its people. Virtually everything done was done by resident citizens, starting small, growing into full-fledged entrepreneurs, building their home community.

Guthrie, Oklahoma is the only intact territorial capitol in the United States. It is intact because development bypassed it and it became almost a ghost town after 1910, when the capitol was moved to Oklahoma City. It could have continued to dwindle away, become a vestige and possibly even disappeared.

Now there are 75 to 100 downtown buildings undergoing restoration in a multi-million dollar effort. As this restoration work continues the Arts and Humanities Council plans to bring in big-time entertainers to perform amid the frontier ambience.

What happened? Local people saw the potential and provided the spark. One was a woman who owned downtown property, had some of it renovated and moved downtown to live, thus starting a trend. Another major mover was a local bank vice president. In the mid-1960s he began to emphasize restoration and renovation. The bank has been an important factor in financing the comeback.

In the case of Guthrie we see a community with resource potential, but it needed a spark to take advantage of that potential. Through the vision and leadership of local citizens the initiative has now been provided.

In the above examples, the deciding factor was not the natural or historical resources. It was the human ingenuity and vision that counted. Most importantly, local citizens provided the key leadership.

The Role of the Community in Accessing Tourism Resources

We noted in Chapter 3 that tourism attractions are primarily accessed through communities. We also noted that many who have an interest in the development of recreational features do not always recognize the vital role of communities in providing recreational access. A discussion of tourism resources should refresh this understanding.

Tourism resources come to a focus in the community. Real resources—natural features, historical resources, hospitality facilities—are spatially sited and managed by local governmental units. Services are provided by people who identify with communities. The infrastructure, which makes it possible for the human systems—whether for residents or tourists—to function, emanates from communities.

This provides yet another view of the community as a tourist destination area. Without the basic community in place, there would be limited opportunity for positive tourism experiences. The means for accessing tourism resources by living away from home, or the ability to reach these resources through knowledge and by physical means, would be limited or lacking altogether.

THE WORST OF ALL WORLDS IN TOURISM RESOURCE USE

Many North American communities suffer from what can best be characterized as "the worst of all possible worlds in tourism resource use." They lack realistic tourism industry goals and a workable policy for tourism development and management. Their malady consists of a syndrome of drastic underdevelopment of tourism resources (Rosenow, 1979).

Such a syndrome includes the following: Many communities have potentially appealing attractions such as unique natural sites, fish and game, historic sites, and colorful folkways. Often these communities lack programs of protection, management and development of these features, even though such development could help the community become a significant tourist destination area and provide needed balance to its economy. Most local citizens resent those few curious and brave tourists who come. Even these tourists are harmful to the resource, because no facilities or management exist. In order to experience the feature, visitors are forced unnecessarily onto fragile natural ecology, or historic sites, or they may consume game wantonly, or intrude into the affairs of citizens. Since the community offers few services, including hospitality establishments, it has almost nothing to sell the tourist and hence realizes little income (OECD, 1980).

What has happened? The resources are consumed, perhaps partly destroyed. Despite this resource loss, the community has realized almost no return; and the visitor has achieved only limited satisfactions. *This is the worst of all worlds in tourism resource management and use.*

In such settings a tourist vs. resident animosity often develops. Some communities have organized, not necessarily in jest, such organizations as "Hate Tourists Incorporated!"

The reader can almost certainly prescribe remedial measures. These would include:

—The first responsibility of the community to itself with regard to the tourists is to realize income from them. Tourists, whether 10 or 100 or 10,000, constitute only an irritation unless the community is psychologically and physically prepared to host them. Physical preparation means that the community can sell tourists goods and services, thus developing a tourist industry that will yield jobs, profits, rent and taxes for the host community.

— Resource management, including appropriate protection, must be provided (Blank, 1977). *Preservation and protection is a primary responsibility of the local community.* In cases where the resource is of state or national significance, state and/or national agencies should assist. In any case, adequate resource management requires a constructive, cooperative working arrangement among all governmental levels.

— All of the components of a complete tourist destination area as discussed in Chapter 3 must be present, providing experiences of a quality appropriate to the market and the resources. These, by way of review, include hospitality facilities, complementing features, supplementary activities, and access as well as the overall community structure.

The fact that such communities have resources to exploit means that they have tourism potential. "Development" is clearly indicated, and the manner and pace at which it proceeds will be unique to each setting. *Such development can make the difference between an embittered community that resists visitors, and one that is proud of itself and has a viable tourism industry.*

CARRYING CAPACITY: WHAT DOES IT MEAN?

Carrying capacity management enables us to achieve the best of all worlds: The ability to use tourism resources to advantage and yet keep them.

In Chapter 4 we noted three interrelated aspects of carrying capacity:

—Users have different specifications for the experience that they expect from a given tourism resource (Manning, 1980).

—Use levels are not fixed for a given resource; management techniques can greatly expand use while maintaining quality of the resource and the experience (Walter, 1982). New technologies transform the management alternatives into economic problems—is it economically feasible?

—Some tourism resource use levels may impact upon levels of living quality of community residents.

Chapter 4 dealt with the influence of carrying capacity on the scale of a community's tourism industry. In this chapter we treat the relationships among resources, their management, and the experiences achieved by tourists.

Specifications for the level of experience by recreational/tourism users vary. These levels can apply to any tourism experience and we use wilderness experiences here to illustrate some of the range in desired experiences.

Not all users either want, expect or can undertake a 100 percent wilderness experience. Let us assume that a 100 percent wilderness experience is one in which the recreator/tourist penetrates to an area completely unimpacted by western civilization, and while there encounters no other human beings (West, 1981). It should be obvious that such a level of wilderness recreational experience is achievable by only a very small number, and also a diminishing number.

A substantial number of tourists in the Upper Great Lakes area were found to define wilderness as a place where there are mostly trees (Lucas, 1964). Such individuals apparently are able to achieve and acceptable wilderness recreational experience simply by traveling the Northern highways in thinly populated portions of the Upper Great Lakes area and observing the forest flora. Could we assign this activity a 20 percent value as a wilderness recreational experience?

Some wish to stay for a period in a mountain or northwoods area, but by reason of physical capability or inclination prefer to remain in the comfortable accommodations of well-appointed resorts. They do not wish to penetrate further. Many of the latter accommodations are situated in sites having a picturesque ambience. We might arbitrarily assign a 30 percent value to such a wilderness experience.

Some hike from Pinkham Notch, New Hampshire along Appalachian trails. Rather than "rough it," they may prefer the food and lodging provided by the Appalachian Mountain Club. They might thus achieve a 35 to 40 percent wilderness recreational experience.

Still others push out in paddle canoes into the heart of Quetico Provincial Park, Ontario. Or they might use pack horses in a western wilderness area. In either case they would carry with them simple means of wilderness subsistence. As they cross passes or portages and penetrate deeper, they see less and less of human invasion signs and encounter fewer and fewer other recreating parties. They may thus achieve a 50 percent, 60 percent or even a 70 percent wilderness recreation experience.

A wilderness recreational experience is thus seen as relative, depending upon the wishes and circumstances of the user. Some recreators are fulfilled in a given experience by a level of involvement that would be virtually meaningless to others. Of great relevance to carrying capacity is the fact that as the percentage of "wilderness recreational experience" that is achieved is higher, the number who may be thus accommodated, or carried, falls sharply.

An important principle regarding natural resource use is *to not force users into a deeper nature encounter than they wish.* If all levels of these desires are recognized, and appropriate accommodations provided, carrying capacity can be greatly expanded.

Management of the resource can expand carrying capacity. User areas such as campsites can be "hardened," with little loss of experience for most users. Levels of use can be zoned or rationed. Use can often be diverted away from pristine areas into areas where facilities for handling volumes are available. Commercial service providers can thus reap financial rewards while fragile areas are protected. These illustrate only a few of the many management tools available.

Urban recreational experiences, unlike wilderness experiences, are often enhanced by volumes of people (Perloff, 1969; Walter, 1982). Large numbers of people enjoying themselves at a fair, or theme park, adds to the festive atmosphere. There are limits; few wish to stand for hours in long lines. Even in such situations management is possible: The queue line can lead past entertainment, and alternative activities can be offered.

A community that has good understanding of its market, and has adequately analyzed its resources and their patterns of use, can chart a policy for user experiences and resource management. This will enable the community to achieve an optimum tourism industry income while maintaining the quality of its recreational resources.

THE PROBLEM OF THE COMMONS—A SPECIAL CASE IN RECREATIONAL/TOURISM RESOURCE MANAGEMENT

The focal attraction upon which many tourism destination areas depend for primary tourism appeal often involves a publicly owned and managed resource. This is the case of major public parks and their accessing communities; of wild rivers, and the communities that provide river floating experiences; of canoeing waters and their canoeing outfitting communities; of fishing lakes and their resorting, and fishing outfitting/supplying communities; and of major historical features and their food and lodging (and sometimes interpretation-supplying community). There are among the many examples that could be cited (Hardin, 1977).

In these cases, the tourism industry often becomes exploitative upon the commonly owned resource. Costs of ownership and management of the resource—lake, river, scenic wonder, historical site—are shared by the society at large. The society pays these costs because of perceived contributions to general welfare of public reservation, maintenance and management of the resource feature. But economic benefits accrue specifically to those firms situated there that take advantage of the fact that tourists who come to enjoy the commonly owned recreational resource will need to eat, sleep, have transportation, and may need rental equipment and guide services. These operations tend to view the resource as their own, demanding management that is to their own specific advantage. Worse yet, if allowed, they may exploit the resource. That is, the resource has no cost to them, and the more users that they can feed into the resource, before another operator does the same, the better off the individual firm. Meanwhile, competing operations also attempt to exploit the resource. The result is a strong tendency to overuse the resource by putting excessive people and activity pressures upon it.

Even the public agency responsible for management of the resource sometimes becomes caught up in the local zeal to expand use, and sometimes overuse, of the resource. This occurs because managers are often local residents. Secondly, it occurs because the agency sees its role and importance as growing in proportion to the user numbers.

Two solution approaches are suggested to this "problem of the commons." The first is objective administration of the public recreational/tourism resource by the appropriate public agency. Use is clearly one goal, but this use should be viewed in the context of larger public welfare, and the yielding of quality experiences over time. Despite the observation about public managing agencies made in the paragraph immediately above, it is fully acknowledged that many public managing agencies work hard at maintaining the resource and providing for a quality recreational experience.

The most important solution to the problem of the tendency to overuse a public recreational/tourism resource may lie within the overall thrust of this chapter. An optimum tourism industry requires development of a full set of complementing and supplementing components. Given such development, a complementing set of facilities can divert use pressure from the publicly owned focal attraction to other related and equally satisfying activities.

We observe here that some tourism operations can be exploitative upon a common recreational resource. But the best solution is not that the community reduce its tourism industry. Rather, it is more desirable to strive for a balanced development that complements the common resource while also diverting use pressure.

A REVIEW OF RESOURCE MANAGEMENT MECHANISMS

What are the means available to a community to adequately manage its tourism resources, not only to preserve them for continued viable use, but to enhance the nature of their appeal? These mechanisms are reviewed briefly in this subsection. This treatment is not intended to be comprehensive; individuals needing more detailed information will need to refer to local legislation and other reference sources.

Many suggestions made here will be recognized as nontraditional and not even considered in most

texts on land use and resource management. While these non-traditional mechanisms may be difficult to institute, where they function, they are observed to be the most effective possible controls available.

Citizens will protect what they appreciate. Community appreciation on the part of citizens may be the most effective long range mechanism for management of resources for quality. By "appreciation," is meant that citizens have a sophisticated understanding of the characteristics of the community's resources and the living quality thus made available, and they wish to maintain and enhance it. This is in contrast to a chauvinistic attitude that simplistically assumes that "I and my community are naturally superior," or, at the opposite extreme, an attitude that views with contempt those familiar features and peoples with which one grew up, failing to see value in appreciating and protecting their appeals and beauty.

The appreciation suggested here builds community pride. It is an ethic that allows those holding it to enjoy the community's living quality, but that is willing to share it with others. At the same time it zealously seeks to maintain and enhance community resource and living quality.

This pride in quality of community and life style appears to function in a number of the communities used as examples earlier: Frankenmuth, Michigan, New Glarus, Wisconsin, and Lancaster County, Pennsylvania. More than the force of law (see "Formal tools" below), this community spirit directs the architecture, maintenance and aesthetics of those communities.

In Chapter 12, informational and educational programs are suggested as part of the means toward developing a constructive community mind-set.

The formal tools of government: planning and zoning, codes, taxation, and others. Most local governments employ zoning for enhancing public health, safety, and morals. Some also employ it for aesthetics. Building codes have related purposes.

Land use can be nudged in appropriate directions by tax classifications. Utility systems of power, water, and waste management are usually regulated. These regulatory tools apply the force of law, where public good is perceived to require control of private actions, usually in the management of a piece of real property.

Most such public legislation such as zoning and codes is only effective when there is widespread public understanding and appreciation of the objectives. Zoning and codes that are not understood are often circumvented and rendered impotent. This means that these legal mechanisms must be based on an agreed-upon community policy, one that is understood and that clearly goes in a direction desired by community citizens. Here again is a major role for community communications and education.

Public ownership: the ultimate zoning. Public ownership of sites having unusual value for many citizens is commonly practiced. Public recreational parks, areas of unusual geology and ecology, and historical monuments are among the more common examples.

Once the unusual qualities of a given site are recognized, it frequently happens that steps are taken to place it in public ownership. Such procedure is often in the public interest. But it should also be recognized that even public ownership does not guarantee preservation. The agency controlling the site must be given a clear charter concerning its management. Further, the general public must also appreciate the site, and not only avoid violating it, but also be jealous of its special character to the extent that they work to preserve and enhance this character.

Private investors and developers need a community spirit. Developers of hospitality services, home and other real property in a community play an inordinately large role in shaping its character. If they understand the community and

are imbued with pride for its qualities, they can make a difference, just as can governmental agencies. The long-run interest of developers and investors depends strongly upon community quality, but sometimes short-range interests and exigencies obscure that view.

The formal tools of government—zoning and codes—have a necessary place. But they function best when investors and developers have caught the spirit of community pride and a concept of the community's future. This harnesses the powerful ingenuity of the community's citizens. Where it occurs, what results can be better than what any bureaucrat or formal planner could have ever imagined!

AN EMBARRASSMENT OF RICHES — CAN A COMMUNITY HAVE AN OVER-ENDOWMENT OF TOURISM RESOURCES?

Spectacular recreational features can contribute greatly to the richness of human life. But to citizens of the community having these features, they may— at least in the short run—be viewed as a curse.

This effect occurs because outstanding features are often viewed by the larger society as belonging to all. Instead of being considered a community resource, they are thought of as a state, national or even a world resource to be enjoyed, used and developed by governments and entrepreneurs of the larger system. When these features are "discovered" this attitude tends to take control from the local community. Exploitation of the feature may result in submerging of the native culture, denial of many formerly acccepted residents' rights to use of the feature and a merger of the local economy with that of the larger system.

Demands of environmental/preservationists may compel larger governments to reserve areas of the community's land. This often removes it from the tax base, although in-lieu payments are sometimes made. It also restricts use of the area by local residents.

Outside entrepreneurs may view the area as having investment potential. Their purchases of land preempt it from local citizens' use even more than does governmental reservation. When facilities are developed, managers and technical personnel are imported. These people may quickly dominate the community power structure.

Usually there is a secondary response by both outside and local entrepreneurs. This consists of smaller developments, operations and facilities that are designed to complement or supplement the focal attractions and the major facilities, and take advantage of the markets that they create. Often these secondary developments are of lesser quality, and may even amount to community clutter.

Numerous other effects may occur. Not only people who come to work in the new facilities, but the tourists themselves have a profound influence upon the local culture. Further, some of the thus created tourist destination areas that depend heavily upon long-distance travel, may be subject to boom and bust. This introduces instabilities in the local economy that were not previously present.

The effect of this development, nearly all of which is initiated from outside the community, can be compared to what was discussed as the "worst of all worlds in tourism development." Here again, resources are committed to tourism, but the local community may realize only a small return from this tourism, at least initially. There is also a great difference: the "worst of all worlds..." is a case of underdevelopment; the case discussed here usually involves substantial development.

Some authors (Rosenow 1979) have referred to similar situations as "Ugly Tourism." Its worst features are most likely to occur in a third world situation where there is a clash of very different cultures. It can and does occur in communities of the first world.

Communities can mitigate the above-noted possible ill effects by taking timely and appropriate action. This consists of setting up and actively implementing a tourism industry policy as discussed in Chapters 11 and 12. To carry out the policies communities would need to continuously monitor activities underway, and get relevent information to citizens, policy-implementing bodies, and local investors. They may also need to employ the tools of land management and control as noted in the immediately preceeding subsection. A community implementing a constructive approach toward management of a major resource can usually exert a major influence in guiding its development. When such a demonstrated positive policy is lacking, other nonindigenous units of the society may move in and exercise control because the local community defaults.

State and national governments may also share the blame for disruption to a local community resulting from development. Seldom do state and national govermental units give adequate attention to the local community. Rather they concentrate upon acheiving control of a specifically-delineated tract of land. This approach often fails to realize that proper enjoyment of a specific site may be strongly contingent upon the way in which the community complements and provides access to it. In the case of a preserve, designated because of special natural, historical or other ambience, the public's needs might be much better served by creating a large "park-like" area rather than concentrating attention solely upon a specific site.

Few communities with rich endowments are able to act in a fully prescient manner. Inadequate forecasting ability creates the first difficulty—our view of the future is severely limited. Further, the tools of resource management are particularly difficult to apply in an *ex ante* situation. Only when there is an obvious threat will citizen resource-owners place restrictions upon themselves and hence upon other owner/investor/developers. Most citizens want to take personal advantage of any possible windfalls that may occur, and since many small communities feel need for income and employment, they are more inclined to encourage rather than restrict potential investment from any source. Resources can be positively managed, but such action requires responsible, fully informed citizens.

The greatest difficulty from the development of strong resource endowments usually occurs in the shortrun—while the community's economy and society is adapting from one economic base to a more tourist-oriented system. After adjustments have taken place—the new immigrants have become old residents, present residents no longer recall the resource uses, and new sets of employment skills have developed—the community may apperar to operate "normally." The transition period may be relatively short in some cases. In other situations transition is ongoing, and has been observed to extend over the span of a full century.

In contrast to communities having national or world-class tourism attractions are those having less ostentatious features. The latter case is illustrated by the examples of Frankenmuth, Michigan and Guthrie, Okalhoma, described earlier in this chapter. In these, the community features, at least initially, have limited attracting power. The attracting power had to be developed. The process of this development is one of the main thrusts of this book. Development of less obvious features consists of the investment of a community into itself. Because development is often initially slow, outsiders can seldom gain from this process. The community and its citizens, on the other hand, stand to gain in many ways: improved living quality, pride in their community and its amenities, and from the jobs, profits, taxes and rents generated by an improved tourism industry.

Here a caveat is in order: Once a community develops its tourist attracting power it assumes a position alongside those having previously-existing, high-level attractions. At this stage there is possibility for claims upon the community by the larger society. There may be eagerness for investment by non-local entrepreneurs. At such a point the community's tourism industry could assume an autonomous life of its own—unless community leaders monitor the course of events continuously, and act to provide direction through an adequate set of tourism industry policies.

COMPARATIVE ADVANTAGE REVISITED

At this point, the discussion of comparative advantage from Chapter 4, the examples of community tourism industry development in Chapter 6, and the resource development and management discussion of this chapter can be brought into simultaneous focus.

Suppose that the two Missouri recreational communities discussed in Chapter 6 (Branson/Table Rock and Lake of the Ozarks), had elected not to allow substantial tourism-related new investment in the region. They might instead have feared that this would have interfered with their agricultural industry. What might have happened? We might hypothesize that, instead of strong population growth and expansion in their tourism industry, they would have continued to experience the decline then underway that continued in the other rural areas such as Mark Twain Lake/Hannibal. It is even probable that their agricultural sales would have grown more slowly had there not been the tourism industry development. They provide examples of moving appropriately on a comparative advantage opportunity.

Suppose Frankenmuth, Michigan citizens had insisted that they were basically an agricultural service community. Alternatively, they might have worked at becoming an automobile industry satellite community. Would they have experienced a greater and more stable economic growth? (Recall the instability of the 1970s and 1980s in the U.S. automobile industry.) Would their living quality and pride of community have been better?

Comparative advantage is not fixed; it is instead highly subject to management. Comparative advantage in the tourism industry appears much more dependent upon development than upon a static endowment of resources. This development is a function of public and private investment, of the aroused and expressed ingenuity of the community's citizens.

Questions for review and further study

1. Explain the relationship between development and a community's existing tourism resource endowment.

2. What conditions produce "the worst of all worlds" with regard to tourism resource management?

3. What do you understand "exploitation" to mean? Why do some tourism firm managers attempt to exploit commonly owned tourism resources?

4. Explain how the nature of the recreational experience desired by users can greatly influence or change the carrying capacity of a resource.

5. How can comparative advantage among TDA's be altered by developmental activities?

6. In what different ways can community tourism resources be created?

7. What steps can be taken by a community to avoid exploitation of the "commons"?

SUGGESTIONS FOR FURTHER READING

Dillman, D., & D. Hobbs. (Eds). (1982). *Rural Society in the U.S. , Issues for the 1980s.* Boulder, CO: Westview Press. (Part 7, Natural Resources).

Murphy, P. (1985). *Tourism, A Community Approach.* New York: Methune. (Section 2).

Rosenow, J., & G. Pulsipher. (1979). *Tourism, the Good, the Bad, and the Ugly.* Lincoln, NB: Century Three Press. (Chapters 6 and 11).

Shelby, B., & T. Heberlein. (1986). *Carrying Capacity in Recreational Settings.* Corvallis, OR: Oregon State University Press.

TEXTUAL REFERENCES

Blank, U. (1977). Minnesota's Water Resources and Its Recreation and Tourism. *Minnesota's Water Resources in the Year 2000.* St. Paul, MN: Water Resources Research Center, University of Minnesota.

Hardin, G., & J. Baden (Eds). (1977). *Managing the Commons.* San Francisco, CA: W. H. Freeman.

Liu, J., P. Sheldon, & T. Var. (1987). Resident Perceptions of the Impacts of Tourism. *Annals of Tourism Research . 26*(1). Elmsford, NY: Pergamon Press.

Lucas, R. (1964). The Recreational Use of the Quetico Superior Area. (U.S. Forest Service Research Paper LS-8).

Manning, R., & C. Ciali. (1980). Recreational Density and User Satisfaction: A Further Explanation of the Satisfaction Model. *Journal of Leisure Research, 12*(4). Arlington, VA: NRPA.

OECD. (1980). *The Impact of Tourism on the Environment.* Paris, France: Organization for Economic Cooperation and Development.

Partners for Livable Places. (1981). *Livability Digest, 1* and subsequent issues. Washington, DC: Partners for Livable Places.

Perloff, H. (1969). *Quality of the Urban Environment.* Resources for the Future, Baltimore, MD: Johns Hopkins Press.

Pilgram, J. (1980). Environmental Implications of Tourism Development. *Annals of Tourism Research, 7*(4). Menomine, WI: Department of Habitational Resources, University Wisconsin-Stout.

Rosenow, J., & G. Pulsipher. (1979). *Tourism, the Good, the Bad, and the Ugly.* Lincoln, NB: Century Three Press. (Chapters 6 and 11).

Simonson, L. (1974). *Plant Tours.* Unpublished doctoral dissertation. Texas A & M University, College Station, TX.

Walter, J. (1982). Social Limits to Tourism. *Leisure Studies, 1*(3). London: E. & F. N. Spon, Ltd.

West, P. (1981). Perceived Crowding and Attitudes Toward Limiting Use in Backcountry Recreation Area. *Leisure Sciences, 4*(4). New York: Crane Russack and Co. Inc.

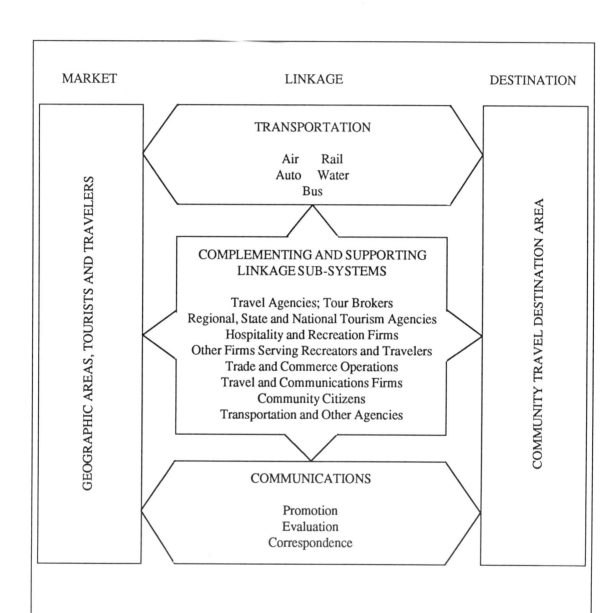

MARKET   LINKAGE   DESTINATION

GEOGRAPHIC AREAS, TOURISTS AND TRAVELERS

TRANSPORTATION

Air   Rail
Auto   Water
Bus

COMPLEMENTING AND SUPPORTING
LINKAGE SUB-SYSTEMS

Travel Agencies; Tour Brokers
Regional, State and National Tourism Agencies
Hospitality and Recreation Firms
Other Firms Serving Recreators and Travelers
Trade and Commerce Operations
Travel and Communications Firms
Community Citizens
Transportation and Other Agencies

COMMUNICATIONS

Promotion
Evaluation
Correspondence

COMMUNITY TRAVEL DESTINATION AREA

Figure 8.1 Overall Community Tourism System: Amplified Linkage Component

EIGHT

The Linkage System

This chapter treats the mechanisms by which communities, attractions and their travel experiences are linked to tourist markets. The linkage system's elements and principles of operation are explained. This discussion includes advertising, but only in a limited way does it treat the "how to" of advertising. The complete linkage system is much broader than advertising. Advertising procedures are discussed in many publications that are readily available to the reader and this "how to" information can be used in an effective way once basic principles of the linkage system are understood. Chapter 9 builds upon this discussion of the linkage systems by expanding upon systems for understanding markets.

THE OVERALL LINKAGE SYSTEM REVIEWED

Figure 8.1 highlights the linkage system. Its two principal components, communications and transportation, have been noted in Chapter 2. Figure 8.1 shows an expansion of the linkage which is designated "Complementing and supporting linkage subsystems." They are summarized below for ready review.

Communication is the Key

People do not go places that they have never heard of. Even while traveling in a specific area, tourists do not do—experience—things that the area offers, but that they know nothing about. The task of the communication linkage is to overcome the all-too-prevalent syndrome debilitating the tourist industry of many communities: that of maintaining their appeal as "well-kept secrets." Favorable experiences in any given destination area depend first upon tourists' knowledge and understanding of what that area offers.

Communication consists of varied kinds of informational stimuli, and must reach potential and actual travelers:

— While they are in their home area;
— While they are at various stages of their travel;
— While they are in the destination area; and
— After they have returned home.

This multi-staged communication pattern is necessary to support the tourist development of a given facility or destination area. Equally, it helps tourists by encouraging the use of facilities and services that are appropriate to their current travel and recreational needs. It also informs and assists their full enjoyment and appreciation of those experiences that they undertake.

The Transportation System

Few tourists go to places that cannot be reached by reasonable means. For that reason, travel volume to a given TDA depends upon transportation convenience. Transportation systems are subject to change due to such factors as new technology, growing affluence and new investments in such things as highways, airports, and waterways. A destination area that fares well with automobile travelers may find that it can tap bus and air travelers only with difficulty, if at all. Air travel may not only reduce the time costs of travel, but the actual dollar costs. Certain kinds of travelers have marked preferences for one type of transportation over another. These and related transportation factors can exert major influence on the market growth of one destination, compared to other areas where the travel access is different. Although transportation systems are part of the larger public infrastructure, many destination areas will need to manage their own transportation access system as a condition of serving their travel clientele adequately.

Complementing and Supporting Linkage Subsystems

In today's setting, a number of complementing operations influence the flow of both information and people between market and destination areas. These operations have a direct, vested interest in tourism; hence they should be regarded as component parts and allies by tourism destination areas and by tourism-related firms. In the next section they are discussed under the headings "Complementing Communicators" and "the Communication Nesting System."

THE COMMUNICATION LINKAGE

The successful tourism destination area takes its cue from tourists' needs. It matches its tourism resources and their development with these needs. Then it communicates to its clientele, "We have what you want ," through an appealing, believable message that builds a powerful destination area image in the clients' minds. The TDA then delivers the sought-after experience. This achievement is the challenge to the communication linkage, and also to the destination services and facilities. In accomplishing this feat, the communication must be two-way and the destination area must constantly readjust both its message and its travel-recreation offering; failure to do so can result in market obsolescence.

Good Experiences: The Premiere Communication Means

"Satisfied customers" top the list, by far, as the primary, positive image-builder for tourist destination areas. As high as 95 percent, and rarely fewer than 50 percent, of the tourists in an area have either been there before, or have had it recommended by someone else who had been there. The communication means operating here is "word of mouth" or memories of one's own experiences (Woodside, 1986). It indicates that effort placed into ensuring that tourists now in an area have a good experience is by far the best means of securing future tourists. Seeing that the area's guests are satisfied customers has implications for:

— The quality of hospitality services and
  facilities offered.
— The quality and aesthetic appeal of the area's
  environment.
— The quality and courtesy of treatment by
  personnel.
— Information access to the area's recreational
  features.

Fulfilling these requirements ensures that tourists know the full range of things to see and do in the area, and can fully appreciate and enjoy those parts in which they choose to participate. Means for providing this access are treated in the section "An Information / Direction / Interpretation System for the Community," below.

Continued Advertising and Promotional Effort: An Ongoing Necessity

A well-designed, continuously updated advertising and promotional program demands major effort on the part of the destination area and individual destination features. Such a program acts as a complement in the image-building process to the delivery of outstanding experiences to actual area visitors.

There is need to continually reach out to new markets in addition to those reached by word of mouth (Bendl, 1987). The more dynamic the destination area's development, the greater the need for aggressive advertising to continually tap new markets. An aggressive advertising program may mean that three to eight percent of a firm's gross tourism income is devoted to that purpose. Among the reasons for ongoing advertising are the following:

— Tastes are continuously changing; this occurs not only as fads in the society, but also because of such happenings as changes in income, travel technology and offerings by competing destinations areas.

— Overall population demographics change; migration takes place; the age-groups change their relative sizes; and occupations, education, family structures and living conditions are altered.

— As the area's ongoing development of its tourism offering proceeds, there may be potential for serving new markets. These must be informed through advertising and promotional effort.

— Without ongoing market image renewal through facility development, and reaching out to new markets or appealing to existing markets in a new way, there is serious likelihood of market obsolescence setting in.

— Domestic tourist destination areas are now in competition for markets with other destination areas

on a world-wide basis. Advertising is one means of maintaining one's destination area image in the mind of this globally oriented travel market.

The advertising/promotional challenge is how to break into the cacophony of enticements and claims with a crisp, clear, appealing message. While a "how to" detailed discussion is beyond the intent of this book, a number of specific marketing steps and approaches are summarized here. They are examples of the type of broad-scale approaches that must be combined with detailed advertising effort to achieve effective communication with the appropriate market. A TDA might do any or all of the following:

— Set up a positive marketing policy based on knowledge of both the market and the tourism destination area. A marketing policy is one part of an overall tourism policy, as discussed in more detail in Chapter 11. As a minimum the policy should include a statement of goals, market targets and evaluation mechanisms. Review this policy at least annually in the light of results achieved (as indicated by evaluation of the advertising conducted) and new market research information that is available.

— Conduct systematic market research. Research informs about what the market wants and how the TDA's tourism offering fits into the market.

— Implement a consistent sales-advertising-promotional program based on sound information. It may include traditional media use plus many of the activities noted immediately below.

— Positive news media reports about your area and its offering can achieve more than paid advertising. Staging newsworthy events and achieving other favorable media coverage rank high on the list of promotional efforts. Ideally this would be reported as general news. Less valuable, but still effective, is news that is written and reported as travel news by travel writers. *The community should take the initiative in generating this news and seeing that it is reported.*

— Take maximum advantage of other marketing systems and complementing tourism elements that share your area's interest and stake in the tourism industry. These include tour operators and agencies, transportation firms and agencies, and hospitality firms; also included are other TDA's in the region, and wider geographic entities such as that of regions and states. The systems and elements are covered in more detail elsewhere in this chapter.

— Cross-selling may offer an effective means of widening the message and extending dollars spent for advertising. Cross-selling consists of promotional efforts of destination areas in cooperation with transportation firms, food and beverage firms, restaurant and motel chains and many others. It may take the form of shared costs for advertising, or it may involve a special offer in which all cross-sellers stand to gain.

— Stage familiarization (FAM) tours for writers, travel agencies, and personnel of businesses having interests. Once they are sold on what the destination area offers, they in turn can sell the TDA to travelers.

— It is uncommon to find literature that is accessibly placed and that clearly tells what the traveler needs and wants to know. Good maps are particularly valuable. Much destination area literature appears written to satisfy egos of firms in the area and/or those of the local chamber of commerce rather than for travelers. Outstanding literature can help your area to stand out.

The above summary is intended to be representative of broader-scale items deserving attention in an advertising program (see suggested additional readings for Chapters 8 and 9). Changes in details and additions to the list will be needed for each different tourism destination area. The most important among these is the need for a specific, positive marketing policy to guide advertising and

related operations. The policy must be systematically executed and regularly reviewed.

The Role of Specialized Advertising Firms

A number of different kinds of firms are able to provide assistance to tourism destinations and to tourism-related firms in the design and conduct of advertising and promotional programs. Among these are 1) agencies that do only advertising; 2) media firms with personnel who can help with planning, design and layout of advertisements; and 3) general consultant firms with units that can help with market studies and advertising program evaluation. All of these are referred to as "ad agencies" in this subsection.

An ad agency can provide effective inputs in ways such as the following:

— In an advisory role—assisting the community or tourism firm to determine what its alternative approaches to advertising might be and to understand the possible scope of such a program.

— Assisting with determining markets to target, and overall market positioning strategies.

— Performing the technical production work of preparing newspaper, magazine, radio and/or TV ads.

The same principles apply in the management of ad agencies as in the case of other consulting and service firms (see Chapter 11). The service of a capable ad agency can be a valuable asset, but the community or firm is advised not to hire such an agency and instruct them to "advertise us." Rather, the community officials must study the community's tourism marketing situation sufficiently so that they know what is needed, at least in principle, and can instruct the ad agency.

We have noted that the ad agency can assist in understanding advertising/promotional needs and possible actions. This advisory role does not relieve the community officials or hospitality firm managers from final responsibility for advertising/promotional decisions.

Information must flow effectively both ways between the ad agency and its client. The decision maker—the client—needs to stay on top of the advertising/promotional action. Such monitoring is needed, both so proper advertising decisions are made and so the community can make needed adjustments and take proper action to complement and support the advertising and promotional program. Failure to do so can result in an ineffective program and wasted advertising dollars.

Communication is Two-way

All true communication flows two ways. For a destination area to know what its clients want, it must receive information from them. Some communication from clients is received in direct oral and written communications. Clients further communicate desires by their pattern of choices—provided they have adequate knowledge of the range of choice available to them. In addition, a large part of the tourist market's needs must determined by some kind of research that is initiated by the tourist firm or community. The research evaluates what tourists do while in the destination area and may also follow up by asking tourists' evaluation after they have returned home. This communication from the market to the destination area forms a major part of the discussion in Chapter 9. The market-destination communication forms the complementing part of the destination-market communication of which advertising and promotion consist.

The two-way nature of communication is underscored by observation of much ineffective advertising effort. Potential tourists simply ignore most messages beamed to them that are not consciously or unconsciously "asked for." Achieving a breakthrough—where the market is induced to actively

seek information about a specific TDA—is one of the first and primary of many marketing tasks.

Complementing Communicators

Fortunately a number of elements have an overlapping interest in developing the tourism industry of most tourism destination areas. This may mean that the communications with the market by these elements can support and complement those of the TDA. In some cases, cooperative efforts may be possible that can generate greater marketing impact than could be achieved by operating singly.

Travel and tour agencies. disseminate information about destinations to travelers, since their business depends upon their being able to sell travel services. They consist of a whole system ranging from those who set up tours, to tour wholesalers, travel retailers (these are the visable part that prospective travelers contact), and tour operators (those conducting the actual travel). A rapidly growing number of travelers, for example long-distance vacation travelers and senior citizens, use this system. For this reason every destination area should establish contact with the travel and tour agency system, using it to augment the TDA's link with the market.

Hospitality firms, such as lodging operations, may be linked into parts of the travel agency system in addition to serving travelers directly. Many are also linked with other hospitality firms through various kinds of ownership, supply systems and reservation systems. All communicate with travelers both formally and informally about destinations. Their reservation systems, in some cases, play a major role in travel decisions.

Telephone networks are not neutral, passive transmitters of communications. Travel and telephone use have a strong positive correlation. Telephone systems may influence the communications to a community by price structures, by the quality of service and by direct communications of their own. Increasing use of 800 numbers is changing some market communication patterns.

Public carriers and transportation firms include airlines, buslines, taxi firms, auto rental agencies, and Amtrak. All of these firms have an obvious vested interest in travel. They communicate with travel clients through media advertising, their own literature, and through their office agents. Cooperative communication in concert with these operations has the potential for mutual benefit for the TDA and the operation.

Automobile manufacturers, their sales agencies, automobile insurers, and auto clubs communicate regularly with travelers. Like the public carriers, they do this through advertising, their own literature and their employees.

Other TDA's in the region are often viewed as competitors. This view arises from a zero-sum concept of the tourist market for the region: What one TDA captures from that pool of tourists is lost to the others. In actual fact, the most serious competition usually comes from other competing states and regions. There may be substantial possibility for gains by communicating cooperatively to create a greater marketing impact and build the destination image of the entire region.

Departments of transportation communicate with travelers through the production of state maps, directional signs and their control of private road signs. As a minimum, each TDA should systematically investigate the treatment of the community and its attractions on the state map and by highway directional signs.

The Communication Nesting System

In communicating with tourists, every community is a part of a geographical/political system consisting of diffcrent levels. In size, these levels extend from the individual tourism operation to the national government. The system is in place and available for use. Starting from the individual operation it may be seen as five-tiered: firm-TDA-region- state-national.

Figure 8.2 portrays the system graphically. The entire rectangle represents the national level. Each quarter represents a state, shown uncluttered in the upper left quarter. Moving clockwise, the regions, tourist destination areas, and firms within the TDA are illustrated in succeeding quartiles, or states.

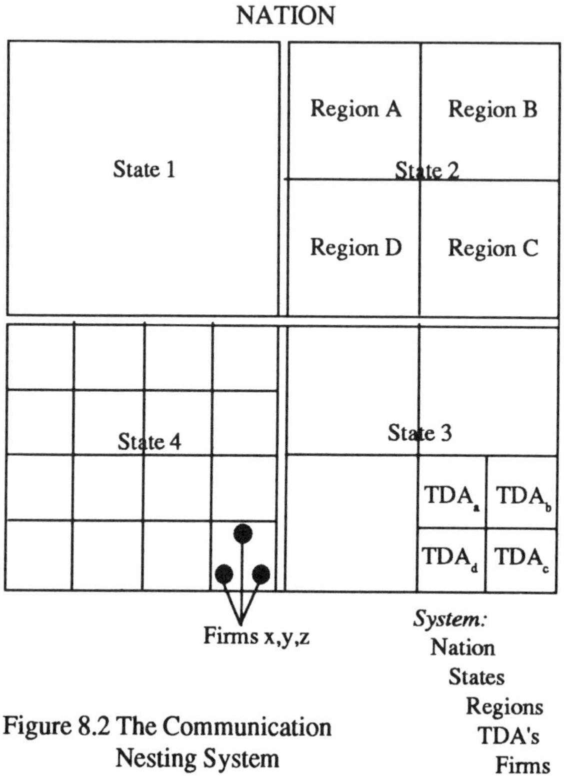

Figure 8.2 The Communication Nesting System

This system is not a hierarchy in the sense of one element being superior to another. Rather, as one moves from the individual operation to each successive part of the system, a progressively wider geographic area is involved. Each level in the system has its job to do; when properly functioning each level supports the others, and is in sync with what is done by the levels above and below it. The several parts, and their separate roles include the following:

At the national level in the United States is the U.S. Travel and Tourism Administration (USTTA). Its major function is to encourage travel to the United States by people living in other countries. It is a part of the U.S. Department of Commerce, and is supported with appropriations by the U.S. Congress.

International tourism to the United States depends upon inter-country relationships; the state of world affairs, especially world peace; the exchange rate of the dollar with respect to specific other currency; and the state of prosperity of each nation, among a number of other factors. Overseas travel to the United States shows a recent strong growth trend. It increased by 40 percent in the 1984 to 1987 period (Wynegar, 1988). Many communities have potential for appeal to foreign visitors and could participate in the growth trend. It is thus to their advantage to establish contact with the USTTA, and operate in other added ways to directly encourage foreign tourists.

Each state has an agency concerned with tourism promotion. In addition to tourism promotion, a few also consider tourism industry development as a part of their charter. States promote themselves as tourism destinations in order to gain the income for travelers' expenditures. Not only does this generate jobs, rents and profits for state individuals and businesses, but since nearly all states levy a sales tax, state decision makers see

tourism as a way of increasing the tax income with only limited added public costs.

While tourists rarely view an entire state as a destination area, the states see themselves in competition with other United States and international destinations for tourists. Ultimately tourists are serviced by specific operations in specific communities. It is the specific attractions of the several substate destination areas that the state ultimately promotes. This forms a basis for cooperative working relationships between each destination area and the respective state tourism agency.

Many states are further subdivided into what are commonly called "tourism regions." These are often formed on the basis of a feature such as a large city, or a geo-physical region dominated by such things as forests, mountains, lakes, and agriculture. Regions are often at least partially dependent upon state governments for their funding. They may also be supported in part by the several smaller governmental units (such as counties) within them, and/or by individual firms. Since they are closer to the individual communities, regions are often in closer contact with attractions and services and can be more specific in their descriptions of what is available.

The individual community or coherent set of communities becomes the ultimate destination of most tourists. This we call a TDA. The TDA has the opportunity to be specific in its advertising/promotional program since it represents only one attraction or attraction's set. Unfortunately few destination areas systematically think through the nature of their focal attraction feature along with the full set of subsystems—activities, information/interpretation, infrastructure, community ambience and hospitality services—that should support it. This is particularly true in the case where a number of smaller cities share one major focal feature, such as a large park, lake, or other travel attraction.

In this latter case there is the tendency for each separate city to operate in isolation, and often in competition with others in the same destination area.

Cooperative effort between the destination areas and regional and state tourism programs should ensure that there is appropriate and accurate representation of the destination in the regional and/or state advertising.

The individual tourism firm or operation is the most frequent point of contact by tourists where money transactions are made in the local community. These firms have an immediate stake in development and marketing of the tourism industry by the community in which they are a part. Within this setting it is the individual operation's obligation and opportunity to so conduct its services to tourists, and its own promotional effort, that it receives its share of the travelers that are attracted by the appeals of the overall TDA. It also has an obligation, in turn as a TDA component, for contributing positively to experiences of tourists that are in the area.

Depending upon the purpose, this nesting system may be viewed either as firm-TDA-region-state-national or the reverse national-state-region-TDA-firm. Within this system, each level has a task to do that cannot be as well done at other levels. Ideally, the several levels function in a coordinated way; without adequate coordination there can be considerable lost motion in an overall promotional effort. The need for coordination of effort and sharing of information is underscored by estimates of some regional tourism officials that as many as 20 separate replies have been made to some individual tourist requests for information. This is costly duplication resulting from inadequate information flow, improper targeting of markets and improper handling of requests for information.

Overcoming the "Well-Kept Secret" Syndrome: An Information/Direction/Interpretation System for the Local Community

Even after tourists reach a destination community, they still will not see and do things there that they never hear of or know about. Tourists who lack information about the TDA will have a limited experience because of this poor information access. This is another major part of the challenge to the communication linkage system. Its job is to overcome the "well-kept secret" syndrome debilitating the tourism industry of many communities.

Information about the community is seldom adequately disseminated, even to visitors who are present physically in the community. Tourists often drive through, eat meals or stay overnight, and then drive on, oblivious to the community's offering of things that they innately would enjoy experiencing (Perdue, 1986). It is to this information inadequacy that this subsection is addressed.

The communication linkage's task is not completed when tourists leave home, nor is it completed when they arrive at their destination area. Within the community the information/direction/interpretation system's job is to reinforce the power of the tourist destination area image. It does this by complementing and enhancing the focal feature, and by enabling tourists to more fully experience the community and its special characteristics.

Positive Action Needed. How badly is improvement needed in the local information system? Periodically, community leaders should try this test: Drive out 10 to 20 miles from the community along a major highway, then turn and re-enter the community pretending to be a tourist—you have never seen it before, or had not seen it for five or 10 years. Ask yourself: How would I know what is unusual about this community? What things are there to see and do? How do I find these? Where can I eat?

How do I find decent lodging? The visitor is usually presented fragmentary, confused, haphazard information rather than a clear welcoming message.

An adequate community information/direction/interpretation system rarely happens by chance. It usually results from deliberate effort that is consistently and positively directed over a period of time. This also usually means that some group or agency gives specific, positive leadership to the effort. Such an effort may well be given priority as an early step in implementing the policy-action procedures as discussed in Chapters 11 and 12.

Major components of a community information/direction/interpretation system are discussed categorically below.

An information center. Every community should have an information center where the communication effort heads up physically, and where travelers can go directly to satisfy their detailed information needs. Considerable ingenuity may be required in the establishment of an information center. The arrangement will need to be different depending upon the character of the community, its size, and the resources available for this purpose.

What should the center provide? It should have access to all needed information about places to eat, sleep, and things to do. Interpretations of the community—what it is about, its attractions and special features—can add much. This may be done with displays, dioramas, video tapes and slides. Real, live people should serve as hosts.

When should these services be provided? The answer to that is simple: When tourists need it. Who needs a visitor information center that closes at 5:00 pm and on weekends? Recognizing the times when visitors need information is a part of the marketing problem of defining what tourists want.

In smaller communities the information center may be operated in association with another public or private office or business. It should be clearly marked and accessible.

Larger communities may find that a single information center location lacks access to many tourists, simply because of the distances involved and a number of different access routes. This suggests a multi-sited system for providing primary information. Inaccessibility of a single information center may be solved in a number of ways:

— Signs giving clear directions to the information center location can be placed at all community entrances. Both large and small communities should do this.

— Unstaffed information stations may be located at major entrance points. These can describe what the community is about, display maps and provide literature. Telephone connections to the headquarters center may greatly increase the usefulness of such unstaffed stations, but they may also increase the management required.

— Computerized, video display information stations are increasingly employed at points where travel converges and/or where people congregate. Some versions of these programs can also be set up to operate through television sets in lodging rooms and/or hotel lobbies.

— Where air travel is important, there should be an information center at the airport. Communities having major airports where travelers change planes without leaving the airport have a special challenge: The travelers are there physically; can these people be given a sufficient community experience that they are motivated to stay over, or come back on another trip?

— Largely overlooked is information and interpretation on metropolitan beltways. This is the same situation as an airport: The people are there because of the travel node. This time they are going through, but they're present physically. Is there a way to appeal to them so they are motivated to stop, or return when they have the time?

The visitor's entering experience. What is the aesthetic quality of the visitor's experience upon entering your community? This communicates volumes about the community, its inhabitants, and the nature of the experience that can be had there. Does it welcome or repulse the visitor? Does it look as though the community expected visitors? Does it say that the residents are proud of their community? Does it highlight the focal attraction, and entice further exploration by tourists?

Some communities beckon with vistas of a major attraction; with well-managed welcome/information stations; with well-appointed hospitality services or residential areas; with natural areas; or even appropriate, indigenous manufacturing or processing operations. Others repulse with scenes of obvious pollution; poor services for the traveler; unkempt buildings, overgrown with weeds; and/or miscellaneously strewn refuse or junk.

A simple test of the entering experience for residents is similar to that recommended for checking the overall information system: Drive 10 miles or more away, then return, pretending that you have never been to the community before. Ask: Is this community really expecting company (visitors)? Would I want to stay here overnight—or even stop for a cup of coffee?

The community's aesthetics. The entering experience, just noted, deserves special attention as a first impression to the tourist. The overall community aesthetics may also exert a powerful influence upon the tourists' experiences there. The overall community can convey an impression of residents who take pride in their home, who enjoy a good quality of living, and can extend this quality experience to the visitor.

As referred to here, aesthetics has nothing to do with modernness. In fact, much charm may be lost by inappropriate attempts at modernization, especially where part of the appeal is an ambience of a special vintage, or a specific community activity. Examples include the quaintness of a coastal fishing village or of a "wild west" town. Aesthetics refers more to an ambience that is appropriate for the destination area. It also includes sustainable order and management of manmade and natural features.

Genuineness, that is, a basis in the natural, economic or cultural environment, usually delivers a better experience than the ersatz and contrived. In Chapter 3 we also noted the advantages of enhancing indigenous features, although recreational parks and entertainment features may be important exceptions. Congruence with the physical and cultural environment, however, is an important factor in ambience and its imparting a pleasing aesthetic sense.

The community's salespeople. Who sells the community to travelers? The chamber of commerce director? Perhaps. But his or her job is only one part of the community's sales force. *Everyone* who sells goods and services at retail regularly contacts travelers and can therefore be considered a community salesperson (Wick, 1980). True, some such as those in the information stations, and those who operate hospitality and travel businesses, contact travelers most often. But travelers ultimately buy from all retailers. In addition, even the average, run-of-the-mill citizen has much more tourist contact and "sales opportunities" than may be at first recognized. This contact includes visitors in homes, on the streets and gathering places, and the image that business and residential areas give to the traveler. Thus, while some community citizens have specific responsibility for "selling" the community to tourists, all residents share this responsibility.

Citizen salesmanship to tourists begins with pride in the community by residents. Living quality for residents depends partly upon this pride. The concept differs greatly from "boosterism," which is often advocated by community leadership. Rather, it is based upon knowledge, understanding and appreciation of the community—its history of human toils, tragedies, tears, triumphs and achievements; its natural history; and its current people, economy, and recreational offering. Community salesmanship consists of appreciating and enjoying one's community, and being willing to share it as good hosts with visitors (Ritchie, 1966).

Salesmanship: the basics. In Chapter 7, pride was treated as a factor in resource management. In this chapter, community pride is suggested as a factor in "selling" the community to visitors. Further, we broaden the concept here to the basics of good salesmanship generally. Key points in good salesmanship include:

— Deliver a superior product; whether a good or a service, the product should give satisfaction to the buyer.

— Display the product properly, and make it appropriately available. This is the equivalent of knowledge and physical access as we have discussed regarding tourism resources.

— Know the product well; be able to explain it to advantage so the buyer understands what it will do.

— Recognize and welcome prospective customers as having needs that you may be able to serve. Determine thoroughly what their interests and needs are.

— Know customers' needs; interpret the product to them; explain how they can use it to satisfy their needs.

— Be able and available to provide backup service so that expected full performance of the product is achieved.

The above principles work equally well whether the product is a restaurant meal or a pair of shoes. Adaptations of the above principles to the business of selling the community may be noted:

— Recognize especially people who are tourists. Good hosting communicates to the tourist,

"We are proud of our community, and pleased to have opportunity to share it with you, the visitor."

— Find out the tourists' interests and needs. Help them understand how the goods and services that your operation provides will help fulfill their needs; explain community services, and community things to see and do that will meet their needs and expectations and will give them a rewarding community experience.

People who have received full measure from the services of the individual firm, and who achieve a rewarding community experience, will be back. They will also tell others.

Literature and maps. Literature provided locally can lean strongly toward details of what there is to see and do. Since the visitor is already present, a "lure" is not necessary. Instead, the tourist needs to know what is available and how it can best be found and experienced.

Good community/area maps are particularly lacking or elusive in most communities. They can be one of the most positive devices for explaining, comprehensively, the full range of things to see and do, as well as beginning the process of community interpretation.

Unless placed accessibly, literature and maps are of little value. In addition to placing them at formal information stations, literature should be available at all major points where tourists contact the community. This means placing them in many private business places. Proprietors and employees in each such business place should not only know the literature and maps well, but use this material to "sell" the community.

Public media. Newspapers, radio, and television can be major instruments contributing to citizens' education in community appreciation, awareness and living quality. The media can also contribute to visitors' knowledge of the community and things available for them to enjoy. Media managers and employees will need to have training in this work in a way comparable to the training that must be given to all other community salespersons.

Signing. Signs provide travelers with needed information about travel directions and services. Interpretive signs add to understanding and appreciation of the area, and hence to the travel experience.

Unfortunately, signs can be obtrusive. This raises the question of how and where to use them. The problem can be summarized from results of traveler surveys: Travelers are repulsed by a clutter of signs, by neglected signs, by unnecessary signs and especially by signs that block aesthetic views. But travelers rate well-designed, well-placed signs giving information that they need as highly as they rate a good scenic overlook (Gunn, 1965).

Some states reduce the obtrusiveness of signs on the landscape by the use of information boards and sign kiosks at rest stops. Controlled commercial advertising may be permitted by the use of this device.

Some communities provide sign bays where information about attractions and accommodations may be presented in an organized way at a convenient drive-off place. This avoids cluttering large sections of the roadside. Such drive-offs appear best located near the intersection of local access roads with major highways and interstates, or just before entering major communities. These may be part of a multi-sited community information system, as noted earlier in this chapter.

Within the community, directional signs at every entrance should tell where community information center(s) can be found. Well-marked road junctions and street signs are essential. Businesses and attractions need point-of-sale signs. The challenge is to provide necessary information while welcoming the traveler, and to do so tastefully and in a manner befitting the sought-after destination area image.

Interpretation: what's so great about it?
Increasingly, travelers get enjoyment from looking behind the community facade. They wish to relive the dramatic parts of the community's history, and gain insights into a new part of the world through experiencing the natural, social and economic system of another community (Sharpe, 1976).

Museums, restorations, industry tours, and guided or self-guided nature trails and community tours can be important parts of interpretation. Other important parts consist of interpretive signs, dramas in public areas, the use of video tapes and slide shows, literature of many kinds, and above all, the human communication system discussed under "salesmanship."

All of the above are parts of the local information access to the community. Lacking an adequate system, visitors pass through or pass by, yet have no way of knowing what is in the community to see and do and enjoy. Without an information system, most attractions and tourism resources simply remain "well-kept secrets."

THE TRANSPORTATION LINKAGE

Except for a scattering of adventuresome travelers, few will go to places requiring arduous travel. Transportation thus becomes part of the linkage. The transportation component is apparently, but not necessarily, more tangible and physical in nature than communications, and it too requires management.

Key principles applying to transportation and its major component parts are discussed in this subsection.

Basic Travel Model

Figure 8.3 gives a simple travel formula in the form of a gravity model (Isaard, 1960).

The model simply says that travel between community 1 and community 2 is directly proportional to their populations, and inversely proportional to the distance between them, multiplied by a constant. In other words, the larger the populations of each community and the closer together they are, the more travel there will be between them; the smaller their populations and further apart they are, the less travel (Darragh, 1983).

$$T_{1,2} [\text{travel}] = K \frac{P_1 P_2 \ [\text{populations}]}{D_{1,2} \ [\text{distance}]}$$

Figure 8.3 Gravity Model: Travel Between Two Communities

The constant K when stated as simply as in Figure 8.3 represents a wide variety of things (Smith, 1985). Some of these are illustrated by studies of commercial lodging guests in Minneapolis-St. Paul (Johnson, 1973).

— *Travel interaction follows trade.* K values for North and South Dakota were three to four times higher than for Iowa. Minneapolis-St. Paul is a major supply and shopping center for the population of the Dakotas. The Iowa population and businesses, though as close or closer than those of the Dakotas, trade mainly with larger Illinois cities.

—*Travel follows immigration.* K values are also larger for North and South Dakota because there is relatively more migration from the Dakotas into Minneapolis-St. Paul, compared to Iowa.

—*Tastes in preferred vacation areas affect the K.* The fun-in-the-sun areas of the Southwest had relatively high K's, reflecting Minnesotans' desire to escape the cold by vacationing and retiring in the Southwest, and then returning for visits to Minneapolis-St. Paul.

—*Distance has an inverse influence as a power that is larger than one.* K's were consistently smaller for more distant destinations.

—*Competition of other destinations—operates to lower K for destinations that are further apart.*

—*K values varied by season.*

The above are some of the more prominent factors operating to influence travel, in addition to population and distance.

The Time-Money-Effort Effect

Most travel has a cost in terms of time, money and effort. In the case of general sightseeing trips, multi-destinationed wandering through an area is the major motivation; travel cost has only limited impact upon any one destination. Most travel, however, has a more narrow destination focus. In such cases, travel costs may be a major factor in the decision whether or not to undertake the travel to a given destination.

Figure 8.4 shows graphically the combined effect of time, money and effort upon possible travel choices by a hypothetical traveler. This traveler lives in city A which is at the intersection of two interstate freeways, I-101 and I-202. All of the points along the dotted lines are regarded by the traveler as equivalent in combined time, money and effort costs. He can travel 300 miles to points w, x, y or z, which are on the interstate freeways; he regards each as being equally accessible. This travel one-way, using his own automobile, costs $60 and requires 6 hours.

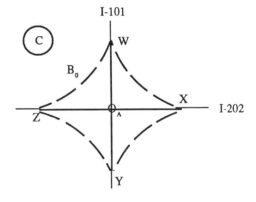

Figure 8.4 The Time-Distance-Effort Effect

There are two other travel choices that the traveler regards as equivalent. He can travel to village B, which is off the freeway. It is only 250 miles but requires 7 hours of driving, costing $50. City C is 500 miles distant; however, he can reach it by air in only 3 hours total time, at a cost of $100. Travel to city C is equivalent to the 6 or 7 hour automobile drives even though the dollar cost is higher because he regards air travel as safer than surface automobile travel. In addition, he does not have to undertake a fatiguing drive, it requires less time, and he can further use the time spent on the plane.

Because of the multiplicity of travel destinations and travel modes available, potential travelers to a given tourist destination area will weigh total costs of travel in a manner such as the above. Increasingly, costs other than dollars and miles traveled are factors that swing travel decisions. Some residents of Chicago may regard an air trip to Europe as costing less than a one and one-half day's automobile drive of 700 miles into a neighboring state. Further, it yields much more in terms of prestige.

Dollar cost is important in travel decisions, but often is secondary to other considerations. Senior citizens may prefer a bus tour because it is leisurely and secure, and because they can be with a number of their friends on the trip. Many travelers prefer the convenience of arrangements for travel and destination stops made by a travel agent to the problems of personal arrangements. These factors all bear upon the perceived total costs of travel.

Technology

Ongoing changes in travel technology act to expand the travel horizons available to many tourists, thus increasing competition among tourist destination areas (American Geological Society, 1986). This technology may be of at least three kinds:

— Physical means of moving people, such as that occurring to cause the shift from trains to autos to planes.

— Travel organization and arrangements, such as by travel agent systems, and tour buses.

—Hospitality arrangements, such as reservation systems and fast food, and hybrid arrangements such as ocean cruises.

Travel technology increases travel by lowering costs. This travel-increasing effect of new technology is illustrated in Figures 8.5 and 8.6. Figure 8.5 shows the supply curve for travel to a given TDA and the demand curve of a specific tourist segment. The perceived travel costs are higher than any point on the tourist segment's demand curve and no travel will occur. Figure 8.6 illustrates the situation in which perceived travel costs have been lowered through new technologies and, depending upon demand for travel to competing destinations and perceived costs, travel may now occur.

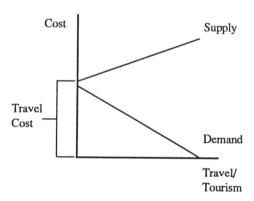

Figure 8.5 Pre-Technology Travel Cost

What could have occurred to lower travel costs as in Figure 8.6? A transportation innovation such as the introduction of jet aircraft produces such lowering. Long-distance travel, because of jet aircraft, now competes with short-distance travel for some travel segments. This is because jet travel costs less in time, effort and sometimes money. Some destinations are greatly benefitted. For example, jet aircraft were introduced just before the admission of Hawaii to statehood. The new technology plus added awareness produced explosive growth in travel to Hawaii.

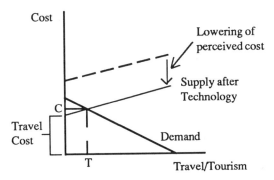

Figure 8.6 Cost-Lowering Travel Technology

Travel arrangements also lower perceived costs for certain tourist segments. Many might have presumed the worry, hassle and security costs of a trip to Latin America as prohibitively high when all arrangements had to be personally overseen. Now that travel agents arrange Latin American trips, the "costs" have dropped drastically. Travelers will participate in such tours who would previously have dismissed travel to those destinations as unthinkable. Figure 8.6 also illustrates such a situation.

Laws governing and regulating travel and transportation businesses can be another factor of change related to technology. For example, deregulation of air carriers changed both the frequency of service and fares into many destinations.

One might contemplate what might happen should fast, convenient rail transportation become

available. It could revolutionize patterns of travel between destinations less than 500 miles apart.

TDA's need to watch all travel developments with the intent of taking advantage of them where possible, and minimizing possible adverse effects where necessary.

Is Getting There Really Half of the Fun?

Most tourist destination areas can be reached by a variety of travel combinations. Destination areas may thus feel that the exterior travel access of the market to them is mostly out of their hands, and beyond their control. In many respects this view is unfortunate, since the mental image of the traveler of any given destination includes more than just the destination experience; it includes as one experience the travel to the destination, the destination itself, and the return home travel.

Because of the inability of tourists to separate the experience of "getting there" from the experience of "being there," tourist destination areas need to be directly concerned with the "getting there" experience (President's Council, 1966). In a far too brief overview, some important related factors are noted here:

Highway access includes the quality of the roadbed, its people and traveler services, and its information and signing. These factors exert impact upon tourists using major routes connecting the destination with significant market areas.

Air transportation includes the convenience of schedules, costs and the people services provided. Adequate air access may be a major factor in whether or not a given destination area is able to remain abreast of emerging market trends. In some settings general aviation (private aircraft) may be as important as scheduled commercial service.

Other transportation services include tour
buses, rental autos and the service of travel agencies. These operations are often important not only
as key parts of the external linkage, but as means of
reducing the seasonality of travel.

Internal Transportation Systems

These provide the means by which the tourist is
able to circulate among facilities in the destination
area. In many destinations the system may be much
more than simply people movement: it may
contribute vitally to the destination experience.
Consider applicability of the following:

— The entering experience has been noted
before; it is a part of the local transportation
system. Each community should ask if this experience provides the visual access, thrill, and destination image that the community wishes to achieve.
The provision of vistas of the focal attraction may
be possible; sometimes interpretation is appropriate;
adequate information should be provided to
travelers. The experience should say "Welcome;
you're in a special area!"

— Roads can be designed with sensitivity to the
traveler's experience, destination image and
ambience that is sought. For example, in a mainly
natural, outdoor area, a 100-foot right-of-way road
having all vegetation stripped may enhance travel
safety, but virtually rapes the environment and
deprives travelers of experiencing the natural
beauty. A less-severely manipulated roadway with
over-arching tree canopies might be preferable. At
least, the latter can be incorporated into designs at
rest stops, interpretive stops and other drive-offs.

— Access to local activity and experience
points includes visual access, possibly interpretation
and information, and parking.

— Not every community can have the cable cars
of San Francisco, but systems offering equal
romance may be possible. In numerous communities, steam trains now combine transportation,

visual access and a recreational experience. Among
the examples is the Roaring Camp and Big Trees
Railroad in the Felton/Santa Cruz, California area.

Questions for review and further study

1. Why do communities retain many of their
potential tourism resources as "well-kept
secrets?"

2. Advertising appears to be a less important
factor than "satisfied customers" in
generating tourists to a TDA. Why then do
most firms and communities continue with
aggressive advertising programs?

3. Which part of the communication "nesting
system" appears to you to be the more
important or necessary? Explain your
answer.

4. What major challenges confront a traveler
upon nearing and entering a strange
community?

5. How does the average person-on-the-street
operate as a part of the community's tourism
sales force?

6. Explain the effect of cost-cutting travel
technology upon travel.

7. What are the major factors influencing travel
between two communities?

SUGGESTIONS FOR FURTHER READING

Evans, J., & B. Berman. (1982). *Marketing.* New York: MacMillan Publishing Co.

Gunn, C. (1988). *Tourism Planning.* New York: Taylor & Francis. (Chapters 4, 5, and 6).

Koth, B. (1987). *Tourism Advertising: Some Basics.* (CD-FO-3311). St. Paul, MN: Minnesota Extension Service, University of Minnesota.

Schmoll, G. (1977). *Tourism Promotion.* London: Tourism International Press.

Wahab, S., L. Crampon, & L. Rothfield. (1976). *Tourism Marketing.* London: Tourism International Press.

Weaver, G. (1986). *Tourism USA.* U.S. Department of Commerce. (Chapter 4).

TEXTUAL REFERENCES

American Geographic Society. (1986). Transportation and Urban Growth. *Focus.* *36*(2). New York: AGS.

Bendl, P. (1987). Seven Myths of Tourism, or How to Stop a Tourism Development Program Before You Start. *Proceedings of 18th Annual Meeting, TTRA.* Salt Lake City, UT: Bureau of Economic and Business Research, University of Utah.

Darragh, A., G. Peterson, & J. Dwyer. (1983). Travel Cost Models at the Urban Scale. *Journal of Leisure Research. 15*(2). Arlington, VA: NRPA.

Gunn, C. (1965). *A Concept for the Design of a Tourism Recreational Region.* Mason, MI: B. J. Press.

Isard, W. (1960). *Methods of Regional Analysis: An Introduction to Regional Science.* New York: John Wiley and Sons, Inc.

Johnson, D. (1973). A Market Analysis of the Lodging Industry in the Twin City Metropolitan Area. Unpublished masters thesis, University of Minnesota. St. Paul, MN.

Perdue, R. (1986). The Influence of Unplanned Attraction's Visits on Expenditures of Travel-Through Visitors. *Journal of Travel Research, 25*(1). Boulder, CO: Business Research Division, University of Colorado.

President's Council on Recreation and Natural Beauty. (1966). *A Proposed Program for Scenic Roads and Parkways.* Washington, DC: PCRNB, U.S. Department of Commerce.

Ritchie, J. (1966). Measuring Effectiveness of Tourism Hospitality Awareness Campaigns. *Proceedings, 17th Annual Meeting, TTRA .* Salt Lake City, UT: Bureau of Economic and Business Research, University of Utah.

Sharpe, G. (1976). *Interpreting the Environment.* New York: John Wiley and Sons, Inc.

Smith, S. (1985). U.S. Vacation Travel Patterns: Correlates of Distance Decay and the Willingness to Travel. *Leisure Sciences, 7*(2). New York: Crane Russack and Co.

Wick, N., & A. Bateman. (1980). *Hospitality Awareness Training Manual.* Rapid City, SD: Agricultural Research and Extension Center, South Dakota State University.

Woodside, A., & E. Moore. (1986). Word of
    Mouth Communications and Guest Retention in
    Competing Resort Hotels. *Proceedings, 17th
    Annual Meeting, TTRA.* Salt Lake City, UT:
    Bureau of Economic and Business Research,
    University of Utah.

Wynegar, D. (1988). 1988 Outlook for
    International Travel. *1988 Outlook for Travel
    and Tourism.* U.S. Travel Data Center.

Good tourism marketing consists of determining tourist's needs and providing services that satisfy those needs. New Hope, Pennsylvania. Photo credit: Uel Blank

NINE

The Tourism Marketing Setting: Complex, Dynamic and Shifting

"One man's meat is another man's poison" applies as aptly to tourism as it does to food. Some individuals travel to participate in the raucous revelry of a major sporting event; others are attracted by the resounding splendor of a great orchestral performance. Some seek to hike or canoe into the primitive isolation of a vast wilderness area; others opt for the opulence of the finest hotels amidst the company of hundreds or thousands of other people. Opportunities for snowmobiling and/or skiing in frigid winter air compel some to travel; others prefer to luxuriate on a sun-drenched ocean beach. Many travel extensively to view awesome nature wonders of waterfalls, canyons and mountains; others seek an understanding of how different human societies live, work and play. Still others travel only to visit relatives.

These examples represent wide contrasts in tourism-recreation styles. The operating problem of sorting out target market groups is rendered all the more confusing by the fact that all of the travel-recreational activities listed above, plus many more, may be undertaken by the *same individuals* at different times and circumstances of a given year, and/or at different periods of their lives.

Constant shifting in demand patterns adds further to the marketing challenge. These changes are, in turn, produced by changes in many other background factors, including population demographics, economic and social patterns, and the technology of travel and communication. We examine details of some of these patterns later in this chapter.

International travel responds not only to the above-noted factors but also to international conditions. Such events as war or threats of war may profoundly curtail travel abroad. The threat of terrorism drastically cut European travel from the United States in the year 1986.

Fast, affordable travel, combined with the availability of package tour travel, has expanded travel competition. Almost every area of the world is now in competition with every other area for certain portions of the U.S. travel market. This competition extends to local tourist destination areas. These are important developments but they are only illustrative of the many factors operating to produce shifts in travel demand.

This chapter helps equip communities for dealing effectively with the dynamic nature of social, economic and technological systems as they impact upon the tourism industry and its markets. Treated are guiding principles for analyzing the market and securing a match between the community's tourism offering and appropriate market segments. The intent is to provide basic understanding of principles that can be used over time to build and maintain a viable community tourism industry.

TOURISM DEMAND GALORE

Twenty years of U.S. travel data highlight dramatic growth in travel. In 1967, the year of the first travel census, 140 million people made 250 million trips that were 100 or more miles from home. By 1987, the number of person-trips in the United States had grown by 360 percent to almost 1.2 billion (USTDC, 1987). Growth in person-trips was rapid in the 1970s but appears to have slowed during the decade of the 1980s.

What will be the future course in numbers of people traveling and dollars that they spend? There is good reason to expect continued growth, particularly in money spent for travel. In addition, *the market can be expected to both broaden and deepen.*

Travel markets will *broaden* in the sense that a wider spectrum of the population will be involved. In the early 1960s when median family incomes were barely $5000 annually, travel 100 or more miles from home was largely limited to those families having incomes above the median. This means that half of all households seldom undertook such travel. It does not mean that families in the lower half of the income range did not recreate; rather, they did it in the local community, at home, and in the homes of relatives and friends. Such a pattern of tourism-recreation required little travel and little interaction with the commercial economy. Later in the chapter we will examine the pattern of growth in family income that makes extensive travel possible for a larger proportion of families.

There are almost limitless other aspects of the broadening travel demand. For example, retirees are traditionally regarded as people sitting passively at home; now many retirees have health, good incomes and travel more than at any time in their lives.

Tourism-recreation demand *deepens* as tourists expand the range of the travel and recreational activities that they undertake. To explain the concept concretely: Instead of only hunting, fishing and visiting relatives, tourists not only engage in those activities, but also take charter flights to Las Vegas, take weekend vacations in a metropolitan hotel, have a growing interest in ecology and nature generally, and try new variations of old sports such as charter fishing and game farm hunting. Some take trips to exotic locations to engage in sports such as golfing and tennis that are readily available at home. Because families are increasingly more widely scattered, many must travel more and further simply to visit relatives. In one of its many manifestations, this travel shows up as an increasing proportion of people who use air travel. In 1971, only 49 percent of the U.S. population had ever flown. By 1987 this proportion had risen to 72 percent (Benincasa, 1988). This deepening represents changes in lifestyle patterns produced by changes in income, education, occupations, travel technology, and new recreational offerings, among other underlying factors.

Growth in both the quantitative and the qualitative dimensions of tourism-recreation demand would appear to guarantee a ready market for any kind of tourist service. Hardly! Yes, the tourism industry of some communities will flourish. But that of many others will fail to develop. In some cases, currently flourishing community tourism industries will atrophy.

The dynamic tourism market will have a differential impact upon communities in the future as it has in the past. While opportunity abounds, failure to interpret market demand properly and to remain abreast of it in the community's and firm's tourism offering can have dire consequences for the tourism industry of that community and firm.

A MARKETING APPROACH TO COMMUNITY TOURISM INDUSTRY MANAGEMENT

How does the community take advantage of the strong demand for tourism services?

An effective marketing approach starts with understanding of travelers' needs. It asks how these needs can be fulfilled by the TDA. Finally, it designs a sales program that will best communicate with its tourist clients (Wahab, 1976).

In contrast, an early, apparently instinctive, first step on the part of almost all communities is to raise money and immediately begin an advertising effort. In Chapter 5 the reasons for this common first response were discussed; advertising is easier than systematic study and development, and it is seen as less likely to directly create competition for existing businesses. Advertising occupies a major role as noted in Chapter 8, but it is only one part, and not the first priority of an overall marketing program.

The first community marketing step consists of developing a marketing policy. The policy should fully recognize the fact that a viable community tourism industry depends upon meshing tourism demands with the community's tourism offering. This tourism offering includes all community tourism elements: hospitality services, things to see and do, price, place availability, etc. A goal is appeal that matches felt needs, the provision of eminently satisfactory experiences for those who visit. Such a marketing policy is the pivotal feature of an overall tourism industry policy as discussed in Chapter 11. Included in the marketing policy are four parts listed in summary form immediately below.

Have a thorough understanding of tourism markets, including overall tourism-travel-recreation markets and those segments specifically applicable to the community. This is the community market information and communication necessary to provide symmetry in the community's communication with the market. This market understanding can be achieved only by systematic, comprehensive, and ongoing research programs, as discussed later in this chapter.

Thoroughly evaluate the community's tourism resources, natural, man-made and human attractions, services and facilities. The first question to ask is "How do these satisfy market needs, or how can they be developed to satisfy market needs?" Developmental priority is most appropriately placed upon those tourism features in which the community has the best comparative advantage.

Position the community in the market by fitting its tourism product to the market. Positioning will include targeting to those market segments having the best effective demand for the community's tourism attractions and services; marketing mix approaches; pricing policies; sales strategies and programs; and evaluation of developmental and sales efforts.

Conduct a sales program based upon the market information gathered, and designed to achieve the desired market positioning. Advertising programming procedures are noted briefly in Chapter 8, but not treated comprehensively. Handbooks and materials providing much helpful sales suggestions are available in many forms (see Suggestions for Further Reading, Chapter 8). The limited treatment of promotion, advertising and sales techniques must in no manner be interpreted as minimizing the necessity of well-designed and executed advertising and promotional efforts. The thrust of this publication is upon enabling communities to move off in the right direction toward the end of developing a viable community tourism industry. Unfortunately the provision of a detailed road map for all aspects of the journey is beyond its scope.

The marketing approach to tourism industry development is almost exactly the opposite of an advertising or selling approach. The philosophy of marketing is to fulfill client/customers' needs and wants. It determines these needs, develops products, facilities and services to satisfy them and *then* develops and executes appropriate sales programs. In contrast, the selling approach begins with an advertising program to sell what the community has. In its least effective form this approach is carried out without systematic analysis of what the community offers as a tourism experience, and without organized information on patterns of consumer needs in tourism-recreation.

TOURISM RESEARCH PRINCIPLES

Research is a means of getting information—that is, of asking questions. Market and product research, to the end of meeting market needs, is emphasized here. Market research is one of the major communications means feeding information about the market to the tourism destination area.

The tourism research policy should be a priority part of a community's tourism industry development policy. It can be viewed as an integral part of the marketing policy, or as a direct, necessary marketing complement, depending upon how the overall policy is organized. To date, few tourism destination areas have instituted anything like an adequate tourism research program, although some states and cities appear now to have a good start. Chapter 11 discusses these policies further.

A whole syndrome of factors accounts for this failure to institute needed tourism research programs. Recent emergence of the industry has not allowed time for adequate support systems such as research to be developed. Research in the tourism industry is particularly difficult since the industry is made of parts of a large number of business types as defined by the Standard Industrial Classification (SIC) Codes; it is not definable as one class of business. Tourism, travel and recreation cross-cut a large part of the warp and woof of not only economic but social and public life, adding to the difficulty of definition and comprehensive understanding. Some of the early research was inadequately conceived and executed, yielding poor quality information. Fortunately with the establish-

ment of the U.S. Travel Data Center and the Travel and Tourism Research Association (TTRA), these difficulties are being overcome. Good quality tourism information is now available from research. The Research Handbook prepared by TTRA is particularly recommended (Ritchie, 1987).

Three aspects of tourism research deserve special note:

— What is the proper question to ask?
— Is the research procedure such that it will yield objective, adequate and accurate information?
— What kinds of tourism research are most useful?

All Tourism Research Starts With a Question or Problem

Research is conducted in response to a problem or question. What recreational experiences does the market want? What parts (segments) of the market want what mix of experiences? What defines the geographic market areas most relevant to our tourist destination area? How effective is our "hosting" treatment of guests? What community tourism resources can best be developed to serve the needs of emerging tourism demand? The list of possible questions is virtually endless. In turn the initial question needs to be refined, and re-refined, and subjected to scrutiny: Does it really state the relevant problem that we need to deal with, and about which we need information?

The question, or problem statement, is of paramount importance since it determines the kind of information that will be sought, and the direction that the research will take.

As an example, let us assume some questions for the Mark Twain Lake/Hannibal area in Northeastern Missouri that we reviewed in Chapter 6. The reader will recall this as a relatively rural area with almost a century-long history of population decline. Suppose the area stays firmly with its agrarian heritage and asks, "How can we become a great agricultural producing area?" Alternatively, it might ask, "How can we capture manufacturing plants from the Chicago or St. Louis areas?" The Mark Twain Lake/Hannibal area has a new recreational resource, along with outstanding Mark Twain memorabilia. It thus might appropriately ask, "What are the tourists' needs that we can fulfill with our tourism resources through the development of our tourism industry, thus building a balanced local economy?" Pursuit of each of these questions separately could yield very different results for the community.

Research Procedures

Well-designed, objective research procedures can provide the insights needed to make key decisions. These decisions can set the community's tourism development and marketing program off on the road to success. Detailed research procedures, in common with detailed sales techniques, are beyond the scope of this book (Gitelson, 1986). This, however, does not lessen the crucial necessity of proper tourism research procedure. Inadequate research procedures may yeild not only little useful information, but worse yet, information that is wrong and misleading.

Information about research procedures is now readily available (Weaver, 1986; Ritchie 1987). In addition, experienced leadership is recommended if a substantial research project is to be conducted. Such advice and/or assistance may be had from professional consultants, tourism extension specialists of state land grant universities, or others versed in social science research such as the faculty of institutions of higher education. Because of complexities of both tourism itself and tourism research procedures, it is recommended that tourism research leadership only be entrusted to competent persons having understanding of both.

Research requires not only good design and execution but also honesty and objectivity. This requirement may limit the role of a local tourism-related agency in the conduct of its own research. Many such tourism-related groups have a "community booster approach." This is not inappropriate, but may prevent them from facing adverse facts objectively, and research findings are almost never fully positive. Failure to adequately consider negative findings by any research effort is the operational equivalent of a solitaire player who slips cards up his sleeve.

Kinds of Tourism Research

Seven kinds of research are noted briefly here. They represent a classification of tourism research according to function; what is it supposed to accomplish and for whom? The research policy of almost every destination area should include the first four kinds discussed. The reader should recognize that there are many other kinds of research that could be listed under a functional classification; further, there are a number of other useful ways to classify research. The simplified treatment given here allows us to retain a focus upon the use of research to help meet market needs.

Impact research determines quantitatively the current tourism industry and the broad characteristics of its market. Such studies typically determine how many tourists come, what they spend and for what purpose, where they come from and by what travel means. Many specific refinements are possible, depending upon the methods used for gathering data. Good impact research has proven to be a powerful tool in community education. Many businesses discover that they are involved in tourism to a much greater extent than they realized. Many communities also discover than they have larger tourism industries than had been commonly supposed. Impact research also provides good guidelines for setting up studies to gain an in-depth understanding of market needs. Impact research is often advised as one of the first research projects to be undertaken. The findings need to be updated regularly; better still, impact can be continuously monitored as an ongoing evaluative means.

Market research is a term for a wide range of related research. It might be used to determine market segments, market tourism needs and factors in decision-making of touring units, among many other questions. It is used to guide both the development of facilities and services and the conduct of information-advertising-promotion-selling programs aimed at the traveler.

Product research classifies and evaluates the community's tourism resources. Included are natural, man-made and human resources. Facilities and services that have potential for serving tourists are also included. The information is used to match resources and their potential with market needs.

Evaluative research asks what happened as the result of action taken. The action may have been a specific marketing program, a new service, or a new or refurbished facility. Evaluative research provides guidelines toward further improvements, updating, developments, and revisions.

Research of competing areas and/or facilities adds to market and product research. It investigates other TDA's that the clients of a given TDA may travel to. Often it asks how effectively these other TDA's fulfill the clients' needs. Research of competition can uncover techniques used by successful operations that may be adapted and used locally. It may also reveal unfilled market niches.

Feasibility research predicts the potential success for a proposed new feature, facility or service. Feasibility research is now conducted for most proposed new elements of the National Park system. Much more commonly, feasibility studies are done to help guide the siting of new restaurants, lodging facilities and resorts. Most feasibility

studies bring together market, product, area and business management data, focusing it upon the proposed facility.

Operating research guides organization, management and operating decisions of a facility or service. The variety of questions treated and methodologies employed is almost infinite. Questions dealt with may range from "How do we maintain the fragile ecology of a wilderness area?" to "What is the best work space layout for a specific food service?" to "Are employee task assignments efficiently allocated?"

MARKET CONCEPTS AND PRINCIPLES

Marketing is any activity involved in the sale or rental of a product or service. Marketing aspects requiring the development of strategies include product, price, promotion and place. It is repeatedly pointed out in this book that *good marketing* puts first emphasis upon the *consumer* and the *consumer's needs* rather than upon the selling function. The premiere *tourism marketing* principle, then, is to focus upon serving tourism/recreational needs and achieving customer satisfaction.

In Chapter 2, basic demand curves were discussed. Here we use variations of these curves to illustrate the application of other marketing concepts and principles that will assist the community in the development of an appropriate tourism industry.

Income Elasticity of Demand

In the dynamic U.S. society, many families have experienced changes in income. Details of this general phenomenon are treated in the next major subsection of this chapter. What happens to the purchasing pattern of a family or an individual as real income expands? People are observed to buy relatively more of some things, and relatively less of others. This is the concept of income elasticity of demand: the change in the amount of a given good purchased relative to changes in income.

Income elasticity of demand was noted as an important driver of the sector theory of economic development. It drives development, because as incomes rise due to production efficiencies, families buy relatively less of the production of farm, forest and mines, relatively more processed and manufactured products, and more services. Tourism, as a service, benefits from this demand growth.

To briefly explain income elasticity numbers: Items having an income elasticity of one will be bought at a rate that is a constant proportion of consumers' income. Such items are illustrated by line 'a' drawn through the origin in Figure 9.1. Items that are purchased at a rate that increases faster than consumers' income are called "superior goods" and are illustrated by the more horizontal line 'b' in Figure 9.1. Purchases of some goods increase relatively more slowly than incomes. These are referred to as "inferior goods" and are illustrated by the more vertical line 'c' in Figure 9.1. Tourism and recreational services are commonly thought of as superior goods hence profiting relatively more from income increases. We note below, however, that many frequently purchased tourism-related goods and services have income elasticities close to one or unity.

In the current setting, those items of tourism that exhibit patterns of the highest income elasticities of demand are often expensive experiences such as sit-down restaurant dining, the higher-priced lodging accommodations and the more exotic, expensive recreation destinations.

Many tourism, recreation, and hospitality services are now so much a part of our way of life that the more commonly used services now have

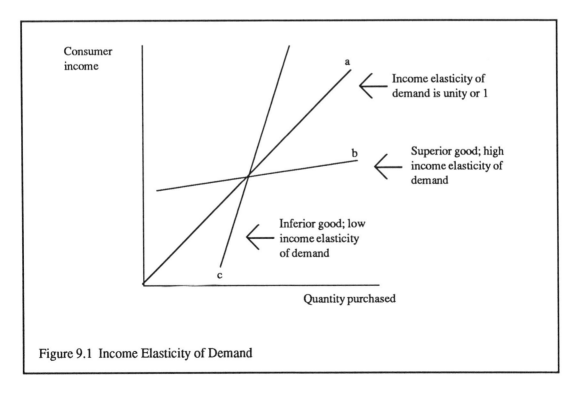

Figure 9.1 Income Elasticity of Demand

an income elasticity of approximately one. In other words, their use increases at a rate proportional to changes in consumer income. This is the case for a series of recreational expenditures maintained by the U.S. Department of Interior, where dollars as a percent of personal consumption expenditures fluctuated narrowly between 6.6 and 6.9 percent in the 1970 to 1984 period (U.S. Statistical Abstract). Similarly, the income elasticity of food purchased away from home was found to average .98 over a 50-year period. It fluctuated from a low of about .5 to a high of about 1.5 over that period, due to vicissitudes in the U.S. social and economic setting (Blank, 1982).

Income elasticity of demand reveals important insights into our lifestyles and economic system. If widely used tourism and recreation services have an income elasticity of only one, what major items enjoy superior status as having high income elasticities? Since about 1960, two items stand out: housing and health care. U.S. citizens value housing highly, and the proportion of our incomes spent for that purpose has risen steadily. Similarly, advances in medical technology have added much to health care costs, and at the same time they hold out promise. Everyone values health, and is willing to spend for it.

Price Elasticity of Demand

Is price competition among tourism-recreational services good or bad? The individual producer would prefer to be able to set prices at what is regarded as a favorable level and not be concerned that competing services have more price appeal. Price competition that attempts to eliminate competitors can be destructive. On the other hand, price competition can have long-run good effects; under conditions of price-elastic products, as noted below, it can expand markets, employment and the industry.

A number of tourism-related services have been observed to expand beyond what was initially considered the market potential. Among these are

airline passenger miles, winter ski resorts in the Upper Great Lakes and country music groups in the Tennessee-Missouri-Arkansas region. What was happening here? Apparently several factors were operating, among them price elasticity of demand, and Say's Law, which is discussed below.

For many tourism-recreation services, price elasticity of demand operates benignly. That is, a reduction in price causes a relatively greater increase in consumption or use. The result is a greater total revenue. This effect bodes well for expansion of the tourism industry of most communities.

Figure 9.2A illustrates the price-quantity behavior of a price-elastic product. At price P_1 the quantity Q_1 is consumed. At a price P_2, that is 20 percent lower, a quantity Q_2 that is 80 percent larger is consumed. In this example, the result will be a 44 percent increase in dollar volume of sales. Airline passenger-miles appear to be an item that is price elastic

Figure 9.2B illustrates a price-inelastic product. In this case when the price is dropped 25 percent from P_1 to P_2, the quantity consumed increases by

A. More price elastic

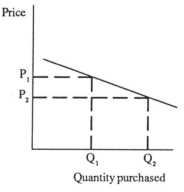

Figure 9.2A Price Elasticity of Demand

B. Less price elastic

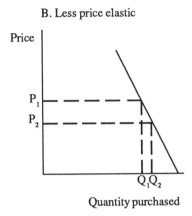

Figure 9.2B Price Elasticity of Demand

A. Complementing products

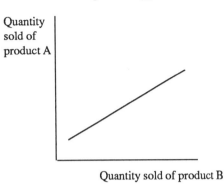

Figure 9.3A Cross Elasticity of Demand

only 10 percent. Despite the increase in sales, total sales revenue in dollars will diminish to only 82.5 percent of its former level. Staple items such as basic foods are classical examples exhibiting this price-consumption behavior.

Figures 9.2A and B will be noted as ordinary demand curves, having slopes on the curves that are dependent upon the relationships between prices and amounts consumed of the product.

Time may have a major effect on price elasticity of demand. In the short run customers often appear very insensitive to price: the product will appear to be price inelastic. For example, a late-night traveler who is experiencing difficulty finding a room may rent a quite expensive room. But for the next day, or on later travel, that tourist may be much more careful to engage a room earlier in the evening, or reserve ahead in less expensive accommodations.

Cross Elasticities

Some products go together as *complements*: When one is purchased, there is a likelihood of the complement also being purchased. Figure 9.3A illustrates the graph of complementary products. Examples are boats and motors, motel rooms and meals, air fares and car rentals, camping trailers and campground rentals.

Other products *compete* with each other: the purchase of one will reduce the likelihood of the other being purchased. Figure 9.3B illustrates the relationships graphically. Examples are campground rentals and motel rooms, golfing and fishing, and cross-country Amtrak tickets and airline seats.

B. Competing products

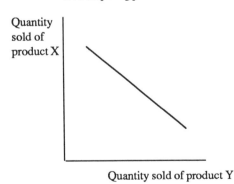

Figure 9.3B Cross Elasticity of Demand

Say's Law; Critical Mass

Rapid expansion in some tourism-recreation related products has been noted, such as the offering of fast foods in certain locations and country music entertainment in some TDA's. Expansion in both the offering and market response sometimes appears to proceed beyond what might at first be expected. Why? In addition to price elasticities, it is suggested that a combination of Say's Law and critical mass effects are partly responsible.

Say's Law, in part, observes that "Supply creates its own demand." That is, to be somewhat ridiculous, no one went to see the Mount Rushmore monument when it was not there. Once created, this spectacular monument has generated a large visitation.

Say's Law appears to operate in conjunction with the critical mass effect. With no country music evening entertainment, no one can enjoy it. When there is only one such facility, only a few people know about it, appreciate the form of entertainment and talk about it. As more such places of entertainment are established, both the "availability of supply" and "word of mouth" factors operate to generate demand.

A single food service at a travel node has been observed to experience difficulty with sales volume. After the establishment of a number of others in the same area, astonishingly, all operate profitably. The "critical mass" effect operating in this situation was knowledge on the part of travelers that they could go that particular travel node and have a selection of good, dependable food services.

The good news of this principle is that addition of tourism services in a community may sometimes act as complements to those already existing rather than competing with them.

Market Segmentation

No one tourism service or tourism destination area appeals to everyone. The market is made up of different parts, each with its own needs and responding to specific appeals. *A specific market segment is made up of those customers who may be treated similarly with regard to such things as communications, the appeals that reach them, and their patterns of tourism-recreation need fulfillment.*

A unique market segmentation pattern applies to each TDA (Etzel, 1982). This is because its location and product mix differs from that of every other TDA. Among common kinds of market segments may be noted the following:

— Geographic location—where do customers live?
— Income—median? Upscale?
— Travel purpose—business, pleasure, convention?
— Season—when are they free to travel?
— Personality—innovators, security seekers (Schewe, 1978)?
— Travel mode—family automobile, air, bus, Amtrak?
— Family composition—singles? Couples with young children?

Differentiating the Product

What's so special about our community, why would anyone come here to visit, and what would they do after they get here?

These questions pose the major challenge of tourism product differentiation: *how can the community's tourism facilities and services provide a tourism experience that is unique from all others?* At the same time that it is unique, it must be appealing, so travelers will come in the first place, and satisfying, so they will return and tell others.

A unique, genuinely indigenous tourism product has the advantage of greater market power: Travelers must go there, specifically, to get the experience. This factor may give an advantage in advertising and promotion; terms such as "only," "oldest," "first," etc., may be truthfully used.

To the extent that the appeal is powerful, it may also give a degree of monopoly price advantage: the price does not have to be fully competitive, since no other TDA provides a strictly comparable experience.

What are means available for product differentiation? All facets of the community's tourism industry and its management can have a bearing. For the sake of simplicity, we note three possible avenues:

First, all TDA components, as noted in Chapter 3, provide significant means for differentiating the tourism product. The focal attraction may be the most crucial component along with its complementing activities. In the specialized Gull Lake fishing region of Minnesota, one community offers 54 holes of golf; they cannot guarantee that fish will bite, but they can guarantee a good meal and a good game of golf! Ambience can stand out: What community do you know that greets the visitor with the neat tidiness of Switzerland's countryside?

Second, hosting and services offered make a difference. People like to be treated as *people*. Some resorts specialize in children's programs, so both children and adults can have an enjoyable experience.

Third, promotional/advertising programs can differentiate the TDA, provided it adequately makes good—or better—on its promises.

The above are not really three separate ways to differentiate the tourist destination area. These and other possible avenues must be operated in concert. They are all needed to reinforce each other to build a powerful destination image and deliver an outstanding experience.

UNDERSTANDING UNITED STATES TOURISM DEMAND

Major United States Tourism Demand Shifters

Successful community tourism industry development and marketing depends first upon a broad understanding of those factors that "drive" tourism, producing shifts in demand. While a specific attraction may involve only a small, specialized part of the overall market, it is important to know what the prospects are for expansion or contraction of this market segment. Fortunately, these broader patterns may be followed relatively easily and at low cost using data that are regularly published by federal and state agencies. Some of the more important "demand shifters" are discussed immediately following:

Family income; per capita income.
In Chapter 6 the spectacular growth in U.S. per capita income over the past century was cited. This real income growth impacts dramatically upon the way that U.S. citizens live, work, and play. It was the major factor in mass tourism that became perceptible in the 1920s, and that grew explosively in the period following World War II.

Income continues to broaden the market to an increasingly larger share of the population. In Table 9.1 it will be noted that the median family's real purchasing power increased by 37 percent in just the 1950-1960 decade. More recently, income

Table 9.1
Median U.S. Family Income, in Current and Constant Dollars. 1950-1986.

Year	*Current Dollars*	*1986 Dollars*
1950	$ 3,300	$15,200
1960	5,600	20,800
1970	9,900	27,900
1980	21,000	28,000
1986	29,500	29,500

Source: Current Population Report, Series P-60, No. 157.

growth has slowed, and some even forecast re-trenchment. But there have been periods of rapid and slow growth in family income before, and the period until 2000 will very likely bring continued increases. U.S. income deserves continuing monitoring.

Education. Education is closely interrelated with income. Improvement in human capital (the ability of people to perform) usually means that the individuals involved have greater earning power. Important because of its effect on earnings, educa-tion also influences tourism in other significant ways. Education changes world-views and cultural tastes influencing not only how much traveling indi-viduals do, but how they travel, where they go, and what they do. Education operates to both broaden and deepen the demand for tourism. As shown in Table 9.2, the average years of schooling and proportion of citizens with college education have continued to increase in recent years. About 20 percent of the present U.S. population has com-pleted four or more years of college.

Population growth and age structures. During the 100 years of the 19th Century, U.S. population increased by 14 times. This furious growth rate has not continued in the 20th Century. In the decade of 1970-1980, U.S. population grew by about 11 percent. In 1987, U.S. population was about 245,000,000, and some demographers are lamenting the fact that births may in the near future fall below the Zero Population Growth rate.

Immigration into the United States, both legal and illegal, appears to at least equal the population increases due to births. This latter factor alters the character of the population, but its long-run impact upon tourism may as well be positive as negative. Positive impact could occur because of highly motivated immigrants whose rapid income gains translate into increased travel within a few decades.

As important as sheer numbers of people is their differential location in the nation (discussed elsewhere) and their age structure. Thanks to the post-World War II baby boom, the United States now has a very high proportion of its population who are in their most productive, middle-age years.

Table 9.2
Educational Attainment in the United States, 1960-1985

Year	Percent completed 4 years high school	Percent completed 4 years college	Median years of schooling
1960	24.6%	7.7%	10.6 years
1970	34.0	11.0	12.2
1980	34.6	16.2	12.5
1985	38.2	19.4	12.6

Source: *Statistical Abstract of the United States*, 108th Ed. U.S. Department of Commerce, 1988.

Also because birth rates declined rapidly after 1965, we are now experiencing an actual decline in the numbers of teenagers: Table 9.3 shows that the 5-17 year-old group will have diminished by 8 percent in relative terms during the 1980-1990 decade. This means that we have a disproportionate number of our population in their best earning years, and with a declining proportion of dependents. This factor will drive tourism demand strongly and with less emphasis upon child-related services than was the case in the 1970s.

have a larger number of people who are relatively free to travel when they wish, with good health and good incomes, than ever before in history, and their number is increasing. The numbers of U.S. citizens 65 years and over will have increased by about 18 percent in the 1980s decade, Table 9.3. This segment particularly buys off-season travel, winter vacations, bus tours and many package tours. In addition they participate in nearly the full gamut of tourism/recreation possibilities, from wilderness hikes to theme parks. Their availability to travel

Table 9.3
Proportion of United States Population by Indicated Age Groups, 1970-1990

Year	Ages 5-17	Ages 25-34	Ages 34-54	Ages 65 & Over	Total U.S. Population
1970	25.7%	12.3%	22.7%	9.8%	205,052,000
1980	20.7	16.5	21.3	11.3	227,757,000
1990	18.2	17.5	25.3	13.6	250,410,000

Source: *Statistical Abstract of the United States*, 108th Ed. U.S. Department of Commerce, 1988.

There will continue to be large numbers of juveniles in the population over the coming decades, despite falling fertility rates. These children are being born to the large numbers of World War II baby boomers who are now in their child-bearing years. The family pattern will differ greatly from that of the 1970s. In place of average-income families having three to five children, it appears that there will be affluent families, both parents earning good incomes, having only one to two children.

Retirees. Retirees represent a tourism market segment that adds to the comments about population segments made immediately above. We now

during slack seasons makes them a particularly sought-after market by facilities that can adapt to their needs.

Discretionary time. In recent decades, the average hours worked per week have not changed greatly; in fact, between 1970 and 1985 the average hours worked weekly by manufacturing employees increased by about one hour. At the same time, other, more important, changes have occurred in such things as vacation time, long weekends, and mandated hours on the job. There has been a trend toward more vacation days per year and toward multiple vacations, where the vacation time is split into two or more periods and taken at different times of the year. Long weekends allow for a number of mini-vacations a year, for those finding such travel suited to their lifestyle. A growing number of people can exercise a degree of discretion over their exact work times; many have greatly expanded freedom to travel.

Occupational and industry patterns. Occupational and industry patterns may substantially impact the tourism industry of a given community and geographic area. Only a few of the many types that might have relevance are noted here as examples. A growing proportion of the work force is composed of professional workers. Such individuals are more likely to travel as a part of their work; they attend conventions, provide technical services, conduct training and many other activities that may require travel. Industry organization, operation, and spatial distribution abets the need for travel. Increasing use of technology requires increases in training, consultative services and other group meetings.

Women in the work force. In quantitative terms women are no longer moving into the work force; they are already there. In 1986, 44 percent of the labor force consisted of women (see Table 9.4 on the following page). A large shift that currently continues is in the employment of women with young children. In 1986, 55 percent of the women having children who are 6 years old or younger were employed. This proportion had increased from only 14 percent in 1950.

Women in the family who are working may reduce travel flexibility because of work schedules. On the other hand, their added incomes along with time on the job act to increase demands for commercial services—air travel to get there and back in a hurry, food away from home as well as lodging, and weekend travel to get away from the stresses of the job—and they have the money to pay for it.

Differential rates of inter-regional population and economic growth. Interregional differences may be pronounced. They may also swing sharply from decade to decade (Sofranko, 1980). Since 1950, the dominant pattern has been a shift of population from the Midwest and Northeast to the South, or "Sunbelt," states. In addition, populations of many southern states, particularly those bordering Mexico, have been augmented with an ongoing influx of Hispanic peoples.

Interpretation and prediction of future population migrations are best based upon understanding of why the differential shifts occur. Two major factors are involved in the net migration to the South. One is the flight to a supposedly more benign climate, where living quality is perceived as better. This pattern demonstrates aspects of the "Quality of Living Theory of Community Development" as described in Chapter 6. Another migration "driver" has been a quest for employment, leaving the "rust belt" of the industrial Midwest and the depressed northeast for the South where many footloose industries have relocated.

Regions rarely stay "down" for long periods. Thus, countering the above trends is revitalization in the economies of many formerly midwestern "rust belt" and northeastern "mill town" communities. For example, in 1987, Massachusetts reported one of the lowest unemployment rates in the nation. Further, many Northerly-located communities are consistently reported as offering residents some of the best living quality available anywhere in the nation.

Table 9.5 on the following page shows large differences among states in population growth rates during the decade of the 1970s. In that decade the populations of Nevada and Arizona grew by 64 percent and 53 percent, respectively. During the same period Ohio's population increased by only 1.3 percent, and that of New York actually declined by 3.7 percent. Most of these differences are due to migration. Such data must be used with care. There tend to be time lags: Population continues to

Table 9.4
Women in the Workforce, 1950-1986

Year	*Women as % of total work force*	*Women labor force as % of female population*	*% women who are in the labor force having husband and children under 6 years of age*
1950	29%	31%	14%
1970	37	43	30
1980	42	51	45
1986	44	55	55

Source: *Monthly Labor Review*, February 1986

Table 9.5
States Having Highest and Lowest Rates of Population Change, 1970-1980

States with highest growth rates		*States having lowest growth rates*	
State	*Percent change 1970-1980*	*State*	*Percent change 1970-1980*
Nevada	63.8% gain	New York	3.7% loss
Arizona	53.1% gain	Rhode Island	0.3% loss
Florida	43.5% gain	Massachusetts	0.8% gain
Wyoming	41.3% gain	Ohio	1.3% gain
Utah	37.9% gain	Connecticutt	2.5% gain

Source: U.S. Census of Population, U.S. Bureau of Census, U.S. Department of Commerce

move into a former booming area even after its employment base has ceased to grow. This underscores need to understand economic trends in addition to simply reviewing population numbers. In addition to "rust belt" and other examples given above, we have, in other chapters, noted fluctuations in the fortunes of agricultural and mining communities that led to population migration.

Rural-urban population shifts. Throughout most of the 200 years of the United States' existence, a movement of population from farms to the city occurred. Now, with barely three percent of the labor force classed as farmers, this population movement is virtually spent. But other intra-state shifts may have important implications for travel-recreation markets. Currently 78 percent of the population lives in urban places; and 60 percent live in cities having populations of 500,000 or more. Movement to the suburbs by the more affluent has been followed by a movement of some affluent to concentrate in the downtown area again. Along with these population shifts is a strong move to exurbanize large areas around employment centers, converting them into large-lot bedroom areas. High amenity areas—forests, hills, and water—particularly are becoming exurbanized. In some cases settlement is so dense that new urban areas, just outside metropolitan centers but in formerly rural areas, are created. There are also numerous settings where relatively remote rural areas are becoming populated with people who forfeit urban incomes because they wish to live in the chosen area. This latter, as well as many of the previous patterns, relate closely to the Quality of Living Theory. Each of the above patterns also represents differing life styles and will be found to have different travel-recreation demands.

The items discussed immediately above operate to widen and deepen the tourism market. They are necessary for background understanding of the demand for tourism services of any area, and they must be reviewed regularly, since many change surprisingly quickly. It should also be emphasized that the above are only some of the major representative kinds of information. Variants of the above, or even completely different kinds of national and state information, may be relevant for any given tourist destination area. Further, while this is essential information, it is by no means sufficient for a complete analysis.

Where can information on U.S. Tourism Demand Shifters be obtained? Most all of it is available as secondary data in regularly published documents such as those of the U.S. Bureau of the Census, state departments of economic development, and university extension publications. It is suggested that researchers look first in the *U.S. Statistical Abstract.* Its bibliographical references will lead to other sources. In any event, each community has the responsibility for assembling and interpreting the information that is relevant to its own tourism industry.

United States Tourism Demand: Activity and Travel Patterns

In addition to the evolving pattern of major demand shifters in the United States, there should be understanding of the mega-patterns in travel and recreational activities (Ottersbach, 1985). The activity and travel patterns relevant to a given destination must be selected with a view to applicability. Examples of some of the principal patterns are noted below:

Frequency of travel. Earlier in the chapter we noted that 1.2 billion person-trips were made by U.S. travelers in 1987. This amount of travel is an average of almost five trips per person per year. The amount of travel varies by region of the nation, and by socio-economic and psychographic characteristics, as has also been previously noted. One example of this variation among travelers comes from use of the airlines. Eighty percent of airline revenue is reported to be generated by only 30 percent of the flyers (Vervaeke, 1987). Growth in travel volume has been noted as slowing. Even so, in the 1980-1987 period, all person-trips were up about 13 percent.

Mode of travel. Air, auto, bus, water, rail, or combinations of these travel modes may be employed. Passenger-miles traveled is increasing at approximately twice the rate of person-trips, reflecting longer trips and increased use of air. In 1986, passenger-miles of U.S. intercity travel totaled 1.4 trillion, up 35 percent from 1976. Twenty-two percent of the 1986 passenger-miles were traveled by air, compared to 15 percent 10 years earlier (USTDC, 1987). Bus and rail travel now accounts for only about two percent of all intercity passenger-miles in the United States. Rental automobiles represent a growing element. Auto rentals relate closely to air travel; some rental firms report 70 percent of their business from customers who also have used air travel (Vervaeke, 1987).

Services used. All who travel must use *transportation* means. Most also make use of commercially-available *food services.* Other commercial services, however, are used in smaller and quite varied proportions, depending upon the type of travel and traveler (Dardis, 1981). Business travelers who stay overnight use *commercial facilities* in a high proportion. Other travelers stay overnight using varied accommodations, so that less than half of the nearly six trillion person-nights are spent in commercial establishments. In many settings the proportion may be lower than one quarter. What other over night facilities are used? As an example, a recent Ontario study found that 60 percent of all nights away from home were spent with friends and relatives and another 15 percent were spent in private cottages (Ontario Travel Research Section, 1987). Automobile and equipment rentals, sightseeing tours, package tours, and many others may be among the services that are used.

Purpose of travel; kind of trip. Travel purposes were discussed in Chapter 2. Travel purposes relate closely to travel segments and the travel/recreational needs of these segments. Trips may be described in a number of ways, as was done in Table 2.1. There we saw that about two-thirds of all

U.S. person-trips were for vacation travel.

Among the trends that we might note, business and convention travel is becoming increasingly important as a travel purpose. In 1987 an estimated 18 percent, 211 million, of all person-trips were for that purpose, up by 30 percent from 1980.

A recent study categorized U.S. pleasure travel into eight trip types. These findings are shown in Table 9.6. The approach to trip categories and descriptions is somewhat different from that taken in

Table 9.6
U.S. Pleasure Travel Market: Trip Types 1985

Type of Trip	Percentage share of trips
Visit to Friends and Relatives	41%
Close-to-Home Leisure Trip--to beach, lake or park	21
Outdoors Trip--camping, hunting, fishing, hiking	12
City Trip--shop, entertainment, dine	8
Touring Trip--sightsee, general interest	7
Resort Trip--to resort or resort area where many activities are available nearby	6
Theme Park--special event or exhibition	4
Cruise--trip on cruise ship to enjoy on-board activities and stops points of interest	1
Total (468 million trips)	100%

Note: Person-trips by people 16 years and older, at least 100 miles one way, one night away from home, and using either commercial accommodation or transportation.

Source: Tourism Canada, *U.S. Pleasure Travel Market,* Tourism Canada, Department of Regional Industrial Expansion, Ottawa, 1986.

Chapter 3. Even so, visits to friends and relatives were found, at 41 percent, to be by far the most important reason for pleasure travel. Close-to-home leisure trips, such as to the beach, accounted for another 21 percent. These findings, in addition to adding documentation, provide added insights into travel patterns.

Activities. What do people do when they travel? Activities are closely related to purpose of travel and to facilities and services that are available, and/ or that are used by travelers. Activities may be classed in very broad categories, such as outdoor recreation (National Research Council, 1975), entertainment, and shopping. But to be usefully translated in terms of the tourism-recreational resources and services of a given destination, the classes must designate specific activities, such as horseback trail riding, paddle canoeing, attending historical pageants, visiting night clubs, cold water fishing, cross country skiing and similar detail.

Activities relate to felt needs. These are often determined by the tourist's previous experiences. They also are strongly determined by what is available—(Say's Law). Equally important, activities bear upon whether or not the tourist views the TDA as one that should be visited again and recommended to friends.

Recent data about one kind of activity—outdoor recreation—are available from studies of the President's Commission on Americans Outdoors. Finding of this study are shown in Table 9.7. Included are activities that are engaged in when close to home as well as when away. The data, thus, do not represent tourists alone. Two activity types stand out particularly; these are:

Spectator outings (76% participate often). including sightseeing; driving for pleasure, picnicking; visits to historic sites; attendance at zoos, fairs or amusement parks; walking for pleasure; and attendance at outdoor concerts, plays or other outdoor performances.

Table 9.7
U.S. Oudoor Recreation Activity Groupings

Activity Group	Percent Participating Often
Spectator Outings--sighteeing, picnic, attend concerts, walk for pleasure	76%
Water and Golf--swim, sail, golf	48
Ball Games and Running--play ball, attend ballgames, jogging	41
Fish, Hunt, Horsepower--fishing, hunting, power boating, ORV, recreation vehicle camping	37
Observing Nature--backpack, tent camping, canoeing, bird watching	31
Winter Sports--ice skate, skiing, sledding	11

Source: Market Opinion Research, *Participation in Outdoor Recreation Among American Adults and the Motivations Which Drive Participation*, President's Commission on Americans Outdoors, 1986

Water and golf (48% participate often). including sailing/windsurfing; swimming outdoors in ocean, river, lake or outdoor pool; and golf (power boating is included in another category).

Where is information on travel patterns, activities and related factors obtained? It is not as regularly reported as are demographic/socio-economic data, but fortunately a large part of it is available in reports of the U.S. Travel Data Center and the U.S. Department of the Interior, National Park Service. Valuable parts of this type of information are also often provided in special studies and reports, such as those supplying the data for Table 9.6 and Table 9.7 (Goeldner, 1981; Calantone, 1987). Some of these studies may be proprietary. These may be prepared by universities, special commissions, market research firms and transportation companies.

UNDERSTANDING THE COMMUNITY'S TOURISM MARKET AND TOURISM RESOURCES

Researching the Market Demand for the Local Tourist Destination Area

The immediately preceeding sections treated general U.S. patterns. Such general information provides essential background information and is especially necessary for spotting trends that can be taken advantage of. But data about the community's specific market are the most essential information of all. Thorough understanding of the TDA's current market provides the starting point. The follow-up step is more difficult: that of reaching out to find new markets, and making them a part of the community's tourism clientele.

What are our current markets? This is the first step in researching the market for the local tourist destination area (Weaver, 1986; Ritchie, 1987). The community and its business managers need answers to such questions as: Who now visits our community? Where do they come from, and what are their other characteristics? What are their tourism-recreation needs, and how well are they satisfied with what they receive from the local TDA?

An impact study has been recommended as the initial community research project. Such a study not only can tell how much tourism the community has, and who sells to tourists; it can provide much essential information about tourists. While it is wise not to overload an initial study, many questions about the market can be answered.

The next step is to use information gained from the impact study to refine questions about the market. What added information will help us to more nearly meet clients' travel/recreation needs? This insight forms the basis for designing additional studies of the existing market.

What is the community's potential market? Market research that proceeds beyond the current tourism market has four major bases:

— Knowledge of the current market—its needs and characteristic.
— Transportation access knowledge as discussed in Chapter 8. Travel patterns will indicate population concentrations, routes, and current interactions between the local tourist destination area, and market communities.
— Knowledge of U.S. demand-shifting mechanisms and travel/recreation trends.
— Evaluation of present and potential community tourism resources.

The above four knowledge bases will help identify target market locations and target market populations. The next step is to conduct investigations into the new target market area. Answers to such questions as the following are needed:

— What market segments best fit the community's tourism experience?
— What are the specific tourism/recreation needs of these market segments?
— How can the community and its tourism services best communicate with the market segments?

The Community's Tourism Resources, Tourism Product and Product Mix

What development and management is appropriately applied to the community's tourism resources to produce its best tourism product? Tourists' needs and uses determine tourism resources. These needs also indicate the appropriate directions for resource development. The relevant overall question is, "How do the community's resources mesh with tourists' needs?"

A tourism resource has been defined as anything that can contribute positively to a tourism/recreational experience. This definition, we have noted, goes beyond simply those features providing recreation. When we look at what can be considered as a community tourism resource, we come up with a restatement of the community's tourism components as discussed in Chapter 3:

— Focal attractions—having major image-creating, travel-inducing capability.
— Hospitality Services—having ability to service the needs for food, lodging, etc.
— Other things to do—that complement and supplement the appeal of the focal attractor.
— Communication/transportation systems—providing access.
— Basic community—people, ambience, infrastructure, and other economic and social features and institutions.
— Others—location and climate.

So comprehensive a list makes the task of evaluating community tourism resources appear impossible: It encompasses the entire community. Fortunately there are well-designated starting points. A starting point makes the search possible and invariably indicates the best directions for added effort.

Start with current tourists. What facilities are used by those tourists who presently come to the community? This will identify tourism resources by our definition—those things that tourists use. What are tourists' activities? What services do they depend upon? This starting point suggests that impact study and beginning stages of market studies and community resources studies can be operated as parts of the same research project.

Analyze the product mix(es). A tourist or tourist segment uses more than a single tourism resource. Each segment uses a range of tourism resources—attractions, activities, hospitality services, transportation—but in proportions that differ from other segments. *The pattern of kinds and amounts of tourism resources used by each segment is called its product mix.* The product mix should be determined for each major market segment.

Catalogue, classify, and analyze all of the community's parts having possible tourism relevance. The start will be provided as just noted. In its full ramifications this seemingly simple task becomes complex. In one metropolitan area, a year's reconnaissance effort produced about 200 classes of community tourism resources containing an estimated 12,000 separate items. Further, it was estimated that the task was not more than two-thirds completed (Blank, 1969). While many communities are smaller, the task should still be viewed as one to be carried on sequentially and on an ongoing bias. In addition to the fact that every community has much more in the way of tourism resources and potential tourism resources than residents suspect, there is the difficulty of coming up with a market demand-resource synthesis that identifies developmental potential (Var, 1977).

What is to be done with the information gathered?

— Put it into systematic order.
— Use it for community analysis, in developing marketing programs and for feasibility possibilities.
— Make it available in educational workshops for people who are involved as community hosts.
— Develop a reference handbook for placement and use at all points contacted by tourists.
— Use it in preparation of tourism information literature.

How is developmental potential recognized?
Major features used by tourists are easily identified as a tourism resource. But how are features having tourism potential but not currently used transferred out of the "well-kept secrets" status? What added development is appropriate to upgrade the experience from resources that now have limited tourism use? These questions call for the exercise of true genius on the part of the community—its public leaders, its entrepreneurs, its citizens generally. Such development identification is not alone the task of the community development committee, the county government, nor of the city council. Rather it is the task of these leaders to stimulate the community's genius so that development and use of resources occurs. This process is treated further in the two concluding chapters.

Sometimes major resource potential lies hidden. The case of Orlando, Florida is instructive. Most investigators would look first to Florida's magnificent seacoasts for tourism sites. But Orlando is not on a coastal site. The reader will recognize Orlando as the site of the 27,000-acre Disney World. Orlando's selection was no accident (Zehnder, 1975). It resulted from systematic search over a period of time for a suitable site by the Disney Corporation. They noted the following:

— It had a central Florida location, accessible to both east and west coasts where millions of tourists visited annually.
— It shared the benign Florida climate.
— It was in an area predicted to experience substantial population growth, yet was still relatively lightly populated in the 1960s.

The above attributes, combined with the entrepreneurial genius of Disney, made Orlando into one of the premier destination locations in the world. Disney World is a case of development by an agency outside the community, but communities can learn from the analytic procedure. It adds to the examples of smaller communities—Branson,

Frankenmuth, New Glarus, plus others—that illustrate successful procedure.

POSITIONING THE COMMUNITY IN THE MARKET

Here is where we put it together, building upon all that has gone before (Woodside, 1982). Market positioning involves a precise determination of the community's market niche. The basic "positioning" process involves the following:

— Getting a fit between appropriate market segments (community tourism customers) and the community's tourism product mixes.
— Tailoring the product mix(es) as indicated from study so the best possible fit is achieved for serving needs of significant market segments.
— Communicating and/or selling to the targeted market segment or segments. The task is to create active awareness on the part of the market segment to the fact that the community provides tourism experiences that they want.
— Market positioning requires sequentially working forward and backward from market segments and needs to resources and product development to achieve the best possible fit. For each market segment there is an optimum product mix consisting of attractions, facilities, services, etc. Such an optimum product mix provides the best possible satisfactions for the tourist, and best possible income return to the tourism area.

The tourist destination area is required to do not one job of market positioning, but a series. Further, the community has not one product mix but a number. Every community appeals to more than one market segment. Each of these segments is served by a different product mix—the proportion and degree to which each segment uses lodging, food services, recreational and entertainment facilities, etc. There is, then, a mix of product and marketing mixes. This is necessary to adequately employ its tourism resources, and to provide a full season of tourism industry activity. Examples may help to explain:

The bulk of mid-summer tourists may be families. Some will use motel accommodations; some will use camping facilities. These two different types of overnight lodging users may also have different food service needs and different activity patterns.

Tour-bus loads of senior citizens may visit in the summer, but senior citizens can also be induced to visit at other seasons, such as during fall months when families with children do little traveling.

Communities having living amenities may have second home condominiums and single family cottages. These second home users require a different product mix compared to other tourists who primarily use motel lodging.

When special events are staged in a community, such as a musical celebration, or a historical pageant, those who come especially for the event use facilities in a different proportion compared to others coming to enjoy the community's focal attractor and its supporting features.

OBSOLESCENCE II—REVISITED

A healthy tourism industry today does not guarantee a viable tourism industry for tomorrow. Tourism destination areas can be observed to rise and fall in relative market favor and in their economic viability. In Chapter 3, we saw how a series of social, economic and technological developments conspired to cause relative market decline in many northern resort areas. Some communities in these areas, along with other communities, have been able to recover from their decline:

Traverse City, Michigan, is reported to have had a train arriving or departing every hour in the first decade of the 1900s. After World War II, the relative market decline that impacted many northern resort areas also affected Traverse City. During the

1955 to 1970 period it struggled hard. Traverse City has excellent natural appointments of scenery, climate and water. It also has good market location relative to the population of the industrial midwest. It has now rebuilt its tourism industry based on excellent hospitality facilities, and featuring convention/conferencing, cultural appointments, and activities fitting both summer and winter sports enthusiasts. Its tourism product and market differs radically from that of 1900.

Spa areas such as Saratoga Springs, New York, and lesser ones such as Excelsior Springs, Missouri, at one time were meccas for not only the sick, but for other upscale visitors who were mainly vacationing. Their popularity suffered drastic decline, and that of Excelsior Springs continues at a low level. Saratoga Springs, after a long hiatus, has partly recovered. It has a performing cultural offering, and summer and winter sports.

Waterville Valley, New Hampshire, is isolated in the central mountain region of New Hampshire. For 92 years it had a single hotel and a group of cottages catering primarily to summer guests of middle-income means. This business became obsolete. Waterville Valley has now come back. It has a well-appointed conference center, is growing in popularity as a place to live, has winter sports and outstanding mountain scenery. The tourism industry of Waterville Valley, like that of many New England communities, appears to be generated at least partially by Yankee pragmatism. In light of the discussion of the work ethic in Chapter 5, one would expect the stern Yankees to reject tourism. But, lacking good soil for agriculture, and seeing their manufacturing operations decline, they recognized that income could be generated from tourists based on the appeal of their natural resources. They have realized their comparative advantage in "working" tourists instead of the rocky soil. Accordingly, they work at expanding their sales package to tourists to capture dollars.

Failure to adapt facilities, services and marketing programs summarizes a major part of the decline pattern of the tourism industry in the destinations used as examples, and in many others. Changes in marketing demands, traveler demographics, travel and other technologies, and patterns of competing areas occur continuously. Thus, avoiding obsolescence requires ongoing alertness to changes that impact upon the community's industry.

Continuously updated information about markets, market trends, and feedback from the local industry provides the means by which attractions, facilities, services, and marketing programs may be adapted and readapted as needed. This is in fact observed to occur in many popular, growing tourism destination areas. There is a continual updating of the product and the marketing. Such areas do not persist in appealing only to yesterday's markets; nor do they offer facilities designed for the 1930s or the 1960s to a 1990s market. Avoidance of decline demands intelligent use of an ongoing flow of accurate, up-to-date information.

Questions for review and further study

1. Describe three kinds of "deepening" of travel and tourism demand that now appear to be occurring.

2. Explain why "filling needs" is more appropriate as the basis for a TDA's tourism marketing program rather than "selling."

3. Do you think that the demand for fast food will become more or less income elastic? Explain your answer.

4. Whom in the community should know about U.S. patterns of tourism and recreational activities? How would you ensure that they have this information?

5. Select a community (your home community, or another with which you are familiar); explain in detail its tourism product mix for family vacationers.

6. As a leader of the above community, what would you emphasize to avoid your community's become obsolescent as a TDA?

7. What role(s) is the local tourism bureau best equipped to perform with regard to the conduct of tourism research for the TDA?

SUGGESTIONS FOR FURTHER READING

Evans, J., & B. Berman. (1982). *Marketing*. New York: MacMillan Publishing Co.

Ritchie, J., & C. Goeldner (Eds). (1987). *Travel, Tourism and Hospitality Research, A Handbook for Managers and Researchers*. New York: John Wiley & Sons.

Wahab, S., L. Crampon, & L. Rothfield. (1976). *Tourism Marketing*. London: Tourism International Press. (Part III).

Weaver, G. (1986). *Tourism USA*. Washington, DC: U.S. Department of Commerce, Chapter 3.

TEXTUAL REFERENCES

Benincasa, L. (1988). 1988—Outlook for Air Travel and Related Business. *Proceedings 1988—Outlook for Travel and Tourism-13th Annual Travel Outlook Forum*. Washington, DC: U.S. Travel Data Center.

Blank, U. (1982). Interrelationship of the Food Service Industry with the Community, in A. Pizam, R. C. Lewis and P. Manning (Eds). *The Practice of Hospitality Management*. Westport, CT: AVI Publishing Co., Inc.

Blank, U., & E. Numrich. (1969). *Recreational Services and Facilities of the Twin Cities Metropolitan Area*. (working paper). St. Paul, MN: University of Minnesota.

Calantone, R., C. Di Benedetto, & D. Bojanic. (1987). A Comprehensive Review of Forecasting Literature. *Journal of Travel Research, 26*(2). Boulder, CO: Business Research Division, University of Colorado.

Dardis, R., F. Derrick, A. Lehfeld, & E. Wolfe. (1981). Cross-Section Studies of Recreational Expenditures in the U.S. *Journal of Leisure Research, 13*(3). Arlington, VA: NRPA.

Etzel, M., & A. Woodside. (1982). Segmenting Vacation Markets: The Case of the Distant and the Near Home Travelers. *Journal of Travel Research, 20*(4). Boulder, CO: Business Research Division, University of Colorado.

Gitelson, R., & D. Kerstetter. (1986). The Focus Group Interview, an Untapped Resource. *Visions in Leisure and Business, 6*(3). Bowling Green, OH: Appalachian Associates.

Goeldner, C. (1981). Where to Find Travel Research Facts. *Journal of Travel Research, 20*(1). Boulder, CO: Business Research Division, University of Colorado.

National Research Council. (1975). *Assessing Demand for Outdoor Recreation*. Washington, DC: Committee on Assessment of Demand for Outdoor Recreation Research, National Academy of Sciences.

Ontario Travel Research Section. (1987). *1985 Ontario Travel Survey*. Toronto, Ontario: Ministry of Tourism and Recreation.

Ottersbach, G. (1985). Travel Patterns: Insight from a Regional Perspective. *Proceedings, 16th Annual Meeting, TTRA.* Salt Lake City, UT: Bureau of Economic and Business Research, University of Utah.

Ritchie, J., & C. Goeldner (Eds). (1987). *Travel, Tourism and Hospitality Research, A Handbook for Managers and Researchers.* New York: John Wiley & Sons.

Schewe, C., & R. Calantone. (1978). Psychographic Segmentation of Tourists. *Journal of Travel Research, 16*(3). Boulder, CO: Business Research Division, University of Colorado.

Sofranko, A., & J. Williams (Eds). (1980). *Rebirth of Rural America: Rural Migration in the Midwest.* Ames, IA: North Central Regional Center for Community Development, Iowa State University.

United States Statistical Abstracts. (1988). 108th Edition

U.S. Travel Data Center. (1987). *1986 National Travel Survey.* Washington, DC.

Var, T., R. Beck, & P. Loftus. (1977). Determination of Touristic Attractiveness of the Touristic Areas of British Columbia. *Journal of Travel Research, 15*(3). Boulder, CO: Business Research Division, University of Colorado.

Vervaeke, W. (1987). 1987 Outlook for Auto Rental. *1987 Outlook for Travel and Tourism.* Washington, DC: U.S. Travel Data Center.

Wahab, S., L. Crampon, & L. Rothfield. (1976). *Tourism Marketing.* London: Tourism International Press. (Part III).

Weaver, G. (1986). *Tourism USA.* Washington, DC: U.S. Department of Commerce, Chapter 3.

Woodside, A. (1982). Positioning A Province Using Travel Research. *Journal of Travel Research, 20*(3). Boulder, CO: Business Research Division, University of Colorado.

Woodside, A., & E. Moore. (1986). Word of Mouth Communications and Guest Retention in Competing Resort Hotels. *Proceedings, 17th Annual Meeting, TTRA.* Salt Lake City, UT: Bureau of Economic and Business Research, University of Utah.

Zehnder, L. (1975). *Florida's Disney World.* Tallahassee, FL: Peninsular Publishing Co.

Major tourism projects require decisions and positive actions on the part of a large number of individuals, firms and agencies. Stowe, Vermont. Photo credit: Vermont Travel Division

TEN

Getting It Together — The Matrix of Decision Making

This chapter and the two that follow treat three facets of the question: "What are the principles involved in achieving constructive, positive action toward community tourism industry development?" This chapter deals mainly with a single project, showing how the interacting participants operate toward a positive end. The two following chapters treat the community's approach to overall tourism industry development.

Progress toward tourism industry development begins with recognition of a problem and/or opportunity in the community's tourism resources and economy. Usually development progresses project by project. In a project of significant scale, positive action requires inputs from an interacting set of agencies, firms and individuals. Community leaders need to understand both the sequences and interdependencies involved. This chapter discusses the principles relating to these facets of achieving constructive tourism industry development.

THE PROCESS OF DECISION MAKING

Individuals make decisions throughout their waking hours. In a somewhat more complex manner, organizations—collections of individuals—also make decisions. Decisions may be negative—to do nothing; or positive—to take specific, concrete action. Without these positive decisions, nothing

would ever be done. Positive actions toward tourism industry development flow from positive decisions. If tourism industry development is a goal, then we need to understand the process by which positive decisions take place. Further, we need to know who the relevant decision-makers are.

The decision process is closely analogous to research procedures. Both research and the decision process start with a question or recognition of a problem. In its simplest form, the decision process consists of five interrelated stages:

Problem/Opportunity Recognition and Definition

This first step in the decision process comes about in response to such questions as, "Why is our community losing population?" "How can we diversify our community's economy with other industries?" "Are we allowing resources to go to waste that could create jobs and/or improve our living quality?" and other related questions.

Many community leaders have difficulty recognizing that the future might be different from the past. In Chapter 5, a number of reasons for this common myopia were discussed. Related to failure at recognizing problems in the current economy is failure to see the opportunities in the tourism industry (Naisbitt, 1982). So long as problems/opportunities in the tourism industry remain unrecognized, a start will not even be attempted.

Information Gathering and Analysis

In the preceding chapter, good information was noted as necessary to the process of tourism industry development and promotion. If an individual or community leader recognizes a problem, the next step is to get more information that will shed light on the problem and lead to a workable solution. When information has been gathered and analyzed, it often leads to a further question or to a restatement of the problem. For example, the leadership of a community might recognize that the closing of a local processing or assembly plant will leave many residents unemployed. This was the case in the New Glarus, Wisconsin example discussed in Chapter 3. Community leaders might then look for information that will help answer such questions as: "How can we find ways to replace the lost income and keep the unemployed citizens in the community?" or "Can other products be produced using the resources that we have?" Added information, carefully analyzed, indicates the best directions for action. It is easy to understand that the question-information gathering chain might be an extended and complex process. Through the period while this process is underway there is uncertainty. This is a time of questing.

Information-gathering, at least in the initial stages, may be relatively informal. An early step might be to discuss the idea with other citizens. Then there might be contacts with experts in specific fields, use of library or archives resources, visits to other sites, and possibly formal research or study.

Decision

Based upon the information gathered and analyzed, the community leaders—or a single entrepreneur—may make a decision for a future course of action. In the search for information, it might have been noted that other communities had developed a viable tourism industry based upon ethnic uniqueness, or some other resource. The leaders might note, as did New Glarus, that they had a substantial Swiss (or Dutch or French) heritage and decide to amplify and make available this heritage and ambience.

Action

A "decision" is impotent without implementing action. In fact, a decision for positive action of any kind is never actually made until action to effect that decision has been taken. Another way of viewing the relationship between the "decision" and "action" stages is to recognize that until there is action, a state of uncertainty exists and the "decision" itself is subject to revision. During this uncertainty period, certain prerequisites remain unfulfilled, or key information is lacking.

Decision and action, while they may be discussed separately for purposes of exposition, are closely linked in what might be thought of as a decision-action chain. In fact a decision, such as that suggested above, to develop jobs through building a tourism industry based upon the community's ethnic heritage, is not a single, simple decision. In reality it poses a whole series of problems, questions and opportunities.

The entire tourism product mix is involved. Development of each part of the mix requires specific information, and the several thrusts collectively result in an interrelated series of decision-actions: "What services and facilities are needed?" "How do we ensure that they are appropriate and compatible?" "Who should do what?" "How financed?" Many components both inside and outside the community will thus become involved in the decision and action. This process is the matrix of decision making.

Bearing of Responsibility: The Real Decision Maker

Who underwrites the cost, reaps the rewards, or bears the consequences of failure resulting from a given decision? This question, more than any other, determines the true decision maker in any given case. The true decision maker may be the city council or a county commission. Its members will be blamed or credited for poor or good results from a decision to establish and underwrite the cost of a new tourist information center. An appointed building and program development committee may have been named to make recommendations, but if the council/commission accepts the committee's recommendations, the council/commission remains the one primarily responsible. Consultants and advisors who are paid to provide technical information and work out details do not alter this situation. The agency hiring them must understand and oversee the project and bear the final responsibility.

The bottom line is that there is no place to hide for a community body that undertakes tourism industry development leadership. It must lead. This leadership entitles it to credit for successes, but it must also accept blame for errors or failures.

Private entrepreneurs ordinarily undertake more narrowly focused aspects of a larger project. They provide a hospitality service or a recreational facility that contributes as a part of the whole. They bear responsibility for the success or failure of their operation; they pay the costs, and can reap the profits or suffer the losses. As one part of a larger community project, they are dependent upon the other components for a part of their individual success or failure. In turn, they also contribute to success of the overall community tourism industry. They not only add services for tourists but provide the major means for generating jobs and community income from tourism. Suggestions for stimulating action on the part of private entrepreneurs are discussed further in Chapter 12.

The above five stages are a part of every decision, however simple. Often they are performed so routinely that they are not recognized. Take the everyday problem that everyone who goes to school or work faces upon arising in the morning: "What shall I wear today?" Information is immediately needed: "Will it be cold and rainy, or hot and sunny?" Knowledge about the weather influences the decision about footwear, headgear and many items of outerwear. If the improper decision is made, the individual suffers the consequences.

Decisions and actions about tourism development by a community, its agencies and citizens are more conscious, deliberate and complex, but follow the same stages as the simple "what to wear?" problem (Murphy, 1983). This knowledge-action sequence forms one axis of the matrix of decision-making.

PROBLEM RECOGNITION: DETERMINANT OF WHAT TO DO

What will a business manager, a city council or other community leader or group recognize as a problem or opportunity in tourism industry development? A problem is recognized when there is a conflict between a belief (a concept of the world or one's community as it is) and a value (a concept of how the world or one's community should be).

A few case situations will illustrate how beliefs and values dominate and may distort recognition of problems.

— County commissioners of a rural county, having mainly a small farm economy, might look with disdain upon tourism and tourists. Their view of the world as it is, and ought to be, prizes the worth of tangible physical production of the kind that they have wrought by wresting a living from the reluctant soil. They question tourism: "How can it be an industry since it produces nothing?"

— The resort operators around a lake form an association to advertise their area's recreational opportunities. If fishing has been the original reason that brought most tourists, this activity feeds upon itself, building a self-reinforcing image of the area as a fishing vacationland. These fishermen went home and told friends about the fishing there. Naturally operators find that most who come want to fish. Understandably they develop an image of their market as that of fishermen. Meanwhile the lake's ability to deliver satisfactory fishing experiences declines because of continued angling pressure. Concurrently, the general vacationing public expands into a wide variety of other recreational activities. The association will continue marketing to fishermen, ignoring other vacation market opportunities.

—In some large cities, tourists spend more for shopping than for all other purposes combined. Contrasted with this fact is the image held by many retail merchants: That tourists spend money mainly in hotels and restaurants and at such places as major sports stadiums. Unless they have objective information telling them otherwise, retail merchants may regard themselves as "not a part of tourism," and thus refuse to participate in programs to develop and market the city's tourism industry.

In these examples, faulty understandings of the real world (beliefs) caused some tourism industry opportunities to be overlooked. In other cases concepts of what the world should be (values) led to conclusions that were less useful to the community's ends of improved economic opportunities than might otherwise have been the case. These community and/or business leaders either failed to recognize a problem/opportunity when one existed, or incorrectly identified it.

Beliefs about the world, including the tourism industry, are developed through observation. For this reason they can be altered by information. *Once more, the critical need for good information is underscored.*

Concepts of how the world should, or should not be—values—are less easily managed than beliefs. Values develop out of the overall process of maturation and living and are a more deeply held part of each individual's psyche. Because values are subjective in all individuals, it is usually inappropriate to regard a given value as "right" or "wrong." It is, however, appropriate to point out conflicts between two or more values held by the same person or group. For example, a leader in the community that is suffering economically because its population is dwindling, might have as a value the need to retain community youth who might otherwise leave because of poor local employment opportunities. If there were good opportunities for job expansion through tourism industry development, a value that the tourism industry was an inappropriate economic activity would conflict with the value of retaining the young people.

In the Waterville Valley, New Hampshire example (Chapter 9), we observed a value accommodation. Some "Yankees" apparently yielded in their sturdy disdain of leisure to their pragmatism. Recognizing that tourism generates income, they worked at developing the tourism industry.

Once a tourism industry opportunity is identified, information helps to refine and restate it. Dedicated pursuit and analysis of information bearing upon the problem/opportunity and its solution can lead to ingenious approaches that, in the case of tourism, contribute to greater traveler satisfactions and hence to a more viable tourism industry.

EVERYONE GETS INTO THE ACT

It has been noted that the decision process forms one axis of the matrix of decision making. In a tourism-related project of any scale, another axis is formed by the many and varied participants, each of whom must travel its own path through the decision process. The action undertaken by each contributes a part of the community's product mix.

Many projects can be observed as the lengthened shadow of one person, or only a few persons. We noted leadership roles in examples given for New Glarus, Wisconsin: Frankenmuth, Michigan; Guthrie, Oklahoma; and Baltimore, Maryland. These community leaders displayed vision. Often, in addition to serving as a catalyst, they continue to exercise lead roles. While much is owed to these initiating leaders, nothing would happen without added inputs and leadership on the part of many other individuals, groups and agencies.

The interconnectedness of the world leads to participation by a staggering number who become involved in even relatively simple projects. If a historical site is to be more fully interpreted, the local historical society and the state historical agency usually take part. Moving people to it may require road construction. Land may need to be rezoned by the local planning-zoning agency. Private hospitality businesses will need to provide services—and on and on. What happens in the social-economic-environmental arenas related to such an activity is somewhat comparable to an ecological chain where a lower organism becomes food for another organism, which in turn becomes food for or is symbiotic with still another organism. The relationships bear out the truth of the comment that "When any part of the world is moved, everything else rattles."

TIME HORIZONS: GESTATION PERIODS

Action toward implementation of most tourism projects does not take place suddenly, and actors seldom operate in coordinated unison. A consequence is that the gestation period for a project from the conception of the idea to the point where there is a visible activity may be quite long. The time to maturity, where significant tourism income is generated, may also extend into years and decades. Some examples will serve to illustrate the case of the real world timing:

The Case of the Boundary Waters Canoe Area

Many people who have enjoyed the area do not realize that the Boundary Waters Canoe Area (BWCA) has been in the process of formation throughout the entire 20th Century. It is a million-acre area of northern lakes and forests in Northeastern Minnesota that is managed by the Superior National Forest as a wilderness area primarily for paddle canoeists. Prior to 1920, there was interest in designation of the area. In 1926, a 640,000 acre area was established by proclamation of the Secretary of Agriculture. Legislation in 1948 provided for acquisition of private holdings within the area. Again in 1978, legislation further defined the area and restricted the use of motorized equipment.

The Gateway National Park and St. Louis Waterfront

For more than 50 years the St. Louis, Missouri waterfront area has been in the process of becoming the significant tourism attractor that it now is. National legislation authorizing the Park was passed in the 1930s, but it was not until nearly 30 years later that the Sarinen-designed arch, symbolizing the nation's gateway to westward expansion, was completed. During the 1980s the Laclede's Landing Redevelopment Corporation was busy assisting the conversion of what remained of the old waterfront warehouse area into a hospitality-recreation complex.

The above two stories could be repeated in varied form in many communities throughout the United States. Definition of the problem requires time. Recognition and definition of the opportunities is ongoing as the specific tourist destination area and its market take shape. Thus the time horizon of the matrix of decision making adds yet another dimension to the development process for a tourism-recreation project.

THE KNOWLEDGE-ACTION CONTINUUM

We have noted the problem-solving process which proceeds from recognition of a problem or opportunity to action that will help solve the problem or take advantage of the opportunity. We have called this the decision process. When the decision-maker consists of more than one individual, another step must be added: that of communication/information exchange and education. In most community decision systems, such as those consisting of firms, bureaucracies and the legislative body of a community (such as the county commissioners), this educational step may be involved and lengthy. It interacts with, and is in addition to, what may already be an involved and lengthy knowledge-gathering/research stage. Much communication can be thought of as legitimation: squaring information and proposed actions with beliefs and values of significant community individuals. Communication and education are required at every stage of the process. This communication must be external, with community and other citizens, and internal, among board members, staff and subcommittees.

By portraying the community decision process as a continuum, further understanding can be achieved (Ballman, 1981). Table 10.1 portrays the decision stages. For the sake of simplicity it omits responsibility-bearing.

Here we rename the community decision process the "knowledge-action continuum" to recognize the critical roles of knowledge management and action generation. Movement along the continuum flows in both directions, as indicated by the arrows at each end. For simple exposition, decision making can be thought of as moving from left to right. Actually all stages are interactive with all other stages, with continual feedback from each stage to others. For example, problem recognition is often initiated by some community leader, but its complete definition requires study, which often alters the statement of the problem. Communication is required to expand the problem to the community level. Once the several individuals and organizations of the community consider the problem, their resulting feedback may again alter and redefine the problem.

THE MATRIX OF DECISION MAKING

The knowledge-action continuum expands into a matrix when it is recognized that within the community there are many individuals, firms and agencies that must make inputs into the project. There may be more than one city and more than one county involved. Beyond the local interests there are also the state and national interests. Derived from this we have the simple matrix shown in Figure 10.1.

The operation of this matrix and its expansion in complexity beyond that portrayed in Figure 10.1 can be shown by example. Assume the case of a community where a problem/opportunity in recreational industry expansion is identified by a proposal to develop a 30,000-acre water impoundment on a local stream.

Table 10.1
The Community Knowledge-Action Continuum

Problem Recognition	Study Research	Communications Teaching Interpretation	Decision-Action Construction Production Publication

| Decision Makers | Knowledge-Action | | | |
	Problem- Identification	Information- Generation	Education and Communication	Decision-Action and Application
National-level				
State-level				
Local				

Figure 10.1 Simplified Decision Matrix

The most directly affected federal agency may be the U.S. Army Corps of Engineers. The Corps may initially see the project as one of flood control and power production. Without funding support from Congress, the Corps cannot proceed beyond preliminary investigations.

The State Department of Natural Resources will probably have jurisdiction over streams and wildlife. In addition, it may have jurisdiction over parks, wildlife preserves and water sport accesses.

The local community may see opportunity and need for expansion of its tourism/recreation industry (Getz, 1978). One agency of local government will be responsible for land use zoning, another for taxation. Much of the land will be privately owned. Each owner is a decision-making unit. Some owners will oppose the loss of home-sites and farming land; others will welcome the opportunity for a ready land sale.

The above illustrates a part of the complexity of the overall decision process faced in undertaking a major development project. But there is much more. For example, the exact nature of what is done in dam construction and development of the area for use will evolve from a multi-layered decision process. Local leaders, having a vision of tourism industry expansion made possible by the addition of a new major water facility, will impact their state and national legislators in support of the project. They will also interact with the state and national-level bureaucracies involved. There will be studies done by local, state and U.S. agencies and groups. In a greatly oversimplified view, out of this will come a decision-action series defining the reservoir/lake and its uses. These, in turn, trigger a further set of decision-actions concerning development of the resource: roads to be built, private investment opportunities, boat accesses, and many others that are related.

Each level—national, state and local—is not a unified decision-making system but consists of a multiplicity of different systems. There are, at the simplest conceptual level, governmental decision-units and private operations. There is the national government, and private firms operating on a nationwide, or international level; there is state government, and private firms whose operations are confined within the state; and there is local government, local private entrepreneurs and citizens.

At each level, the governmental decision system and private operators are far from a monolithic unit. A few simple examples illustrate the great complexity:

— The national-level lawmaker and fund-provider is the national legislature. This body's decisions determine active involvement of national agencies. Such a decision often evolves sequentially; an initial small appropriation is made for study. If study results are favorable, additional provisions are made for land acquisition and the construction of dams and other needed facilities.

— The Corps of Engineers may be the unit involved in actual dam construction. The U.S. Forest Service, in the Department of Agriculture, or the Bureau of Land Management in the Department of Interior, may own land in the area and be involved in land transfers, land management, and developmental operations. The National Park Service may have a role in heritage preservation and/or natural resource preservation, management and interpretation. The U.S. Soil Conservation Service may be involved regarding management of the drainage basin. These and many others that could be named as possible actors are all separate entities, each with its own set of goals and agenda. Each must work through the decision process separately, from problem identification, study of the situation and communication within the agency, to an appropriate decision-action for the given bureaucracy.

— National-level private decision makers may consist of one or more operator/investors involved in theme parks. One or more international lodging firm may consider whether a hotel, motel or resort property would be a profitable venture. A fast food chain and a sporting goods chain may also consider the potential of the site. Each of these must specify the problem/opportunity in its own terms; conduct the needed site, market and other research; communicate within the firm; reach a decision and take any indicated action.

— Governmental systems at the state level may include the state legislature's decision regarding enabling legislation and funding support. The Department of Natural Resources may be involved in decisions about a flowing stream, natural and historic preservation, wildlife and fish management, and many related factors. The State Department of Transportation must decide about and act on highway access and signing. Pollution control agencies, health departments, the Division of Tourism and energy regulatory agencies are among the many others that must also act in concert with the project for creation of a lake.

— State-level private investors may have an involvement similar to national-level private operations (Preston, 1983). At the state level there may also be involvement from private interest groups interested in conservation, wildlife, and outdoor activities. These could include the Sierra Club, Audubon Club, Ducks Unlimited, Izaak Walton League, League of Women Voters and ad hoc groups formed for the specific purpose of complementing, supporting or opposing the proposal for an artificial lake (Gondolf, 1986).

— Local governments will play a major role from the initiation through the implementation and operation stages. Among other roles, they have responsibility for local planning, zoning and other land use regulation (Seroka, 1986). In the case of a facility so large as a 30,000-acre lake there will almost certainly be a number of local jurisdictions. These may be county governments, city governments, school districts, drainage districts, levee districts, road districts, townships and similar institutions. Because each has a different purpose and relates to a different piece of geography, each of these units will define the problem differently and must undertake the decision process from its own set of circumstances. Some may favor the impoundment; others may conclude that it will be to their disadvantage; others may be indifferent or ignore the evolving proposal, refusing to recognize it as a problem or opportunity.

— Local private interests are often sharply divided in their identification of a proposal involving a substantial land area, as to whether it represents a problem or an opportunity. A local businessman or politician may envision expanded jobs, profits and taxes through the tourism industry based on the new water resource. Such individuals and their allies will be strong proponents. Others, such as farmers who might be displaced from the drowned stream flood plain, may be dedicated opponents. Local investors may identify opportunities for marinas, lodging, food service, campgrounds and other services; or if local investors inadequately evaluate the opportunities, these investments may be undertaken by nonresidents of the area.

The expanded decision matrix is illustrated on the following page by Figure 10.2. Even though it contains many more cells than Figure 10.1, this illustration is still a vast oversimplification.

Figure 10.2 has the decision-action continuum as its horizontal axis. A representative list of decision units at the local, state and national levels form the vertical axis. It should be emphasized that this list is representative only; many more could be included but they would only clutter the diagram.

Functional operations form a third axis of the Matrix of Decision Making as shown in figure 10.2. Each *function* represents a separate, different path that each of the *decision units* must take through the problem identification/study/communication/decision sequence. For example, the U.S. Army Corps of Engineers will need to consider *feasibility* and decide accordingly. It must consider the *physical engineering* details of dam construction. It must deal with *funding*, and it must consider how it will *organize* the work and *assign personnel* to the project.

A potential private lodging investor must also investigate feasibility for proposed undertakings. This feasibility will consider the physical site, labor availability and financing costs, among other items.

The several decisions do not take place independently; rather, they are interactive. Many decisions feed into another in a recursive fashion. This interaction pattern cannot be clearly illustrated in Figure 10.2, but examples can be given. Local leaders as the result of their study and decisions may work with legislators at both state and national levels, and in concert with key agencies such as the U.S. Army Corps of Engineers and the State Department of Natural Resources. Before a dam can be built, land may need to be rezoned by local authority, state agencies may need to transfer land ownership, and private owners must sell land. These property transfers may involve court action. Before the lake can have meaning in terms of economic gain to the community, there must be roads and a host of services and facilities that can sell services to tourists.

All of the actors and actions described plus many more are involved in the matrix of decision making for a major new community tourism industry resource—in this case, a lake. In a dramatic way they illustrate the complexity of our socio-political-economic system and its functioning.

A similar interacting matrix would be involved in the development of any other major tourism attraction or service, be it a pageant, a trail, a historical restoration or a public event.

			FUNCTIONS		KNOWLEDGE-ACTION	
			Funding			
			Organizational			
			Personnel			
			Environmental			
			Feasibility			
			Physical Development			
DECISION MAKERS						
GEOGRAPHIC	KIND	AGENCY	Problem	Study	Education-Communication	Decision-Action
National	Governmental	Congress				
		Corps of Engineers				
		U.S. Forest Service				
		National Park Service				
		Soil Cons. Service				
		Courts				
	Private	Theme Parks				
		Lodging Chains				
		Food Service Oper's				
		Resource Groups				
		Rec. Activity Groups				
State	Governmental	Legislature				
		Dept. Natural Res.				
		Health Department				
		Dept. Transportation				
		Courts				
	Private	Facility Investors				
		Resource Groups				
		Rec. Activity Groups				
Local	Governmental	County A				
		County B				
		City X				
		City Y				
		School Districts				
		Special Districts				
	Private	Business Managers				
		Land Owners				
		Land Developers				
		Investor/Developers of Facilities				

Figure 10.2 Expanded Decision Matrix for a New Lake Development

Questions for review and further study

1. Explain why problem recognition and definition are the most crucial parts of decision making.

2. Compare and contrast the responsibilities in the development and construction of a motel building on the part of (a) the building contractor; (b) the owner/investor.

3. With so many conflicting interests focusing upon everything that is done, how is it that anything ever actually gets done?

4. Explain the need for communication with and among the general citizenry of a community when a major project is undertaken in or by the community. Also: What is the difference between a project undertaken *in* a community, compared to one undertake *by* a community?

5. What differences are there in the communication needed for projects that are undertaken by governmental agencies and those undertaken by private firms?

6. By what means can beliefs be changed?

7. What are differences in the approaches to a project on the part of someone forced to act (An unsympathetic official, or a property owner whose property is affected) and an individual who sees the project as a personal or community opportunity?

SUGGESTIONS FOR FURTHER READING

Wallace, L., D. Hobbs, & R. Vlasin (Eds). (1969). *Selected Perspectives for Community Resource Development.* Raleigh, NC: Agricultural Policy Institute, North Carolina State University. (Part II).

TEXTUAL REFERENCES

Ballman, G., J. Burke, & U. Blank. (1981). Meshing Resources and Investments With 1980's Tourism Markets: A Teaching-Research Case. *Proceedings, 12th Annual Meeting, TTRA.* Salt Lake City, UT: Bureau of Economic and Business Research, University of Utah.

Getz, M., L. Nelson, & J. Seigfield. (1988). The Local Impact of State Parks. *Journal of Leisure Research, 10*(2). Arlington, VA: NRPA.

Gondolf, E. (1986). Diagnosing Community Standoffs: A Social Factor Model and the Berm Highway Conflict. *Journal of the Community Development Society. 17* (2). Athens, GA: University of Georgia.

Murphy, P. (1983). Perceptions and Attitudes of Decisionmaker Groups in Tourism Centers. *Journal of Travel Research. 21*(3). Boulder, CO: Business Research Division, University of Colorado.

Naisbitt, J. (1982). *Megatrends: Ten New Directions Transforming Our Lives.* New York: Warner Books.

Preston, J. (1983). Patterns of Non-Governmental Community Action in Small Communities. *Journal of the Community Development Society. 14*(2). Athens, GA: University of Georgia.

Seroka, J. (1986). Attitudes of Rural County Leaders in the U.S. Toward Intergovernmental Cooperation. *Journal of the Community Development Society, 17*(1). Athens, GA: University of Georgia.

A well designed tourism policy offers a major means whereby the community can exercise positive leadership in its tourism industry development. Lake Erie, Ohio. Photo credit: Ohio Division of Travel and Tourism

ELEVEN

Getting it Together—
Tourism Development Policy

Chapters 11 and 12 come fully to grips with the community tourism industry imperative. This imperative holds forth the community's opportunities through tourism industry development. It infers that the community has capability and responsibility for exerting a large measure of control in guiding the course of its tourism industry development. Major advantages can thus accrue to the community and its citizens, and to tourism consumers.

THE COMMUNITY'S TOURISM INDUSTRY: WHO'S IN CHARGE?

Resources for the Future predicts tourism to become the world's largest industry within a few decades (Kahn, 1979). For some communities this future is already a reality; some even suffer from the unfavorable impact of uncontrolled tourism industry growth (Rosenow, 1979). However, for each over-impacted community, there are many others needing the economic diversification, stimulus and other advantages that a healthy tourism industry component can bring.

The book's major thesis is that in the developed world, communities can exercise major positive control over their tourism industry's development. This is especially true for communities in which tourism industry is underdeveloped. But it is also true for those communities that are apparently over-impacted by outside agencies and developers. A first prerequisite is that the community, through its

leaders, look to the future positively and with confidence. Simple as this may sound, we have seen in Chapters 5 and 7 that many communities suffer because they lack such a future outlook.

Beyond a positive view, the community can begin by establishing a tourism policy and an intensive program of information management—the systematic gathering and analysis of information, and its use in a multifaceted community education program. In addition, the policy may have many other components.

The approach of a tourism industry policy is not a planning approach as ordinarily considered. Rather than setting up "plans" and attempting their specific execution, a policy's approach attempts to draw out the genius of the community. Its purpose is to create plans in the minds of citizens, entrepreneurs, and agency staff that they can engineer into positive action. Results thereby achieved may well exceed those even imagined by any system of formal planning.

TOURISM INDUSTRY POLICIES

The Federal Level

The national government of the United States has been slow to grasp the concept that tourism industry development might be a part of its responsibility and also present an economic opportunity.

In the closely related area of national recreational policy, the U.S. government established the Outdoor Recreation Resources Review Commission (ORRRC) in 1958. In 1962 the commission issued its first major report, which led to the establishment of the Bureau of Outdoor Recreation (BOR) in the Department of the Interior. Under the stimulus of BOR and the Land and Waters Conservation (LAWCON) Funds that it administered, most states developed state recreational plans in the 1965 to 1975 period. Unfortunately, when the funds became more restricted, most state recreational planning ceased. Later in the period, an administrative consolidation placed most of BOR's mandates along with those of other agencies in the Heritage Conservation and Recreation Service (HCRS).

A draft of the First Nationwide Outdoor Recreation Plan, *The Recreation Imperative*, was prepared by the Department of the Interior in 1968. It was not published until 1974, and then only as a Congressional document. A second outdoor recreation plan, *Outdoor Recreation: A Legacy for America*, was published in 1973. In 1978 the *Third Nationwide Outdoor Recreation Plan* was published.

The 1978 effort was the last of the series of outdoor recreation plans. However, other reports have followed; examples include the following. In 1983 the Outdoor Recreation Policy Review Group prepared its report *Outdoor Recreation for America 1983*. In 1986 the President's Commission on Americans Outdoors issued a report of outdoor recreation activities, *Participation in Outdoor Recreation Among American Adults and the Motivations Which Drive Participation*. Also in 1986 the National Park Service published the *1982-1983 Nationwide Recreation Survey*.

It was not until 1970 that Congress created the National Tourism Resources Review Commission. Its report, *Destination USA*, was published in 1973. In 1978 the *National Tourism Policy Study* was published. This was followed by the National Tourism Policy Act of 1981 that set up the U.S.

Travel and Tourism Administration (USTTA) and created a new post of Undersecretary of Commerce for Tourism, in the Department of Commerce.

Currently the USTTA concentrates its efforts in promotion of travel to the United States from major overseas markets (Ronkainen, 1987). It conducts limited studies of international travel. In 1986 it cooperated with the Economic Development Administration to support publication of a tourism development manual, *Tourism USA*. USTTA is so drastically underfunded that, as noted in Chapter 5, its budget compares unfavorably to even that of Greece. The first U.S. Travel Census was conducted in 1967 by the Bureau of the Census; it was repeated in 1972 and 1977, but has since been discontinued. Currently no group in the United States generates generally available tourism data at the national level. However, in 1973 the U.S. Travel Data Center was set up as a quasi-public organization to conduct travel studies. It partially fills the gap, deriving much of its income from fees charged for studies and reports that it prepares.

In summary, at the national level the U.S. government gives scant attention to the tourism industry, either in terms of promotion, development or data management. In relative terms, the effort is weaker in the late 1980s than during the decade of the 1970s.

The federal government of Canada has provided more positive support to tourism than that of the United States. A recent substantial effort was the Travel Industry Development Subsidiary Agreements (TIDSA). This was a cooperative funding effort with the several provinces to encourage the development of tourism attractions and services (Montgomery, 1983).

Tourism Canada regularly issues tourism/travel data. It provides a series on domestic travel giving data by origin and destination. It also provides a forum for disseminating tourism data generated by other organizations. In addition, it recently commissioned a research firm to conduct a comprehensive study of the U.S. travel market, *U.S. Pleasure Travel Market* (Tourism Canada, 1986).

Canada has historically enjoyed a larger comparative advantage in tourism than the United States. Its international tourism receipts represent a larger proportion of its gross national product; further, the large U.S. travel market is immediately next door.

Tourism Action At the State/Provincial Level

Some states with high amenity water and other recreational resources have promoted themselves as travel destinations throughout most of the 20th century. During the 1980s many states seized upon tourism as a solution to economic difficulties and greatly expanded their tourism promotion budgets. Overall state promotional spending increased by over one-half (52 percent) in just the 1984 to 1987 period.

To the extent that an advertising program can be considered as a state tourism policy, then most states now have such a policy. This means that the state governments recognize tourism as having potential for contributing to their economies. Their "policy" consists of a promotional program to capture tourism income. Unfortunately, in terms of a comprehensive approach including systematic management, development and marketing, few states have accomplished more than random pronouncements. Few have even developed usable tourism data series. Thus most state governments have progressed little, if at all, beyond the national government in establishing working tourism plans, policies or programs. However, some have made progress; representative examples are listed here without attempting to be comprehensive.

Hawaii has progressed further in organizing and planning of its tourism industry than any other state. Significantly, Hawaii is a relatively small state, and it has a major comparative advantage in the tourism industry. One of Hawaii's first acts upon achieving statehood in 1959 was to initiate a planning program. An important objective was to provide guidelines for tourism industry investment and development throughout the several islands, and to avoid excess concentrations at Waikiki.

In 1970 Hawaii's governor convened a Travel Industry Congress. A result of this Congress was a comprehensive set of goals, *Recommended Goals for Hawaii's Visitor Industry*, published by the Hawaii Visitors Bureau. The Hawaii Visitors Bureau is a private, not-for-profit, quasi-public body having paid memberships. Its budget is derived about one-fourth from private sources and three-fourths from state funding. The bureau has four working divisions: marketing, visitor satisfaction, research and conventions.

Ontario, over a period of decades, has developed tourism industry guidelines and conducted systematic research. In 1977 it prepared the *Ontario Tourism and Outdoor Recreation Planning System* . It participated extensively in TIDSA, treating seasonal industry problems, upgrading tourism plant and developing destination attractions. In 1985 Ontario's Ministry of Tourism and Recreation updated its 1982 Travel Survey, preparing the *1985 Ontario Travel Survey*. This research provides comprehensive data about Ontario residents' travel. It is one of the more complete such data sets available.

New Mexico has established travel and tourism policies through a series of regional meetings, with more than 2000 citizens participating. This policy development was under the leadership of the Board of Economic Development and at the governor's direction. It was published as *New Mexico Tourism and Travel Policy 1979*. Policy priorities were placed upon hospitality to travelers and quality of living for residents. The full list of priorities were hospitality, quality of life, state and local communication, agency coordination and cooperation, traveler services, laws relating to travel, planning, development, marketing, and research.

Florida's programs for gathering data on in-coming tourists are arguably among the leading such operations in the United States. They are also of long standing. For several decades Florida has generated a consistent set of tourism industry data, using techniques that it has developed over a period of continued use. A number of other states have done tourism studies, but none has conducted them so consistently over time.

Michigan's private tourism industry was among the first to recognize the value of educational services to its business managers. In 1946 an organization of private tourism-related firms, the Michigan Tourism Association, appealed to and got from the Michigan legislature funding for three tourism and hospitality extension specialists. These three operated as a part of the Land-Grant College Extension System based at Michigan State University. The program focus has varied somewhat over time. Currently a working relationship has been established between the Michigan Tourism Division of state government and the research and extension education capabilities of Michigan State University.

A number of states have attempted tourism planning using a basically sound approach. That is, they brought a diverse, representative group together to identify problems and opportunities and establish tourism industry goals. Despite these starts, most state tourism planning operations have been inconsistent, erratic, and often a one-time effort lacking in follow-up. Despite some individually laudable planning and development attempts, advertising continues to be the primary state-level tourism industry development effort undertaken.

Cities: Coming on Fast!

Cities have recently moved ahead with tourism programs leading to development of tourism plant and services, in addition to the conduct of tourism selling programs. This progress is all the more remarkable because up until only the last decade or two, few cities regarded tourism seriously as a part of their economy. Little effort was made except to attract conventions to the city. This neglect occurred in spite of the fact that cities are the recipients of at least half of the U.S. tourism travel and dollar expenditures. Now many cities are in the process of making themselves more livable for residents, and more attractive to visitors (Murphy, 1983). In some cases, good tourism data provide the basis for development by the multitude of possible investors and other decision makers. Some examples follow:

Baltimore, Maryland has transformed an area of rotting warehouses around its inner harbor into an area bringing in $1 billion in income annually and 20,000 jobs. In 1950 the Greater Baltimore Committee was created. From 1970 to the mid-1980s, the then-Mayor Schaeffer provided much of the leadership. As with many such projects, there was a long gestation period: In 1976 there was the Tall Ships celebration; then the Science Center and World Trade Center; in 1980 the Harbor Center, a complex of shops and food services; 1981 the National Aquarium; 1985 Six-Flags took over the Old Baltimore Trolley and Electric Company Power Building. Much of this was done by creating a group of quasi-public corporations, backed by city bonding.

Private enterprise was stimulated to add investment. In 1980 there were 1,200 hotel rooms in the harbor area; by 1987 this had increased more than four-fold to 5,300. A nearby area of about-to-be-wrecked homes is now rapidly becoming gentrified. Baltimore conducts an annual survey of its tourism business.

Las Vegas, Nevada has conducted an ongoing, thorough research of its visitor market since 1975. The information makes possible a multi-dimensional visitor profile for use in revealing trends; for casino management; for identifying marketing strengths, weaknesses and opportunities; and other marketing and development planning. Reports are now available quarterly to improve timeliness for managers' decisions. In addition, special studies have been conducted, such as visitor profiles from specific geographic market areas and occupancy trend reports. Once the data are supplied, decisions are the responsibility of private entrepreneurs.

Halifax, Nova Scotia established an 11-member City Tourism Commission in 1980. It consists of four aldermen and seven citizens appointed by the mayor; the mayor is an ex-officio member. The program was established by city ordinance. Responsibilities of the Commission include a tourism marketing program, including research to guide the effort; provision of a comprehensive information service to visitors who are in the city; leadership in the development of tourism facilities and services; and a comprehensive citizen education program in schools, industry, and to the general public.

Minneapolis, Minnesota like most large cities, has had a Convention Bureau for decades. It took a major step forward around 1970 by expanding the operation's charter to form the Minneapolis Convention and Tourism Commission. The tourism division has functioned by systematically studying and working with the community and tourism-related businesses; providing information about services to visitors, including use of literature and electronic information dispensing in high-traffic points; staging of familiarization (FAM) tours; and the conduct of community, employee and business manager education. A comprehensive tourism impact and market study conducted in 1977-78 provided the specific data needed for convincing entrepreneurs, employees and citizens of the tourism industry's value to them. In 1980 a three-year tourism plan was developed, including the development of comprehensive training manuals. In addition, throughout the 1970s and 1980s both Minneapolis and St. Paul have rapidly upgraded their central business districts, adding greatly to

liveability appeal for both visitors and residents.

Why have cities been able to implement tourism programs more expeditiously than states? This appears to be due to the integration of their geography and political systems, to the funding mechanisms available to them, and to the large impact of tourism upon them—once realized. Even so, as of now, relatively few cities have effectively operating tourism divisions. The good news is that if some can, many others can also.

THE TOURISM DEVELOPMENT IMPERATIVE— CAN PLANNING HELP?

Tourism industry development calls for positive action where, in many cases, action has not been occurring. Because of tourism's impact on the entire community, concerted community effort also appears to be called for. These requirements suggest the need for a tourism industry planning effort. We thus need to examine the pros and cons of tourism industry planning. This author, out of a number of decades of direct experience, has arrived at a firm conclusion: We must plan—but for many situations planning, as commonly understood, doesn't work.

The Planning Imperative:

Every community's tourism industry is continually being impacted by a variety of factors, outside investors, changes in state laws, state and federal agency programs. The community's only means for exercising control is to have in place its own set of positive objectives, plans and actions.

There must be a systematic approach to the management of community aesthetics and community resources. We have noted in Chapter 7 the "Problem of the Commons" and the dangers of resource attrition without compensation—"The Worst of All Worlds in Resource Use."

Positive development is neither spontaneous nor automatic. Someone with a vision of the future must initiate, plan and implement it.

Some means of achieving communications and coordination among the many actors, as noted in Chapter 10, is needed.

In summary, achieving and maintaining a viable community tourism industry calls for a positive vision of the future and a method for moving positively forward. It also involves understanding and communication among the many elements involved in the community's tourism industry.

Planning: The Impossible Dream?

But planning can't work! We have seen that many states have discussed the need, but done little concretely (Bosselman, 1978). Why?

A comprehensive plan becomes unmanageable in a large diverse system. There is a bewildering complexity of interests and actors—the matrix of decision-making. This factor operates to emasculate many formal tourism planning efforts.

Planning requires foreseeing the future. But human beings lack prescience. We have seen that few communities have good information about past or current tourism, not to mention knowledge of the future. Since most planning must be based upon information from the past, it frequently treats the wrong issues.

Planning as usually done implies an elite. Planning implies a superior-inferior set, with the superior element being able to plan and impose its will upon the rest of the system. An often-observed practice has been the "protection" of a plan from

general scrutiny until it is complete. It is then "sprung," generating predictably disastrous objection and conflict.

An important element of most community's tourism industry depends upon private enterprise. Most tourism jobs and income are generated by the private sector. But the private sector is responsible to its managers and investors, not to the public or general community leadership. Since the community, as a whole, does not bear the consequences of private enterprise results, it can neither plan nor make decisions for private operators.

Planning by a political entity—city, county, state, nation—is hampered by the shifting currents of public political fortunes. What one administration starts will often be cut off from support by the succeeding one. Planning requires a time horizon. Study and/or planning commissions are appointed; often when they report findings to the next administration the report is promptly buried and forgotten.

Planning, in some sectors, has acquired an unsavory reputation. In the United States we have been subjected to the "Great Communist Scare". We have been warned that "Big Brother" would make all plans for us. Because of this myth, opponents of efforts that they dislike have often been able to cripple the effort by labeling it a "Communist takeover plot." The reality from observing 50 years of centrally planned economies is that communism works badly: It competes weakly with more viable social and economic systems of the western world. Much greater danger lies in lack of vitality and failure to renew within our systems, rather than from external threats.

Planning: Who? What? How?

Now planning's role can be put into perspective by considering three of its aspects:

What determines who can plan? We have said that the only people who can plan are those who have authority to carry out action, and who bear the responsibilities for the consequences of that action. In addition, there are different degrees of abstraction in planning and action. For example, a community does not in a strict sense "plan" a public golf course. Citizens can express felt needs and institute the initiative for a golf course, but usually it is a legislative body such as an elected council that makes the formal decision that there be a golf course. The council and/or citizens may approve, or even vote funding—appropriations, taxes, bonding, etc. Actual acquisition, design and construction will be the responsibility of a designated agency. This agency may in turn hire design and construction help.

Needed is recognition of a crucial planning principle: *No one can make a plan for someone else.* It is possible to suggest, assist and stimulate, but any unit, and *only* that unit (individual, agency, firm), responsible for its own action must make its own plan.

Who, Then, Can Plan?

— The community and its legislators set the framework. It does not usually plan or execute an event or carry out construction. It sets the policy, not the detailed plan and action.

— A public recreation department can plan and carry out events and do construction within the framework of the policies and funding set by the community's legislators or overall executive branch.

— The owner of a business can plan and execute those plans within the scope of resources available.

— An individual may also make plans and carry them out—again, within the scope of resources or power available to the individual.

— An organization such as a club or church may plan and carry out activities within its charter and the range of its resources.

Many actions lie outside the range of the community's ability to directly impact. It cannot plan directly for its clubs, individuals, or corporations. If there is a desire to improve the aesthetics of the community's entrance, what can the community do? It can landscape publicly held lands, if funds are available. Private lands can be zoned, but the degree of planning/zoning control is limited unless the values expressed in the zoning are widely held. Thus citizens and businesses are influenced most by what may be thought of as peer pressure, consensus, and community esprit de corps. These factors are not directly manageable by a community entity.

The Best-Laid Plans of Men and Mice. Planning deals with the future. But, as previously noted, we have information only about the past, and often imperfect information at that. For this reason, much planning is in error; much that is anticipated does not come to pass. Nevertheless, there are major gains to be realized. A good planning process acquires information and sets up organization and communication systems. With these systems in place, the group or corporation is then able to deal more effectively with what actually happens, even though it differs from what was expected and planned for.

Change can be predicted. The *exact nature* of future change cannot be predicted. Change will alter markets and cause obsolescence in any community's tourism system. This calls for planning of a different kind than normally considered: *The tourism system that seeks to avoid obsolescence, rather than developing and ossifying its facility's offering and marketing categories, instead develops a system for managing ongoing change* (Gardner, 1962).

The results from planning depend upon the approach used. Consider two of the many possible types of planning approaches. The *lawyer-planner approach* considers planning as the function of an elite. It protects developing plans from the public to prevent their being "spoiled." Once completed, it attempts to impose the plan upon the system using the force of law. The *educator-planner approach* attempts to build the capabilities of the system. It does this by gathering and teaching information, and building organizations and communication systems. Through this means, the social and economic system is able to articulate needs, develop plans and evolve means for implementation.

In practice, much planning that effectively generates action is a hybrid. It uses the aggressiveness of the lawyer-planner approach, while building communications, understandings and capability on the part of the entire structure in the manner of the educator-planner approach.

TOURISM POLICY: GOALS, INFORMATION, COMMUNICATIONS

In the face of these many considerations, is there a way that a community can act positively and intentionally to develop its tourism industry? Fortunately, such positive action is available.

Because of a need to move forward with tourism development, and because of an apparent planning paralysis, a *tourism policy* is suggested as the most workable way for many communities to initially move forward. A tourism policy declares a clear intent to develop the tourism industry. It indicates community goals related to tourism, and may highlight a wide range of priority concerns. Many of the latter may be interrelated with the goal statement.

A policy's purpose is to indicate direction and perform an initiating and stimulating role in achieving that direction. It achieves this by helping the community to agree upon major common aims through the goal-setting process. It then taps the genius of the society by creating awareness of the opportunities and potentials in tourism industry development on the part of the elements who can decide and act. These are the corporations, agencies and individuals who carry on the work of the community. In doing this, a policy stimulates the matrix of decision making to function constructively.

Characteristics of the Initiating Set

The initiating set for policy making must have the confidence of the community. It must be seen as legitimate, capable and operating in the public interest. It could be a public body, such as the county, city or state government. We observed in the Halifax, Nova Scotia example that the tourism commission and its basic duties were established by city ordinance. In other examples, we have also seen that citizens such as a banker or other businessman has played a lead role. Alternatively, the initiating set can be a private club, such as a civic organization, or a quasi-public body, such as a chamber of commerce. It may even be a special-interest group. The initiating set need not be a large group so long as it meets the above requirements. It is not expected to carry out events or cause brick and mortar to rise; rather it is expected to be the stimulating or catalyzing agent.

The Prerequisites for Effective Policy Development

A legitimate, capable initiating set is the first need. Other requirements may be briefly outlined as follows:

All elements of the community that are involved in tourism must be represented in the process. This generally means public resource and service managing agencies, elected officials, private organizations, business classes and citizen leaders. Not all of these need have membership on a formal body, but they should have liaison and feel that their interests and inputs are considered (Ritchie, 1985). Without broad ownership in the policy-making process, the process will likely fail in its most important role: that of stimulating planning and action in tourism development.

Continuity and consistency over time are necessities. Unfortunately, because of the possibility of periodic leadership change in U.S. political systems, assurance of continuity may be a problem. Continuity problems may be reduced by institutionalizing the policy process, rather than the specific policies and policy-makers. This calls for achieving broad agreement on the need for tourism industry development in order to transcend short-time differences.

Policies must allow for flexibility. There should be an expectation of new information, new learning and change, and hence the need for re-establishing goals and priorities as the system evolves. Regular review can help to ensure needed renewal.

A policy statement need not be fully comprehensive at any one time. The policy should include those items having highest priority at the time. In keeping with flexibility, priorities may be shifted. Sequential focusing upon different aspects of policy

may be a means of extending scarce leadership resources. Few communities have sufficient leadership and resources to treat all aspects of an industry so complex as tourism at the same time.

Timing may be important. Sometimes a triggering event occurs. This opens a window of receptivity to new ideas such as the concept of tourism industry development as a major community economic component. Policies initiated at such times may have significant impact.

Key Policy Components

There are three components that are so necessary to the ends of setting up a tourism development policy that every community should include these in the beginning stages.

Establish goals for the community relating to tourism industry development. Goals point in the direction that the community wishes to move. Goals can be a communication device and integrating mechanism; this is the reason for making sure that all community elements have ownership in the goal-setting process.

The tourism goals should capture broadly the community's hopes and aspirations for tourism and what it can do and be for their community. For this reason many communities may wish to include, as a part of their tourism industry goals, a series of statements about overall ideals of the community as a place to live, work and play. Tourism can contribute to residents' living quality, and a part of the industry's development should deliberately work toward achieving that end. The total statement may also set forth clearly the destination area image that the community seeks to place in the minds of tourists.

To the extent that a "Big Idea" of the community as a place to live and visit can be established in the goal statement, this can act as a rallying point for all residents to build pride in their community, reduce conflict and achieve coordination in development efforts. After basic information is available, a *Concept Plan* as discussed in Chapter 12 may serve as the Big Idea. Beyond the broader views, it may be desirable to include as goals, intentions toward specific developments such as those listed under "Other Possible Elements of Tourism Policy." As with all aspects of policy, goals must be regularly reviewed and updated.

Tourism research: a policy toward data and information. The need for adequate information is so universal and critical that it is included here as a "must do" part of policy to be translated into action. Tourism development actions can be only as good as the information upon which they are based.

If appropriate tourism industry development is a goal, then research and analysis of factors relating to the industry are prerequisites. *Good tourism impact data* can be one of the best means for educating the businessmen and the public concerning tourism's current contribution and its potential contribution to the economic scene. *Systematic information about the community's tourism physical plant and tourism resources* can stimulate the development process, and is needed by current and potential investors and by public resource-managing agencies (Liu, 1980). *Market analyses* complement the resource analyses, serving to guide both developmental and promotional efforts.

Ordinarily, the policy-making body will not itself conduct the research. But in its role as initiator, this group should ensure understanding and support for an ongoing research effort.

Community information and education. A free flow of information and on-going community educational programs are called for as a major feature of tourism policies. Some observers regard the flow of information as so crucial that they have labeled this the "Information Age" (Hobbs, 1987). Educational needs arise from the frequently noted severe lack of understanding about the tourism

industry on the part of most people. A community often fails to act because it lacks information (Roberts, 1979). Good information is a major means for stimulating the genius of the community and its entrepreneurs to act on tourism industry development (Burns, 1979).

Information needs call for a many-faceted program of public education, which may use the public school system, workshops, the media and many other facilities and procedures. This education is one important use of the data that are gathered and analyzed by a research program. The data have little value unless they are made available to relevant individuals. Specific educational programs need to be targeted at industry and business leaders, managers of tourism facilities, employees who work in hospitality facilities, elected officials, agency staff and the general public. Policies regarding community education in tourism need to establish the responsibility for its conduct and oversight. Multiple agencies may be jointly involved in this educational effort.

A community tourism policy that sets forth goals toward which the community can aspire, and that provides for research and educational programs, will help establish the basis for sound progress toward tourism industry development. The educational and communication process will, in fact, have begun with the goal-setting in the beginning stages. In setting goals and helping to establish community tourism research and educational procedures on a regular basis, the policy will set the stage for decision makers of the community to act, as in the "Matrix of Decision Making," toward community development.

OTHER POSSIBLE ELEMENTS OF TOURISM POLICY

A community tourism policy may include many other elements in addition to the three discussed above. Each community will have its own set of priorities that only it can determine. Clearly, those things seen as the most important problems, needs and opportunities should be included as a part of tourism policy and given priority. In each case there must be specific assignments of responsibility and considerations for funding. Included here for review are some of the elements for which many communities may want to develop a specific policy:

Attractions Development

Tourists do not come to a community to look at or stay in the motels, or to use other hospitality services. They come because something there to see and do appeals to them. They use the hospitality services incidentally to achieving the experiences sought, although as noted elsewhere, the hospitality services may be a significant part of those experiences. The primacy of attractions in the tourism industry dictates to each community that it continuously review its attractions against market needs.

Hospitality Services

Hospitality services provide a major complement to the experience offered by attractions. Further, they are among the major means for generating income from tourists. Thus they too must fit the community image in addition to serving needs for tourists to travel and live away from home. Since most hospitality services are provided by the private sector, the community as an entity does not directly make hospitality development investment decisions. Chapter 12 considers means available to facilitate these private enterprise developmental actions.

Activities: Other Things to See and Do

Activities may supplement the focal attractor and provide added incentive for tourists to spend time in the community, thus generating added income.

Recreational activities, evening entertainment, shopping and other related services may in themselves be important income generators. They add importantly to the "sales package" offered by the community to tourists. "Other" things may provide the link to the familiar, in an exotic ambience that travelers often seek. Some such features may be publicly provided, as in the case of trails. Others, such as evening entertainment, may be private operations.

Promotional/Advertising Programs

Most communities conduct publicly supported promotional efforts. Despite this, in many communities, the sum of marketing efforts by private enterprise overshadows that done publicly. Community marketing policy should consider the overall effort, asking how it may be improved, assisted and coordinated.

Transportation Systems

Transportation preferences and technologies evolve continuously. The transportation system and the mix of travel accesses need to be matched with the appropriate market, and with the market's travel preferences.

Community Ambience and Aesthetics

The total community impinges upon the visitor's image of it as a place to visit, and upon the self-image, community pride and living quality of residents. Ambience includes those physical, economic and cultural factors that pervade the overall impression one gets of the community. Community ambience and aesthetics can be managed. An early step is to ask systematically, "What do we want the community to be and what image do we want to project to residents as well as tourists?"

A Local Information, Direction and Interpretation System

The challenge is to reduce the problem of the community's well-kept secrets. Recognition of the place for such a system as part of a deliberate policy will help the system get built into a plan that improves information access to the community. Public, quasi-public and private agencies may all be involved in its implementation.

Community Infrastructure

Those things that make the community run may, in any community, be a weak link in its tourism development. Infrastructure includes the many things that make it possible fo the community to function, serving residents as well as visitors. Infrastructure is primarily a public responsibility.

Financing of Development

Financing may be a part of general policy, or a specific part of each individual project. Policies toward financing might include types of projects that might receive financing assistance, and indicate the source of funds. Tax policies, bonding and loan backup may be among specific policies.

Resource Quality and Resource Management

Environmental and other quality factors bear upon the community's ambience, and hence upon the experience of both visitors and residents. Tourism development may require attention in areas such as environmental quality, zoning and land use, developmental patterns, intensity of use and development and related items.

Assignment of Agency Responsibilities and Coordination of Their Efforts

Every government and every community strives to achieve efficient, coordinated operation of the agencies that serve it. Communication is a first step. A task or project will only be carried out by an agency having the authority, resources and responsibility for doing so.

International and Other Special Market Thrusts

Tapping the potential of international markets may require a policy to be followed up with specific plans and actions.

Seasonality of Tourism

Seasonality poses a limitation to the tourism industry development of some communities. Under some conditions, the community may find it wise to set up a policy to guide development and invest-ment toward tourism expansion in specific seasons, and/or to limit expansion in a given season.

Residents' Living Quality

The community's function as a place to live is a foremost reason for tourism industry development. Tourism provides economic returns enabling residents to live better, as well as making services available that the community might not otherwise be able to afford. Pursuit of tourism as an industry should never lose sight of the goal of its positive contribution to the community's citizens. Some aspects of tourism have been labeled "ugly." A deliberate policy of tourism industry development can enable the community to exercise positive control. Such a policy can not only help reduce the problems of domination by outside elements. It can give citizens and institutions a sense of control over their home's destiny, and enhance their self-worth (Greer, 1987).

TOWARD DEVELOPING THE ENTIRE ECONOMY

To attain an optimum community system that services residents' living quality needs, proper consideration must be given to all resources and economic activities. The major thrust of this book is to indicate opportunities for adding balance and vitality to the economy through expansion of the tourism industry. At the same time, economic expansion investigations should explore all available avenues (Fitzgerald, 1986). Any comparative advantage enjoyed or able to be developed by the community in any industry offers opportunity. This may be by reason of the natural resource endowment, human resources, location advantages or existing human development.

The tourism industry does not operate in an economic vacuum. Rather, it takes place in the full context of the economic, social and cultural life of the community. Every facet makes a contribution to the life of the residents. Every economic component deserves attention toward helping it make its best contribution to the community. Chapter 6 discusses several classes of economic activities, particularly those applicable to smaller communities. Where the comparative advantage factors are favorable, any legitimate economic activity may have a place in a given community. All activities, including tourism, have positive attributes and all have disadvantages. Thus in building the community's mix of economic activities, policies can be developed for taking advantage of positive features, and minimizing negative features of each class of activity.

Questions for review and further study

1. Discuss the benefits to a community from undertaking the process of establishing tourism industry goals.

2. Some units of government, such as a city, appear better able to move forward with tourism industry development compared to more dispersed, larger units such as a state. How would you explain this?

3. What do you see as the factors limiting formal planning for tourism industry development by a TDA?

4. Why is it unwise for a community to hire a consultant to prepare goals for it?

5. While overall economic and social development is assumed to be the community's goal, what are the advantages and disadvantages of considering only tourism industry goals at one specific time?

6. Who has the right and responsibility for planning and developing a community park? Explain.

7. Who has the right and responsibility for developing the community's lodging facilities? How may this differ from the responsibility for a specific lodging facility and its operation?

8. Why do you think so few states mount really effective tourism research programs?

9. Explain why the current period is referred to as the Information Age.

SUGGESTIONS FOR FURTHER READING

Burns, J. (1979). *Connections: Ways to Discover and Realize Community Potentials.* Stroudsburg, PA: Dowden, Hutchinson and Ross Inc.

Gardner, J. (1981). *Self-Renewal: The Individual and the Innovative Society.* New York: Norton Publishers.

Gunn, C. (1988). *Tourism Planning.* New York: Taylor & Francis. (Chapters 1 and 3).

McIntosh, R., & C. Goeldner. (1984). *Tourism Principles, Practices and Philosophies* (4th ed.). Toronto: John Wiley and Sons. (Part IV).

TEXTUAL REFERENCES

Bosselman, F. (1978). *In the Wake of The Tourist.* Washington, DC: Conservation Foundation.

Burns, J. (1979). *Connections: Ways to Discover and Realize Community Potentials.* Stroudsburg, PA: Dowden, Hutchinson and Ross Inc.

Fitzgerald, J., & P. Meyer. (1986). Recognizing Constraints in Local Economic Development. *Journal of the Community Development Society,* 17(2). Athens, GA: University of Georgia.

Gardner, J. (1981). *Self Renewal: The Individual and the Innovative Society.* NY: Norton Publishing Co.

Greer, J. (1987). The Political Economy of the Local State. *Politics and Society, 15*(4). Stoneham, MA: Butterworth Publishing.

Hobbs, D. (1987). Enterprise Development: Is it a Viable Goal for Rural Communities? *Proceedings of Conference on Entrepreneurship and the Community.* Southern Rural Development Center, Mississippi State University, MS.

Kahn, H. (1979). *World Economic Development, 1979 and Beyond.* Boulder, CO: With the Hudson Institute, Westview Press.

Liu, J., & T. Var. (1980). The Use of Lodging Ratios In Tourism. *Annals of Tourism Research, 7*(3). Menominie, WI: Deptartment of Habitational Resources, University of Wisconsin-Stout, Menominie, WI.

Montgomery, G., & P. Murphy. (1983). Government Involvement in Tourism Development: A Case Study of TIDSA Implementation in British Columbia. *Tourism In Canada: Selected Issues and Options.* (Western Geographical Series 21) Victoria, BC: University of Victoria.

Murphy, P. (1983). Perceptions and Attitudes of Decisionmaker Groups in Tourism Centers. *Journal of Travel Research, 21*(3). Boulder, CO: Business Research Division, University of Colorado.

Ritchie, J. (1985). The Nominal Group Technique: An Approach to Consensus Policy Formulation In Tourism. *Tourism Management, 6*(2). Guildfest, UK: Butterworth Scientific Ltd.

Roberts, H. (1979). *Community Development: Learning and Action.* Toronto, Ontario: University of Toronto Press.

Ronkainen, I., & R. Farano. (1987). United States Travel and Tourism Policy. *Journal of Travel Research, 25*(4). Boulder, CO: Business Research Division, University of Colorado.

Rosenow, J., & G. Pulsipher. (1979). *Tourism the Good, the Bad, and the Ugly* . Lincoln, NB: Century Three Press.

Tourism Canada. (1986). *U.S. Pleasure Travel Market.* Ottawa: Department of Regional Industrial Expansion.

The community exists to serve its residents. The tourism industry can add employment and income plus other ingredients of citizens' living quality. Entrance to Frankenmuth, Michigan. Photo credit: Uel Blank

TWELVE

Getting It Together—
From Policies to Plans to Actions

EVERY COMMUNITY CAN!

Every community has a tourism industry. Every community can have an improved tourism industry—well almost every community.

Most communities can have a vastly more rewarding tourism industry. More rewarding, that is, in returns to the economy of jobs, profits, rents and taxes, and also to residents' lives through amenities, living quality and their esteem for the community.

We have seen that some communities apparently have "too much" tourism. They are inundated by travelers, and/or the community is unduly dominated by outside decision makers. These outside interests may be private corporations, or governmental agencies. The citizens of even such communities can regain much control over their own affairs by the approach suggested here, in which they set up workable objectives and work systematically toward achieving them (Kent 1983; Stokes 1980).

While tourism that is invasive to the community is as undesirable as an underdeveloped tourism industry, assistance from beyond the community is not necessarily unwanted. It is, in fact, usually necessary. Properly managed, this assistance can become a resource to aid in appropriate tourism industry development.

We have examined the principles applying to tourism industry development. We have also explored numerous examples of communities where

those principles have been brought effectively to bear. In this concluding chapter we examine the setting for action, and the specific initiatives that generate effective action toward tourism industry development.

FREDERICK—ANOTHER COMMUNITY THAT COULD!

In a 15-year period, Frederick, Maryland went from a community described as "boring and dreary" to one vibrant with new shops, and restaurants and with a growing number of visitors (Hoffman 1988).

This transformation was brought about by instilling citizens with community pride and confidence. Among those giving major leadership were the mayor and the chairman of the Historic District Commission. Citizens were educated in the value of historic preservation. They, and other agencies, were persuaded to invest in Frederick's future.

The city backed up the educational programs and built good faith through a series of positive actions. Trees were planted, downtown cables buried and streets, lighting and safety were improved. Downtown merchants refurbished their historic buildings. The movie theater building was converted into a center for performing arts. The visitors' center shows off the community with guides and tours to historic sites. Underway are plans for a 1.2 mile linear park thru the city's center. As a result most agencies and businesses have remained downtown; the community has re-discovered its identity.

Frederick's renaissance occurred through the stimulation of plans for positive action in the minds of its multifaceted community decision system.

PRECONDITIONING FOR ACTION

Tomorrow Can Be Different From Today!

A full realization, that tomorrow can be different from today, often constitutes the first step forward in any individual and community endeavor. It applies doubly for tourism, since tourism often amplifies the dynamic changes occurring through-out the warp and woof of the economic, social and cultural fabric.

Happy is the community that operates in a *pro active* manner. It is like the healthily-developing community described in Chapter 5, having a dynamically diversified economy, and a leadership that acts creatively to deal with problems as they emerge, converting them to new opportunities.

How can leadership encourage a pro active ap-proach to tourism industry development? A community tourism policy as discussed in the preceding chapter can help the community move in that direction. Examples used in this book demon-strate the basic steps. Through the question-raising and goal-setting process a policy helps to recognize problems and opportunities. In getting communica-tion and information flowing it generates ideas on the part of many in the community to help convert problems into opportunities in tourism industry development. Reinforcement with positive commu-nity action gives citizens and businesses support in carrying out their own positive plans.

Unfortunately, many communities remain too long in a *passive* or *re-active* mode. Communities that passively accept economic reverses over an

extended period can weaken and decline without a whimper. On the other hand, leaders of some communities see every new development as a threat. These developments may be a new state or federal park, a reservoir, a major private investment or a highway relocation. Every such action is opposed rather than seen as a new opportunity. Needless effort is expended in a frontal fight against the "intrusion" rather than seeking ways to manage, adapt to, or take advantage of it.

Confrontation Spurs To Action

Most communities and most citizens are relatively comfortable and conservative. That is they want to preserve what is, and they find repetition of existing patterns easier and preferable to the effort required to undertake new activities and embrace new ideas. This conservatism, which was also discussed in Chapter 5, explains the slow pace of change, and the slowness to develop tourism in most communi-ties. In defense of these communities, conservatism is a means for keeping the pace of change within a manageable rate. But indiscriminate opposition to all change endangers the community's future.

What can cause new thoughts and patterns of action to emerge? Often only a shock or confronta-tion can intervene with sufficient impact so that established patterns cannot continue.

A benevolent form of confrontation occurs from the confrontation with ideas. The leadership in Frederick persuaded citizens and businessmen that historic preservation could be both profitable and aesthetically satisfying. Business leaders in Frankenmuth, MI brought the community to realize the tourism could be profitable.

Other forms of confrontation occur due to a triggering event that produces shock or violence. Often this confrontation is at least partly due to external actors.

New Glarus, WI faced an unemployed work force due to the closing of their cheese processing plant. They were forced to look for new forms of economic base. The dam at Bagnell, MO built by Union Electric Company and forming the Lake of the Ozarks wreaked havoc. It caused almost complete dismantling of pre-existing life styles—mainly subsistence agriculture. In its place there arose a prosperous tourism-based economy (Richards, 1984).

Saulte Ste. Marie, MI suffered shock from the loss of 2000 jobs when Union Carbide closed its local plant. Evaluation showed that Saulte Ste. Marie had a built-in major attraction—the busiest locks in the world, and known to every school-child. There was a period of anguish over the job loss, then initiative arose from an unexpected quarter. A local parish priest offered to construct a tower for viewing the locks, that also incorporated a crypt of sacred history—mass had been celebrated there 300 years earlier by Fr. Marquette. This action exemplifies operation of the "genius of the community." Other developments, by investors, community businesses and the U.S. Army Corps of Engineers, followed.

These confrontations were almost certainly viewed with alarm by many citizens, and officials of the involved communities. The examples reveal a remarkable ability to adapt, evolve and develop on the part of the communities illustrated (Burns, 1979).

BRINGING OUT THE GENIUS OF THE COMMUNITY

A CommunityTourism Development Policy Can be the Mechanism for Bringing Out the Genius of the Community

A community tourism development policy can help initiate developmental action. It enables the community's actors to fill in the cells of the matrix of decision making on a project so the project really

happens (Waterman, 1987). How does it accomplish this?

Goals. Visions of what may be move an organization forward. Shared dreams can move a community forward in tourism development. What can happen that all will support? The goal-setting phase of tourism policy development can establish these goals in the minds of a wide range of the community spectrum, provided it is done using a process of freely flowing communications.

Information. Good information is always friendly, never threatening. It can be achieved with an adequate research program coupled with a communication and education program. There should be opportunity for all citizens to learn and to contribute (Hobbs, 1986).

Confidence. Trust in the community, and its leadership can be built through communication, and with a history of positive actions in which many participate, and from which the community gains.

More ultimate goals. What really do we want our community to be? Employment is necessary, but most citizens want more than that. The community is an extension of one's ego. Citizens want to be proud of their home. They want it to provide a high-quality living experience not just for themselves, but for youth growing up there, and for those who come to visit as tourists. Paradoxically, achievement of this living quality goal can also contribute to achievement of many economic development ends; investors often look for high amenity communities in which to locate new enterprises (Partners for Livable Places, 1981).

The Big Idea—Make It a Challenge

People rally to a concept that appeals to their pride and sense of worth. This suggests that the goal-setting phase of community policy reach out for concepts that will stir positive images on the part of the community.

What "Big Idea" will capture the community's collective imagination? Once conceived, can it be implemented? Perhaps a better question—how can it be implemented?

Such big ideas are many, and variously implemented:

— Texas History, and Cultural Atmosphere—San Antonio, Texas.
— Ozark Culture—Mountain View, Arkansas.
— Horseracing—Louisville, Kentucky.
— The *Song of Hiawatha* pageant—a sacred pageant at a sacred spot, Pipestone, Minnesota.
— Early Ocean Shipping—Mystic, Connecticut.

Ideally, the "Big Idea" will base upon an indigenous resource. This ties it uniquely to the community making it more difficult to duplicate elsewhere, thereby giving marketing advantages.

A big idea that captures the community's imagination can do more. It can divert attention from the many petty, divisive issues that separate citizens and impede their working together. A collectively-held large concept can focus the community's genius toward acting positively. Through this all can enhance their own ego—gaining a more positive self and community image.

The Concept Plan as the Big Idea

What might the community be? This question has been posed before. It is the basic question that goal setting responds to in the first step toward a tourism policy. The concept plan responds as one part of the goal-setting procedure.

Why a concept plan?—Because many have difficulty in visualizing how the community's tourism facilities and services may be developed and be different from the present. A concept plan can fill this void by providing graphic illustrations of the kinds of developments that would achieve the goal statements.

A concept plan, then, puts the Big Idea of the community tourism industry's goals into graphic form. Using word and visual pictures it makes possible an understanding and visualization of the potential. It is not a blueprint; its purpose is stimulate ideas, rather than act as a precise road-map.

Before a concept plant for the community can be developed there must be systematic information available about its tourism markets and its tourism resources. From that stage on, the development of a concept plan is as much community process as it is actual design, writing and drafting. In other words, the concept plan should depict those things that community citizens see as potential. Communication is critical at this stage. Often required are repeated series of citizen consultations and workshops, followed by an attempt to translate suggestions into preliminary statements, followed by further citizen consultations, etc.

Examples of concept plan-guidelines are available from South Central Texas (Gunn, 1973), the Boundary Waters Canoe Area Region of Northern Minnesota (Agri. Ext. Service, 1981), and the Upper Peninsula of Michigan (Blank, 1966). The guidelines are proposed and voluntary, but they base upon sound resource and market studies, as well as having been subjected to scrutiny by local residents.

The end result should be something that has wide community acceptance and agreement. Suggestions and dreams have been translated into written and visual form: "This is our potential for tomorrow!"

Outside Investors—a Golden Lining!

Many conventional views portray non-resident tourism investors and developers as unwanted intervention in the community. There are indeed cases in which outside investment in the tourism industry becomes not only intrusive but invasive. But two important caveats should be noted regarding investment originating from outside the community:

Much outside investment occurs because the local entrepreneurs fail to see tourism development opportunities.

The ability to draw upon financial resources as well as research and design capabilities from beyond the local area can be an asset in developing the community's tourism industry.

A major difference lies in whether the community and its leadership are passive and reactive, or pro active. In the former case, much of the benefits from community tourism investment can accrue to non-residents who perceive an opportunity that is ignored by resident citizens. Such development, occurring in a community that is unprepared, may also be poorly adapted to the community's economic and social fabric.

Each community is part of the larger society. Tourism as well as other export sales are part of the interface with the rest of the world. Thus the rest of the world is vital to tourism and other community economic activities. In most cases there is not only a sharing of markets but a sharing of developmental and investment responsibilities. Even where tourism developments are initiated locally, most communities depend partly upon outside financial and other assistance. They seek roads, parks, water management structures, and financial loans. The challenge, then, is for the community to discover ways for mutually participatory sharing in the development of its tourism resources. Few have the capability to completely go it alone.

Private Initiative and Enterprise: How Can It Be Positively Stimulated to Act?

The community can decide and act on building a park, or a public golf course. Private businesses

and operations, however, lie outside the range of public decisions. These include hospitality services and many others that are essential to an adequate tourism industry. Is there machinery for assisting and stimulating private entrepreneurs to appropriate action?

A first step is shared goals among the community's citizens and entrepreneurs.

The next step, repetitious but vital, is information: Information about resources and their potential, information about markets and their potentials. This step can flow from the research and community information phases of a tourism policy.

Confidence can be developed on the part of investors in a number of ways that extend beyond the goal-setting, information-flow phases. Positive public investment in infrastructure, parks, services, interpretation, information, and aesthetics sends a strong message to investors that the community believes in itself and in a positive future for its tourism industry.

A characteristic of depressed communities is that those living there, who have investment capabilities, lose faith. They send their money outside the community, thereby further perpetuating the local depressed state. We have noted two community examples where local bankers performed a lead role—Guthrie, OK and New Glarus, WI. The New Glarus banker, Waldo, backed tourism projects in the process of converting the community's economy onto a tourism footing. He commented to visiting delegations, "I could have made more money by investing the bank's money elsewhere, but this is my home and it is important to me to see it prosper!" This kind of backing gives strong impetus to other private investors.

Technological assistance to developmental and marketing efforts of tourism firms and investors can sometimes be provided as a public service (Burke, 1982; Blank, 1983). Michigan was noted in Chapter 11 as a state that provided extension specialists in tourism through its Cooperative Extension Service. Many other states have also provided this service through a number of organizational devices attached to their land grant college. Wisconsin, for example, has set up a Recreational Resources Center staffed with personnel having tourism research, developmental and marketing expertise.

A concept plan may be one of the most effective devices available for guiding and stimulating private as well as public action. Such a device synthesizes market and resource information into examples of potential developments and investment opportunities. Agencies, investors and individuals are expected to apply their own individual interpretation to what they conceive and develop.

Communities may provide more direct developmental guidelines through zoning mechanisms. While many view zoning as a negative, constraining procedure, it may also be decidedly positive. The zoning mechanism can provide protection to investment, it can help maintain resource quality, and can help ensure that adequate infrastructure is available to a given development.

Financial incentives of various kinds may be established by the community. The tax system may be used to encourage more intensive use of certain types of prime lands. Tax deferral or temporary tax reductions may also be offered to certain types of investments that the community's tourism industry needs. Another tax device, coming into increasing use, is the lodging or related hospitality service tax. Such taxes if used primarily for the support of a tourism agency can be a powerful tool, making possible adequate tourism promotion, tourism research, and community tourism education programs.

A number of states have enabling legislation allowing the local community to back loans made to local enterprises, including tourism investments. Such backing often allows the borrower to obtain capital on better terms in addition to providing security for the lender.

In summary, a tourism policy provides a means whereby the community leadership can function by helping the community to develop shared goals. These goals become translated into plans and blueprints for actions on the part of citizens, entrepreneurs and agencies (Roberts, 1979). This stimulation of the community's genius may produce results even exceeding expectations.

FROM POLICIES TO PLANNING TO ACTION

This chapter emphasizes policies aimed at initiating and stimulating tourism industry development. We have said that the community policy body, as such, is not likely to undertake specific "brick and mortar" action. Who does, then? Most action projects will be undertaken by businessmen, firms and volunteer groups, or assigned to public agencies. The overall community's role will have been to stimulate and support these entities in undertaking action.

What might be the pattern of action in implementation of a specific project leading to erection of brick and mortar or the staging of an event? We list below a planning-action procedure. This will be recognized as an expansion of the knowledge-action continuum discussed in Chapter 10. Since a number of detailed discussions of planning are available, only a basic outline of the steps are given here (See suggested readings).

Step one: Initiation; the problem recognition stage.

Step two: Set goals and objectives relevant to the specific project. How goals are established depends upon the nature of the unit undertaking the project—whether a private business, a public agency, a civic group, etc.

Step three: Get information needed to help decide how to reach the project objectives. A number of methods may be used including review of other similar projects, and the conduct of systematic research to get information about resources, markets and other factors. Information about physical, social, and cultural factors may be needed, as well as economic data.

Step four: Analyze the specific information relating to the project; make a projection of trends; possibly set up alternate scenarios.

Step five: Develop concepts—what might be the nature of what could be developed? Both physical design concepts and operational concepts are needed.

Step six: Develop strategies—how will the project be carried out? Funding? Who owns? Who will operate? Who is involved in construction and/ or action that is needed?

Step seven: Carry out the plan.

Step eight: Evaluate what has been done. Since most projects have components that are ongoing, this evaluation serves as a feedback into what is being done to direct the further planning and action.

In practice the project implementation often becomes an operation like the matrix of decision making discussed in Chapter 10.

The implementation, step seven above, may consist of multiple operations. Subparts may require repeating all steps, from one to seven, a number of times. These parts may be recursive, that is, they may feed sequentially and iteratively into each other. Alternatively they may form a network in which one or more subparts may need to be completed before another subpart is begun.

TOURISM DEVELOPMENT: A WIN-WIN OPPORTUNITY

Tourism industry development offers to many communities a means for adding balance, economic strength and stability. As with most other economic activities it adds jobs, profits, rents and taxes. Further, the tourism industry promises to continue as an expanding part of our economic and social setting.

Costs? Yes, and these have been reviewed. Every economic activity exacts costs from the society in which it is practiced. Many communities have adapted well to an expanded tourism economic sector.

Tourism development appears compatible with development of many other forms of economic activity—agriculture, manufacturing, commerce— over a wide range of development. Since travel is required by nearly all modern economic activities, tourism is also a complementing input into most other industries, assisting their operation.

In addition to providing employment, tourism makes recreational facilities available to community residents of a quality and type that might not otherwise be supported. The development of a distinctive tourist destination area image can "put the community on the map" and add a priceless ingredient of community pride to residents' self perception. Paradoxically, the upgrading of community amenities and living quality can act additionally to attract other industry types.

Experiences of tourists are enriched by a high-quality tourism-recreation experience.

The community that develops its tourism appeal and offering enriches our store of national resources and enriches the culture.

This is the challenge of the community tourism industry imperative. We need only the vision, will, wit and wisdom to effect it!

Questions for review and further study

1. Why is it necessary for each involved unit of the Matrix of Decision Making to set up its own individual plans—blueprints for action?

2. In what ways can a community operate to encourage and direct private investment in the tourism industry? What obligations does the community have to private firms? What obligations do private firms have to the community?

3. Explain the "Big Idea" that people in
   Frederick, MD appear to hold in common.

4. Show the similarities, and the differences, of
   the "planning process" compared to
   "research procedure."

5. What are some conditions under which a
   community may decline economically and in
   population numbers without taking specific
   action to avoid the decline?

6. How would you explain the "genius of the
   community"? How can it be induced to
   operate in tourism development?

SUGGESTIONS FOR FURTHER READING

Gunn, C. (1988). *Tourism Planning*. New York: Taylor & Francis. (Chapters 9, 10, and 11).

Gunn, C. (1988). *Vacationscape: Designing Tourist Regions*. New York: Van Nostrand Reinhold. (Chapters 7, 8, 9, and 10).

Kaiser, C., Jr., & L. Helber. (1978). *Tourism Planning and Development*. Boston, MA: CBI Publishing Co.

McIntosh, R., & C. Goeldner. (1984). *Tourism Principles, Practices and Philosophies*. (4th ed.). New York: John Wiley and Sons. (Part IV).

Murphy, P. (1985). *Tourism: A Community Approach*. New York: Methuen. (Section 5).

Wallace, L., D. Hobbs, & R. Vlasin (Eds). (1969). *Selected Perspectives For Community Resource Development*. Raleigh, NC: Agricultural Policy Institute, North Carolina State University. (Part IV).

Waterman, R., Jr. (1987). *The Renewal Factor*. New York: Bantam Books Inc.

Weaver, G. (1986). *Tourism USA*. Washington, DC: U.S. Department of Commerce. (Chapter 2).

Wynn, M. (1985). *Planning Games: Case Study Simulations in Land Management and Development*. New York: E. F. & N. Spon Ltd.

TEXTUAL REFERENCES

Agricultural Extension Service and Design Consortium. (1981). *Recreational Concepts for Northeastern Minnesota*. St. Paul, MN: University of Minnesota.

Blank, U., & C. Gunn. (1966). *Guidelines for Tourism-Recreation in Michigan's Upper Peninsula*. East Lansing, MI: Michigan State University.

Blank, U., L. Simonson, G. Ballman, J. Burke, R. Korte, & A. Heikkila. (1983). *Contributing to Tourism Industry Vitality of a Natural Resource Based Region Through Educational and Technical Assistance*. (Staff Paper P83-20). St. Paul, MN: Department of Agricultural and Applied Economics, University of Minnesota.

Burke, J., G. Ballman, R. Korte, & U. Blank. (1982). Using Educational Techniques to Improve Private Sector Marketing. *Proceedings, 13th Annual Meeting, TTRA*. Salt Lake City, UT: Bureau of Economic and Business Research, University of Utah.

Burns, J. (1979). *Connections: Ways to Discover and Realize Community Potentials*. Stroudsburg, PA: Dowden, Hutchinson and Ross Inc.

Gunn, C. (1973). *Tourism Planning in East Texas*. (Information Report 73-1, No. 5). College Station, TX: Department of Recreation and Parks, Texas A & M University.

Hobbs, D. (1986). Knowledge-Based Rural Development: Adult Education and the Future Rural Economy. *National Invitational Conference on Rural Adult Postsecondary Education,* Airlie, VA.

Hoffman, M. (1988, August 5). Maryland City Hums a Lively New Tune. *Christian Science Monitor.* Boston, MA.

Kent, N. (1983). Hawaii: Islands Under the Influence. *Monthly Review Press.* New York.

Partners for Livable Places. (1981). *Livability Digest, 1* (and subsequent issues). Washington, DC.

Richards, R. (1984). When Even Bad News is Not So Bad: Local Control Over Outside Forces of Community Development. *Journal of the Community Development Society. 15*(1). Athens, GA: University of Georgia.

Roberts, H. (1979). *Community Development: Learning and Action.* Toronto, Ontario: University of Toronto Press.

Stokes, B. (1980). *Helping Ourselves—Local Solutions to Global Problems.* New York: W. W. Norlin and Co.

Waterman, R., Jr. (1987). *The Renewal Factor.* New York: Bantam Books Inc.

OTHER BOOKS FROM VENTURE PUBLISHING, INC.

The Future of Leisure Services: Thriving on Change,
 by Geoffrey Godbey

Planning Parks for People,
 by John Hultsman, Richard L. Cottrell and Wendy Zales-Hultsman

Recreation Economic Decisions: Comparing Benefits and Costs,
 by Richard G. Walsh

Leadership Administration of Outdoor Pursuits,
 by Phyllis Ford and James Blanchard

Leisure in Your Life: An Exploration, Revised Edition,
 by Geoffrey Godbey

Acquiring Parks and Recreation Facilities through Mandatory Dedication: A Comprehensive Guide,
 by Ronald A. Kaiser and James D. Mertes

Recreation and Leisure: Issues in an Era of Change, Revised Edition, edited
 by Thomas L. Goodale and Peter A. Witt

Private and Commercial Recreation, edited
 by Arlin Epperson

Park Ranger Handbook,
 by J. W. Shiner

Playing, Living, Learning—A Worldwide Perspective on Children's Opportunities to Play,
 by Cor Westland and Jane Knight

Evaluation of Therapeutic Recreation through Quality Assurance, edited
 by Bob Riley

Recreation and Leisure: An Introductory Handbook, edited
 by Alan Graefe and Stan Parker

The *Leisure Diagnostic Battery—Users Manual and Sample Forms,*
 by Peter A. Witt and Gary D. Ellis

Behavior Modification in Therapeutic Recreation: An Introductory Learning Manual,
 by John Dattilo and William D. Murphy

Outdoor Recreation Management: Theory and Application, Revised and Enlarged,
 by Alan Jubenville, Ben W. Twight and Robert H. Becker

International Directory of Academic Institutions in Leisure, Recreation and Related Fields
 (Distributed for WLRA)

Being at Leisure—Playing at Life: A Guide to Health and Joyful Living,
 by Bruno Hans Geba

Amenity Resource Valuation, edited
 by George L. Peterson, B.L. Driver and Robin Gregory

The Evolution of Leisure: Historical and Philosophical Perspectives,
 by Thomas L. Goodale and Geoffrey C. Godbey

Leisure Education: A Manual of Activities and Resources,
 by Norma J. Stumbo and Steven R. Thompson

Risk Management in Therapeutic Recreation: A Component of Quality Assurance,
        by Judith Voelkl

Beyond the Bake Sale: A Fund Raising Handbook for Public Agencies,
        (Distributed for City of Sacramento,
        Department of Recreation and Parks)

Gifts to Share: A Gifts Catalogue How-To Manual for Public Agencies,
        (Distributed for City of Sacramento,
        Department of Recreation and Parks)

Doing More with Less in the Delivery of Recreation and Park Services: A Book of Case Studies,
        by John L. Crompton

Venture Publishing, Inc.
1640 Oxford Circle
State College, PA 16803
(814) 234-4561